Chinese Research Perspectives on Educational Development, Volume 6

Chinese Research Perspectives on Educational Development

International Advisory Board

Chen Yangbin, *La Trobe University*
Gregory P. Fairbrother, *The Hong Kong Institute of Education*
Gerard Postiglione, *The University of Hong Kong*
Heidi Ross†, *Indiana University Bloomington*

VOLUME 6

The titles published in this series are listed at *brill.com/cred*

Chinese Research Perspectives on Educational Development

VOLUME 6

Chief Editor

Yang Dongping

Deputy Editors

Yang Min and Huang Shengli

BRILL

LEIDEN | BOSTON

This book is a result of the co-publication agreement between Social Sciences Academic Press and Koninklijke Brill NV. These articles were selected and translated into English from the original 《中国教育发展报告 (2017)》 (*Zhongguo jiaoyu fazhan baogao 2017*), 《中国教育发展报告 (2018)》 (*Zhongguo jiaoyu fazhan baogao 2018*) and 《中国教育发展报告 (2019)》 (*Zhongguo jiaoyu fazhan baogao 2019*) with financial support from the New Oriental Education & Technology Group Inc.

Translated by Ji Lingying and Zhang Xin.

The Library of Congress Cataloging-in-Publication Data is available online at https://catalog.loc.gov
LC record available at https://lccn.loc.gov/2021059389

Typeface for the Latin, Greek, and Cyrillic scripts: "Brill". See and download: brill.com/brill-typeface.

ISSN 2212-7488
ISBN 978-90-04-51176-7 (hardback)
ISBN 978-90-04-51177-4 (e-book)

Copyright 2022 by Koninklijke Brill NV, Leiden, The Netherlands.
Koninklijke Brill NV incorporates the imprints Brill, Brill Nijhoff, Brill Hotei, Brill Schöningh, Brill Fink, Brill mentis, Vandenhoeck & Ruprecht, Böhlau and V&R unipress.
All rights reserved. No part of this publication may be reproduced, translated, stored in a retrieval system, or transmitted in any form or by any means, electronic, mechanical, photocopying, recording or otherwise, without prior written permission from the publisher. Requests for re-use and/or translations must be addressed to Koninklijke Brill NV via brill.com or copyright.com.

This book is printed on acid-free paper and produced in a sustainable manner.

Contents

List of Figures and Tables VII

1 Promoting Equity, Improving Quality, and Modernizing Education Governance 1
  Yang Dongping

2 Reform of the Basic Education System in a Context of Diverse Opinions 17
  Yang Mingquan and Gong Pengfei

3 Amendments of Law of the People's Republic of China on the Promotion of Privately-Run Schools and Their Impacts 30
  Wu Hua and Zhang Luhong

4 Practical Paths, Methods, and Reflections on Precision-Targeted Measures to Alleviate Poverty through Education 50
  Zhang Zhaoqin, Feng Qingyun and Wang Chengde

5 "School Education in the Eyes of Parents" Survey Report 70
  Qin Hongyu

6 Report on the Learning and Development of First-Generation College Students in China 95
  Zhang Huafeng, Guo Fei and Shi Jinghuan

7 Studying China's "Super Secondary School" Phenomenon through the "Hengzhong Model" 117
  Wang Shuai

8 The New Policy on "Burden Reduction" for Shanghai Primary and Secondary School Students: Reflections and Recommendations 134
  Liu Hong and Zhang Duanhong

9 Problems and Ways Out for Rural Education – A Discussion Inspired by Dr. Rozelle's Talk 149
  Yang Dongping

10   The Establishment of "Double First-Class" (双一流) Universities in China and Issues to Prevent   166
     Xi Youmin and Zhang Xiaojun

11   A Review of the Changes in Education Funding over the Last Two Decades in China   177
     Hu Ruiwen and Cui Haili

12   Report on "Innovative Small and Micro Schools" (创新小微) in China   197
     Yang Jin

13   The Current Status and Issues of the Compulsory Education: Insights from the National Report on Monitoring the Quality of the Compulsory Education in China   219
     Wei Xiaoman, Li Mian and Huang Fuping

14   Special Education in China: From Ensuring Access to Improving Quality   232
     Feng Yajing

15   Equal School Access for Migrant Children Requires Breaking Down Double Barriers   251
     Lan Fang

16   Research on the Current Development State of Traditional Cultural Education in China   269
     Bao Lige

     Index   291

Figures and Tables

Figures

5.1 Provincial distribution of schools attended by children reported by parents (%) 72
5.2 Comparison of mean values of parental satisfaction in schools of different geographical areas 77
5.3 Comparison of mean parental satisfaction score with school education by parents' education background 77
5.4 Comparison of the mean values of the severity of schools' tendency to teach to the test in 31 provinces 80
5.5 Mean severity of examination-oriented education tendencies in schools as reported by parents of children at different grades 82
5.6 Percentage of parents that reported their perception of the focused areas of their child's school's education 84
5.7 Comparison of parental satisfaction with schools in different areas in public and private schools 86
5.8 Comparison of parental perception of focuses of school education in different areas in public schools and private schools 87
5.9 Parents' expectations of school education 89
9.1 Survey on dropouts in secondary school in poverty areas by REAP 151
9.2 Percentage of population with high school education in middle-income countries 153
12.1 Establishment year of "innovative small and micro schools" 199
12.2 Main reasons for parents to choose "innovative small and micro schools" 209
12.3 Parents' satisfaction rate with their children's school 210
12.4 Parents' satisfaction rate with their children's academic outcomes 211
12.5 Parents' satisfaction rate with their children's school life 211
12.6 Likelihood of parents sending their children back to the institutional system 212
12.7 Students' satisfaction rate with their learning outcomes 213
12.8 Students' satisfaction rate with their school life 214
14.1 Change in the number of special education schools in China, 2012–2017 238
14.2 Change in the number of students with disabilities in schools in China, 2012–2017 239
14.3 Changes in the types of students with disabilities in schools in China, 2012–2017 239

14.4 Change in the total number of special education teachers and the number of full-time teachers in China, 2012–2017   240
14.5 Change in the proportion of full-time special education teachers and administrative, teaching assistants, and supporting staff in China, 2012–2017   241
14.6 Change in the proportion of full-time special education teachers who have received special education professional training in China, 2012–2017   242
14.7 Change in the education level of full-time special education teachers in China, 2012–2017   242
14.8 Change in the proportion of full-time special education teachers with different degrees in China, 2012–2017   243
14.9 Trends in the number of students with disabilities enrolled in university in China in recent years (2012–2017)   245
16.1 Illustration of the traditional culture education   271
16.2 Percentage of teachers with different conceptions of education in traditional culture   275
16.3 Percentage of teachers with different conceptions of the primary role of education in traditional culture   275
16.4 Percentage of teachers with different ideas about the form education in traditional culture should take   276
16.5 Percentage of teachers with different ideas about the chief impediment to promoting education in traditional culture   277
16.6 Provinces where privately-run traditional culture education institutions are located   281
16.7 Types of services provided by privately-run traditional culture education institutions   282
16.8 Student age groups that privately-run traditional culture education institutions served   282
16.9 Course contents offered in privately-run traditional culture education institutions   283

Tables

2.1 The National Education System Survey at the 41st International Conference on Education   20
3.1 Comparison of policies related to for-profit and not-for-profit private schools under the legal framework of categorized management   37
3.2 History of the amendment of the *Private Education Promotion Act*   38

FIGURES AND TABLES IX

4.1 List of annual tasks for teacher training, exchange, and support programs for precision-targeted poverty alleviation   59
4.2 Number of kindergartens in villages under the Gansu Provincial Precision-Targeted Poverty Alleviation through Pre-school Education Support Program   61
4.3 List of annual construction tasks for the "comprehensive improvement of school facilities in poverty areas project" for precision-targeted poverty alleviation   63
5.1 Parents education level and status   71
5.2 Urban-rural distribution of schools attended by children reported by parents   72
5.3 Indicators for parents' evaluation of their satisfaction with school education   73
5.4 Ranking of parental satisfaction with school education   74
5.5 Proportion of parents that were satisfied with schools by detailed categories in urban and rural schools (%)   78
5.6 Comparison of the mean severity of the tendency to teach to the test in urban and rural schools   81
5.7 Attribution of reasons for examination-oriented education in schools by parents with children at different school-age groups (%)   83
5.8 Parents' evaluation of school education focuses in urban and rural schools, % of parents   84
5.9 Comparison of mean parental satisfaction for public and private schools   86
5.10 Comparison of mean parental evaluation of the severity of the tendency to examination-oriented education in their child's current school   87
5.11 Parental evaluation of their child's classroom teachers (%)   88
5.12 Changes that parents expected from schools (%)   90
6.1 Background information and family situations (in %)   98
6.2 Characteristics of subject choices in senior high schools and college-entrance examinations (in %)   99
6.3 Information on college-entrance examination and college/university admissions (in %)   101
6.4 Performance in terms of different learning styles   102
6.5 Interpersonal interactions of first-generation college students   104
6.6 Allocation of time for different extracurricular activities   105
6.7 Proportion of first-generation and non-first-generation college students participating in each high-impact educational practices (in %)   108
6.8 Performance of different types of first-generation college students in their engagement in high-impact educational practices   109

6.9	First-generation college students' evaluation of supportive campus environment	112
6.10	Self-reported educational gains of first-generation college students	114
7.1	Branch schools exported to the whole country under the "Hengzhong Model"	125
8.1	Comparison of "burden reduction" policies of basic education in Shanghai since 2003	139
11.1	Average annual increase rate in China's fiscal and non-fiscal education expenditure, 1995–2015 (at constant prices)	178
11.2	Progress in investment in education in China, 1995–2015 (at relevant year prices)	179
11.3	Trends in the structure of education investment in China, 1995–2005 (at relevant year prices)	181
11.4	Average annual growth rate in fiscal and non-fiscal education expenditure in China, 2005–2015 (at constant prices)	182
11.5	Growth in the amount of education investment in China, 2005–2015 (at relevant year prices, in billions of yuan)	182
11.6	Trends in the structure of education investment in China, 2005–2015 (at relevant year prices)	183
11.7	Trends in per capita income and expenditure of urban and rural residents in China, 2005–2015 (at relevant year prices, in yuan)	183
11.8	Analysis of the structure of per capita consumption expenditure of urban residents	184
11.9	Analysis of the structure of per capita consumption expenditure of rural residents	185
11.10	International comparison of education investment	190
11.11	Comparison of per-student expenditure at all stages of education in China in 2014 and that of OECD in 2011 (PPP dollars)	191
11.12	Analysis of the relation between the annual growth rate of GDP and total fiscal education expenditure, 1995–2015 (all at constant prices)	192
11.13	Analysis of the three major expenditure categories of state fiscal expenditure, 2007–2015	192
11.14	Structure of State fiscal expenditure in the category of social and livelihood expenditure, 2007–2015	194
12.1	Teacher-student ratio in "innovative small and micro schools"	199
12.2	Geographical locations of "innovative small and micro schools"	200
16.1	Measures related to traditional culture education in schools	276

CHAPTER 1

Promoting Equity, Improving Quality, and Modernizing Education Governance

Yang Dongping[1]

Abstract

In the process of rapid urbanization, rural areas are under the great challenge to effectively improve educational quality, which aims at promoting the integrated development of compulsory education in urban and rural areas within counties. The Ministry of Education (MOE) has announced the "core competencies" of student development and the guidance on reforming the high school entrance examination to facilitate the implementation of quality education. At the same time, the serious problem of examination-oriented education and excessive extracurricular tutoring are negatively affecting the well-rounded development of young people. The huge gap in education development between urban and rural areas has become a constraint to improving education equity and quality. The co-existence of examination-oriented education and innovative education has led to a strong contrast between education's ideal and reality. This highlights the reality that the education reform is entering the "deep-water zone" in a landscape of diversified social interests and stakeholders in the education industry. Moreover, our task to promote the modernization of education governance is extremely challenging.

Keywords

education reform – rural education – examination-oriented education – education governance

The year 2016 marks the beginning of the 13th Five-Year Plan. In accordance with the goal of basically modernizing education and completely eliminating poverty by 2020, education development and reform's primary task remains

---

[1] Yang Dongping 杨东平, Director of 21st Century Education Research Institute, and member of the National Advisory Committee on Education.

"promoting equity and improving quality," focusing on the public's pursuit of "a good quality education." In addition, we need to address new issues and challenges of urban and rural education as they arise by improving education governance.

1 The Co-Existence of Quality-Oriented Education and Examination-Oriented Education

1.1 *Core Competencies and PISA Tests*

In September, the Ministry of Education (MOE) published the *Core Competencies and Values for Chinese Student's Development* (中国学生发展核心素养), in response to the worldwide interest in 21st-century skills and core competencies. The core competencies were formulated based on scientific, contemporary, and culturally sensitive principles, aiming at cultivating "all-rounded development" of students. The core competencies cover three broad areas: foundational academic knowledge, independent development, and social participation. Each broad area is composed of two basic competencies, ending up with six competencies, including humanistic heritage, scientific spirit, learning to learn, healthy living, responsibility, and practical innovation. Each of these competencies is broken down into three main elements, with a total of 18 basic elements. Based on this general framework, specific age-appropriate performance requirements for students at each school level can be further developed accordingly. Compared to the consultation draft, the official version of the core competencies framework has been condensed significantly. Specifically, the official version has three fewer competencies and seven fewer basic elements, and thus better reflects the core values.

Following the beginning of the pilot reform of the college entrance examination, in September 2016, the MOE issued the *Guidance on Further Promoting the Reform of the Senior High School Entrance Examination* (关于进一步推进高中阶段学校考试招生制度改革的指导意见). The Guidance requires further improvement of the junior high school's academic assessment system and the comprehensive evaluation of students' competencies to avoid examination-oriented education. The primary approach is to combine the junior high school graduation examination and the senior high school entrance examination into one, which covers all the subjects set by the national curriculum standards. In terms of the admission scoring system, scores of three major subjects, including language, mathematics, and foreign language, will be counted toward the total score, while for the rest of the subjects, students can choose three subjects to be included in the total score. Students are only required to pass the subjects that are not included in the total score. Students will no longer be granted extra points for their performance in sports, arts, and other competitions. Instead, the relevant achievements will be included in the students' comprehensive quality evaluation files, which will be used as a reference in admissions. The comprehensive reform pilot was implemented with the first cohort of students entering junior high school in 2017.

Shanghai's basic education has attracted sustained attention due to its excellent performance in the PISA test. In December 2016, the Organization for Economic Co-operation and Development (OECD) announced the 2015 PISA test results. In the current round of testing, Singapore took first place overall with scores of 564 in maths, 535 in reading, and 556 in science; China, which consists of Beijing, Shanghai, Jiangsu, and Guangdong, ranked 6th in maths, 27th in reading, and 10th in science. Due to the increase in the number of regions participating in the assessment and the different samples, it is conceivable that the four regions' overall level is lower than the results of PISA2009 and PISA2012 Shanghai. Experts believe that what truly reflects a country's competitiveness or region is the percentage of high-level students. In PISA2015, 13 percent of students from the four regions of China and 27.7 percent of students from the four regions of China scored at least one high level in science, mathematics, and reading, just behind Singapore, Chinese Taipei, and Hong Kong.[2]

However, it is well known that Chinese students' achievements are based on "intensive and prolonged" training. The core problem of education in China is still the tendency to place too much emphasis on the examination-oriented nature of knowledge education, and more attention should be paid to the development of students' personality and physical and mental health, and to reducing the burden of academic work.

1.2 *Examination-Oriented Education Is Still Prevalent*

As of November 2016, the number of counties (municipalities and districts) nationwide that had achieved basically developed compulsory education had reached 1,456 in total, accounting for 49.95% of the total. However, this proportion has yet to reach the target of 65% expected to be reached in 2015 and is farther away from the goal of 95% in 2020.[3]

---

[2] "2015 nian PISA ceshi jieguo chulu: Xinjiapo Jushou Dalu dishi, 2015年PISA 测试结果 出炉：新加坡居首大陆第十 [2015 PISA Test Results Released: Singapore Tops, China's Mainland 10th]," China.com, December 7, 2016, http://edu.china.com/second/11087929/2016 1207/30068725.html.

[3] Wu Zhihui 邬志辉 "Zhongguo nongcun jiaoyu fazhan baogao 2016, 中国农村教育发展报告 2016 [China Rural Education Development Report 2016]," press release, December 26, 2016.

In the field of compulsory education, the long-standing problem of examination-oriented education is still rampant. The heavy schoolwork burden, the booming tutoring industry, and the resurgence of the Olympic mathematics fever among elementary school students are damaging young students' physical and mental health, imagination, and creativity, and causing anxiety for many parents. The "starting line" of the academic competition is moving toward younger age. For instance, Olympic mathematics training is even starting in kindergartens. The "super high school" model, known as the "education factory," is still popular. The latest form of examination-oriented education in its digital form in the Internet era makes such training more refined, accessible, and interesting. However, despite the form of the examination-oriented education, it still simplifies education to pedagogy, which further reduces to examination-oriented training, focusing only on grades and knowledge points. In Shanghai, starting from September 2016, all primary schools will implement the "A, B, C, D" letter score evaluation system. This will change the overemphasis on examination points and shift the emphasis from students' grades to their competencies, which is a promising move.

The dangers of examination-oriented education for young people are presented in the warnings of Professor Xu Kaiwen of the Mental Health Education Counseling Center at Peking University. He found that some of the best students suffer from a so-called "hollow heart disease." "These children have a strong sense of loneliness and meaninglessness. They grew up as the best students, the most well-behaved students. They especially need to be praised by others, and they have strong suicidal ideation. They don't necessarily want to kill themselves, but just do not know why to live; what is the value and meaning of living?" According to the survey, 30.4% of the freshmen at Peking University are sick of studying, and 40.4% cannot find meaning in living and claim that they are just living following someone else's logic. While the suicide rate in the country as a whole has fallen dramatically, only the suicide rate among elementary and middle school students is rising.[4]

On the other hand, a variety of bottom-up educational innovations and explorations, both inside and outside the public education system, have become more and more active, and the concept of learner-centered education has begun to take root among educators. The curriculum reform carried out in public schools is developing, and educational innovation exploration

---

4 Xu Kaiwen 徐凯文 "Shidai kongxinbing yu jiaolv jingjixue, 时代空心病与焦虑经济学 [*The "Hollow Disease" of the Times and the Economics of Anxiety*]," Speech at the Ninth New Oriental Family Education Summit Forum, edu.china.com.cn, November 9, 2016.

and advocacy in the private education sector is intensifying. Many influential institutions, groups, and projects are emerging, such as the New Education Research Institute led by Zhu Yongxin, the New School Research Institute led by Li Xigui, the Dandelion Education Think Tank in Chongqing, Wendui Education in Chengdu, the GET2016 Educational Technology Conference organized by Jiemodui, and the LIFE Educational Innovation Project of the 21st Century Education Research Institute, etc. With the popularity of online education and social learning, many parents and educators start running more and more private schools, micro-schools, and social learning institutions. Some experienced teachers of primary and secondary schools are leaving the public education system to run their own ideal education institutions. All these new developments put pressure on and deliver a signal for change in public schools.

1.3 *The Management of Private Education by Categories*

In 2016, China's education legal system entered a new stage of development. The State issued an *Outline for the Implementation of Governing Education According to Law (2016–2020)*, calling for a rule-of-law mindset and method to promote comprehensive education reform and comprehensively modernize the education governance system and governance capacity.

The National People's Congress completed the revision of the *Education Law*, the *Higher Education Law*, and the *Law on the Promotion of Private Education* through a package of amendments. Among them, the amendments to the *Law on the Promotion of Private Education* were extremely controversial during the revision process, and it took three rounds before it was finally passed. It was decided to manage for-profit and nonprofit private schools differently. The law clarified that nonprofit institutions are not allowed to obtain proceeds from running schools. This legally solved the bottlenecks that plagued the development of private education, such as the unclear legal entity of schools, unclear property ownership, and difficulty in implementing support measures. This law also facilitates the government to implement differential supporting policies to these two types of private schools to promote their development. With the current stage of development and characteristics of China's market economy, most private education in China is not funded by donations but by investment. The new law protects the rights and interests of existing private school owners, including the right to receive compensation or rewards in the event of school termination, in accordance with the law. The decision not to allow for-profit education during the compulsory education stage is primarily intended to safeguard the public welfare and equity of compulsory education and to avoid exacerbating class divisions during the compulsory education stage.

2 "Filling in the Gaps" in Rural Education

2.1 *Precision Measures to Alleviate Poverty through Education and Promote the Integrated Development of Urban and Rural Compulsory Education*

In the field of rural education, it is imperative to continue to remedy shortcomings, promote educational equity, and close the gap between urban and rural education. The State Council has adopted a five-year plan to combat poverty in education, requiring improvement of the "shortcomings" in compulsory education in poor counties throughout the country. The "Precision-targeted Poverty Alleviation through Education" campaign has been carried out in various regions. In Guizhou Province, eight education poverty alleviation plans have been implemented; namely, the Student Financial Assistance and Specific Supports Plan, the Plan to Alleviate Poverty and Increase People's Wealth through Vocational Education, the Improvement Plan for the Expansion and Renovation of Schools, the Plan to Promote Information-based Education, the Teacher Quality Improvement Plan, the Plan to Increase Rural and Poor Areas Enrollment with Favorable Policies, the Education Partnership Support Plan, and the Care Plan for Groups with Special Difficulty and Needs. Hubei province has formulated an action plan and 26 supporting implementation plans focusing on supporting the 37 poor counties, 4,821 poor villages, and 767,000 school-age children from low-income families in the province. The Gansu Provincial Department of Education focuses on establishing a system of precision-targeted poverty alleviation policies that reach out to villages, households, and individuals. The department implemented the "9+1" education special support plan for precision-targeted poverty alleviation. The nine special support plans cover pre-school education, compulsory education, ordinary high school education, vocational education, rural teachers' education, education for ethnic groups, student financial aid, higher education admissions, and left-behind children. Together with the *Action Plan to Support Development of Education in the Traditional Revolutionary Regions (2015–2020)*, these plans aim to help low-income families lift themselves out of poverty and break the intergenerational transmission of poverty.

In July 2016, the State Council published the *Opinions on Promoting the Integrated Reform and Development of Urban and Rural Compulsory Education in Counties*, which requires the establishment of development paths in accordance with local conditions, the simultaneous construction of urban schools, efforts to run small-scale rural schools, and guiding the reasonable mobility of students in the light of the actual situation in the east, middle and west part of the country, town types, urbanization levels and local conditions in the villages. The Government set out plans to eliminate large-size class, coordinate the deployment of teachers in both urban and rural areas, reform the policies for guaranteeing the salaries and benefits of rural teachers, reform the policies for controlling dropouts, reform the enrollment policies for children of families moved to new places, and enhance the care and protection of left-behind children. By 2020, the government aims to reach the balanced development of compulsory education in counties and equalize basic public education services in urban and rural areas.

This policy has a strong focus on issues that arise in the rapid urbanization process. Specifically, the trend of concentrating rural schools in towns and cities continues. Meanwhile, many compulsory education schools were forced to be closed or combined. These resulted in excessive schools in cities but not enough schools in rural areas. In 2015, the urbanization rate of primary education reached 69.40%, and that of junior high school was 83.71%, which were 13.3% and 27.61% higher than the population's urbanization rate (56.10%). The urbanization rates of schools were 10.35% and 6.66% higher than in 2011, respectively. Rural compulsory education mainly consists of large-scale schools with large-size classes in counties, rural boarding schools, and small-scale schools in villages. In 2015, there were 111,400 small-scale schools with less than 100 students in rural areas, accounting for 55.7% of the total number of village small schools and teaching centers and 87.9% of small-scale schools nationwide. Of these, 33,900 village school sites have less than ten students. The total number of boarding students at the compulsory education stage in rural areas (towns and villages) is 26,365,000, accounting for 27.8% of the total number of students enrolled in rural areas. The percentages of primary school students and junior middle school students in rural areas studying in boarding schools were 14.4% and 58.6%, respectively. In the western region, these proportions are 21.1% and 67.1%, respectively.[5] Therefore, the challenge of promoting the integrated development of urban and rural education is enormous.

2.2   *Concern on Left-behind Children and Migrant Children*

Statistics show that in the process of rapid urbanization, the proportion of migrant workers' accompanying children who go to school in cities is constantly approaching the stay-behind rate. In 2015, among the compulsory education students nationwide, the proportion of migrant workers' children moving with them reached 40.37%, showing an increasing trend. In the same year, nearly

---

5 Wu Zhihui 邬志辉 "Zhongguo nongcun jiaoyu fazhan baogao 2016, 中国农村教育发展报告 2016 [China Rural Education Development Report 2016]," press release, December 26, 2016.

60% of children were staying behind. In 2015, 13.671 million children at the compulsory education stage moved to cities with their migrant-worker parents, which was 8.42% more than in 2011. Those students accounted for 30.3% of students in schools in urban areas. More than 80% of these students were enrolled in public schools. On the contrary, the number of left-behind children in rural areas is decreasing. in 2015, the number of left-behind children in China was 20.192 million, with a decrease of 8.23% (1,809,800) from 2011. Currently, the proportion of left-behind children among students in rural areas (townships and villages) remains between 27% and 30% and is slightly higher in junior middle school than in primary school.[6]

The central Government is showing concern for left-behind children in rural areas. The State Council issued the first government document on the education of left-behind children at the beginning of the year, namely *Opinions on Enhancing Care and Protection of Left-behind Children in Rural Areas* by the State Council. This document identifies the Ministry of Civil Affairs as the responsible department for this issue and establishes a system of inter-ministerial joint meetings on care and protection of left-behind children in rural areas, consisting of 27 departments and units. It emphasizes the primary responsibility of the family in the guardianship and care of left-behind children. It also sets out the goal of addressing both the superficial and the root causes of the issue of left-behind children, and gradually alleviating the problem from its source. To achieve that, the local government shall vigorously promote the localization of migrant workers, while at the same time guiding and supporting the return of migrant workers to their hometowns to start businesses and find job opportunities.

In November 2016, a joint inter-ministerial meeting announced the statistics of the left-behind children in rural areas: the total number of left-behind children in rural areas nationwide was 9.02 million in 2016. This was over 50 million fewer than the previous number of 61.02 million from the Sixth Population Census data in 2010. It was explained that the main reason for this decrease was a change in the scope. Previously, left-behind children in rural areas had been defined as "children under the age of eighteen with at least one parent away at work." This time, left-behind children in rural areas are defined as minors under the age of 16 whose parents are either both away for work, or one parent is away for work and the other is incapable of guardianship.

---

6 Wu Zhihui 邬志辉 "Zhongguo nongcun jiaoyu fazhan baogao 2016, 中国农村教育发展报告 2016 [China Rural Education Development Report 2016]," press release, December 26, 2016.

Although the proportion of children of migrant workers moving with them is slowly increasing, the policy of strict control of the migrant population in large cities has significantly squeezed the educational opportunities of migrant children in urban areas. The enrollment requirements for migrant children in many places has been raised significantly. Initiatives such as "Limiting Migrant Population through Education Opportunities" introduced in Beijing have abruptly tightened the enrollment for children of residents in Beijing with house registration in other cities. According to a survey, more than 65,000 students from migrant-worker families enrolled in primary schools in Beijing in 2016, with a decrease of about 28,000 compared to 2014. Many non-Beijing school-age children who cannot attend school in Beijing nor return to their hometowns choose to study in private schools in Hebei Province close to Beijing, forming an "education industry belt surrounding Beijing" mainly in cities and counties in Hebei. Migrant children have become "migratory students" who travel long distances between Hebei and Beijing every week.

As a basic public service provided by the Government, compulsory education is the most basic right of receiving education for migrant children. It is an important measure to prevent the intergenerational transmission of poverty, to prevent the solidification of social classes, and to alleviate poverty through education. It is imperative to strengthen the government's public service function, expand the supply of public education services in cities, and lower the enrollment requirements for migrant children. The rigid local population control policies of large cities not only undermine the right to receive education of migrant children, but are also detrimental to the sustainable and healthy development of large cities.

3 New Developments in Local Education System Innovations

China's educational transformation relies not only on top-down top-level design, but also on bottom-up local exploration and practice. In the education innovation practices around the nation, carrying out administrative reform to separate management, operation, and evaluation functions, and solving the long-standing problems of rural education has become noteworthy highlights.

3.1 *Promoting the Separation of Management, Operation, and Evaluation, and Improving the Quality of Education Governance*

With the goal of building a modern education governance system, the city of Qingdao has comprehensively implemented an itemized school management authority system. The city government issued a document proposing further simplification and decentralization of administration, implementation, and expansion of school-running autonomy. Specifically, the government sorted out the list of school management autonomy from three aspects: school cadres and personnel management, financial and infrastructure management, and teaching practice management. The new policy explicitly implemented and delegated management authority to schools in 14 aspects, such as the appointment of vice-principals, internal organization settings and the appointment of middle-level cadres, budget management of financial funds, internal allocation, and student recruitment. The *Measures for the Administration of Primary and Middle Schools in Qingdao City* is the first of its kind in China. In the Wuhou District of Chengdu, a reform of the management system of "school responsible for recruiting teachers and managing funding, and autonomous management" has been implemented in pilot schools. It has delegated to schools the authority to select and hire their own teachers, and has ensured teachers' performance pay through the "all-inclusive funding" system to provide teachers with more incentives. Qijiang District in Chongqing City promotes the autonomy of school districts, and has set up autonomous school district education committees composed of leaders of the district's communities and towns, deputies to the National People's Congress and members of the Chinese People's Political Consultative Conference, social celebrities, parents, and other representatives.

3.2   *Solving the Outstanding Problems of Rural Education*
Some noteworthy cases have emerged in the process of local educational reform, where locally adapted reforms have largely solved some of the long-standing problems plaguing rural education.

Yiyang County in Jiangxi Province has effectively reduced large-size classes in urban schools and solved the issue of "too many schools in cities, but no school in rural areas" by implementing series of measures, including establishing high-quality rural schools, standardizing enrollment process for urban schools, and encouraging rural students returning to hometowns. In 2015, compared with 2012, the number of students in rural schools had increased by 9,400, or 30.68%; the proportion of children left behind has declined, with more than 2,800 parents returned to their children in rural areas. By changing the evaluation system from focusing on the rate of advancement to an assessment of the "dropout rate" and the performance of the bottom 20% of students, the dropout rate in junior middle school in Yiyang County has been significantly reduced, and the proportion of students who finished three-year education in junior middle school has increased by 6.34%. Similarly, Shangli County in Jiangxi Province and Neixiang County in Henan Province have reduced the phenomenon of large-size classes in urban areas by strengthening their infrastructure foundations and running high-quality schools in rural areas.

In Luxi County, Hunan Province, a stipend system has been implemented to motivate rural teachers, with village primary school teachers receiving 14,400 yuan a year more than their urban counterparts. In addition, other measures have been implemented to effectively improve the benefits of rural teachers and retain rural teachers. Those measures included favorable policies in the appraisal system for rural teachers and low-rent housing construction for rural teachers.

Hunan Province is implementing a special training program for rural primary school teachers, which is targeted, free of charge, and aims to train excellent teachers who are willing to work in rural primary schools. Specifically, the program includes three types of tuition-free teacher-training programs: a four-year bachelor's degree program for students with high school degree; a five-year college program for students graduated from junior high school; and a six-year bachelor's degree program for students finished junior high school. Graduates are offered four types of opportunities: going back to the county, work in the township for students from counties, going back to the township, and work in learning centers for students from towns. Students from these teacher-training programs have solid knowledge foundations, comprehensive quality, and are willing to work in counties/towns, whom local people greatly welcome. This program has effectively solved the plight of rural teachers after the "secondary teachers' program" stopped, and can be called an upgraded version of the teacher-training system at the secondary school level.

Through its top-level governmental measures, Shandong Province has successfully broken through the bottleneck of the teacher staffing system. Specifically, on the basis of unified staffing standards for urban and rural primary and secondary schools, the government offered a favorable staffing policy for smaller-scale rural schools. For schools that do not have the standard class size, teachers are provided in accordance with the class teacher ratio; at the same time, the flexibility of staffing is increased, and advanced staffing and flexible staffing are implemented. In June 2016, Shandong Province completed the re-qualification and staffing of primary and secondary school teachers. Under the new policy of stuffing based on class teacher ratio, 37,600 more teachers are allocated to rural schools. The province's total increase in teachers is about 100,000.

4   Development and Reform of Higher Education

As the school-age population declines and university enrollment continues to expand, the total number of students enrolled in higher education reached 36.47 million in 2015, and the gross enrollment rate in higher education reached 40%, higher than the global average for middle- and high-income countries. In June 2016, China's higher engineering education formally joined the *Washington Accord* as the 18th member country. The *Washington Accord* is a multilateral accreditation agreement for undergraduate professional engineering academic degrees that promotes engineering technicians' international mobility through mutual recognition of degrees. Joining this agreement is a recognition of the quality of China's engineering education and an indicator of China's higher education going global.

According to the latest "World University Rankings" released by the QS Global Education Group, in 2016, 65 programs from 7 Chinese universities were ranked in the top 50, 15 more than in 2015. Meanwhile, academic programs from 88 universities were ranked in the top 400.[7] However, the outstanding problem in higher education is the fact that despite the massive scale of the universities, they are not strong enough in academics and research. The university education is still struggling to make the transition from a teaching-focused to a learning-focused classroom.

The public is most concerned about the fairness of higher education admissions and how to increase the proportion of rural students and expand the proportion of students enrolled in the central and western regions. From the 2016 higher education enrollment data, the situation continues to improve through the implementation of targeted enrollment programs for rural and impoverished areas and the adjustment of provincial enrollment allocations, among other measures. Through three special programs at the national, local, and university levels, 90,000 students from rural and impoverished areas were enrolled in higher education institutions, with an increase of more than 20% over 2015. Among the 3,300 students newly enrolled at Tsinghua University in 2016, nearly a quarter came from high schools at the county and sub-county levels. Through the "Strive for Success" program of the self-directed admissions at Tsinghua University and special national programs, 384 new students from

---

7   Zhang Jiawei 张家伟, "Zhongguo 7 gaoxiao 65 ge xueke jinru quanqiu qian 50, 中国7高校65个学科进入全球前50 [Seven Chinese Universities Have 65 Disciplines in the World's Top 50]," *China Education Daily*, March 24, 2016.

rural areas in central and western China were recruited, accounting for 10.2% of the total number of students enrolled.[8]

In 2016, 60,000 students were enrolled through the National Special Plan for Targeted Enrollment in Poverty-stricken Areas. Most of these students were admitted to "211 Project" universities. The college enrollment collaboration plan enrolled 210,000 students from central and western regions, including 140,000 college undergraduates. Those students were from 10 central and western provinces, including Henan, Guangxi, Guizhou, and Gansu, and they were admitted by higher education institutions in 14 provinces, including Beijing, Tianjin, and Jiangsu. Hubei and Jiangsu reduced their enrollment plans by 40,000 and 38,000, respectively. This triggered protests from parents in the two regions, resulting in a major mass incident. However, in fact, the reductions in both provinces are mainly for enrollment plans of private higher education and senior vocational schools, rather than of high-rated colleges or the key universities. The "higher education admissions reduction controversy" has disclosed the problems of regional imbalance of higher education resources and reflects educational governance problems due to incomplete information disclosure and untimely crisis response.

According to the national deployment, Peking University has implemented a comprehensive reform plan, carried out in five aspects: education system, personnel system, governance system, academic system, and resource allocation system. In terms of personnel reform, an attempt will be made to abolish the administrative level of faculty and department heads. Their positions will be delinked from the administrative level, and new recruitment procedures will be adopted. As the department and program heads are all professors with senior professional titles, their salaries will not be affected by abolishing their administrative levels. Therefore, the implementation of this reform will be relatively easy.

More substantial reform in the field of higher education is carried out by the icebreaker of Westlake University, which was founded by famous scientists such as Shi Yigong, academician of the Chinese Academy of Sciences and vice president of Tsinghua University. As the Westlake University's pathfinder, the Westlake Institute for Advanced Study was officially established, positioning itself as a world-class institute of higher education to train doctoral students. The Westlake University, under construction, draws on the scale of the California Institute of Technology and the education philosophy of Stanford

---

8 Wan Yufeng, 万玉凤 "Qinghua: jin 1/4 xinsheng laizi xianji yixia gaozhong, 清华：近1/4新生来自县级以下高中 [Tsinghua: Nearly 1/4 of New Students Come from High Schools below County Level]," *China Education Daily*, August 18, 2016.

University to cultivate innovative and multi-disciplinary talents. The funding sources are mainly donations from foundations and some government subsidies, as well as related education and research funds.

The preparation for West Lake University is one example of the private school-running fever. In recent years, entrepreneurial enthusiasm for running schools has been very strong. A few years ago, Yu Minhong of New Oriental Education took over the Geng Dan College, an independent college of Beijing University of Technology. Chen Yidan, the main founder of Tencent, acquired the Wuhan College, an independent college of the Central South University of Finance and Economics and Law. In 2015, Wuhan College was approved to separate from its parent university and turned into a private undergraduate university, becoming the country's first private university of a public welfare nature. At the beginning of the year, the Lakeside University, organized by Jack Ma and targeted at entrepreneurs, was also in vogue. Ma claims that Lakeside University is not to teach entrepreneurs how to make money, but to discover and train entrepreneurs in the new business civilization era. These new universities, each with its own ambitions and promising prospects, show the tremendous enthusiasm and energy that exists among the public in running schools.

5 Towards the Modernization of Educational Governance and Values

At the end of 2016, the State Council passed the *National Thirteenth Five-Year Plan for the Development of Education*, which calls for continued prioritization of education development. Specifically, the Plan covers topics including the promotion of educational equity, promotion of education and teaching reform, optimization of the education structure, expansion of openness and cooperation in education, encouraging social forces and private capital to run schools and educational institutions, cultivating talents to work for the country, and promoting the modernization of education.

According to the *Outline of China's Medium- and Long-term Education Reform and Development Plan (2010–2020)*, adopted in 2010, China will "generally complete education modernization" by 2020. This goal is a major challenge for China's education. Although China has entered the stage of universalization of education and popularization of higher education, with globalized and Internet-friendly education, our education governance is still trapped in the dual system of urban-rural divide, and actual education and teaching are still on the track of examination-oriented education. Rural education not only needs to "fill in the gaps," but also suffers from confusion and imbalance in the development model. The huge development gap between urban and rural areas constrains the improvement of equity and quality of education. The co-existence of examination-oriented education and innovative education, together with the intertwining of various contradictions and problems, leads to a strong contrast between education's ideal and reality.

In the face of the huge disparity between urban and rural education, we need to continue to emphasize the importance of educational equity. In addition, we need to meet the basic educational needs of rural students, and make up for the outstanding deficiencies of rural education. At the same time, we need to break away from examination-oriented education as soon as possible. Instead, we need to meet the challenges of worldwide educational innovation in the knowledge economy and Internet era. In that way, we can promote educational equity through educational innovation. Within and outside the public education system, education innovations are gradually developing from the bottom up. We can already see the prospect of educational reform. We need to forge a consensus on future-oriented ideas and facilitate the formation of a new educational reality through sustained educational reform. This requires efforts in two aspects: modernization of educational governance and modernization of educational values.

The core theme of deepening comprehensive reform in the field of education and promoting the modernization of the education governance system and governance capacity is to restructure the relationship between the government, schools, and society. The government's role should move from management to governance. Specifically, we need to establish a new education governance structure under the subject of multiple interests through the institutional innovation of "separation of management, operation, and evaluation," which includes entrusted management, purchase of services, and third-party evaluation. It is essentially a reform of the devolution of power from the government to the schools and the society, minimizing the government's management of micro affairs and implementing the schools' autonomy.

Currently, meeting people's demand for high-quality education is to a large extent translated into a demand for individualized, diversified education. This requires the reform of the primary and secondary school system and the fostering of an environment conducive to the emergence of educational expertise and innovation in education, resulting in a move towards educator-run schools. An important aspect of this is to offer more flexibility in running schools and significantly lower the requirements for running schools. The government should support innovation and entrepreneurship in education in the same way that micro and small businesses are supported in the economy. The running of micro- and small-scale schools and homeschooling should be legalized. Against the backdrop of the disappearance of the demographic dividend, there is a particular need to unlock the education dividend through institutional innovation, freeing up educational productivity and improving the quality of education and the population's competence.

What needs to be recognized is that we face not only the challenge of 2020, but also the challenge of 2030 – the challenge from the future. In December 2015, UNESCO published an article: *Rethinking Education: Towards a Global Common Good?* The article proposed to redefine knowledge, learning, and education, indicating a worldwide renewal of educational values. The report is critical of the utilitarian and economistic values that have long dominated education: "The economic functions of education are undoubtedly important, but we must go beyond the strictly utilitarian vision and the human capital approach that characterizes much of international development discourse. Education is not only about the acquisition of skills; it is also about values of respect for life and human dignity required for social harmony in a diverse world." The report emphasizes that education should be based on humanism, with respect for life and human dignity, equal rights and social justice, respect for cultural diversity, international solidarity, and shared responsibility for a sustainable future. "Sustaining and enhancing the dignity, capacity, and welfare of the human person, in relation to others and nature, should be the fundamental purpose of education in the twenty-first century."

For education in China, this rethinking is even more pertinent. We must clean up the strong economicism and utilitarianism. Here, utilitarianism refers to the utilitarianism of the state, which uses human beings as tools, and the utilitarian value of education for individuals as a tool to seek social status in the context of developmentalism and human capital. Returning to the roots and moving towards a human-centered education requires restoring the purpose of education to nurture people, thus establishing the core role of education in society, and making education human-centered.

CHAPTER 2

Reform of the Basic Education System in a Context of Diverse Opinions

Yang Mingquan[1] and Gong Pengfei[2]

Abstract

"Education system" is short for "school education system", which is the product of modern school education development. In recent years, with the advancement of education reform in China, the topic of reform of the education system has been raised frequently. The education system established in 1951 is no longer suitable for the current status quo of China's social modernization and educational development. Therefore, the formulation and promulgation of a new education system have become the consensus on the reform of the education system in academia. The reform of the education system, with the establishment of a lifelong education system as its foresight, needs to clarify the historical context of the development and history of the education system, borrow from the experience of foreign education system reform, and carry out the diversified experiment under local conditions.

Keywords

basic education – reform of the education system – 633 education system – international perspective

The education system, which is short for the school education system, is a product of modern school education development. The education system covers the system of schools of all levels and types and defines their nature, tasks, conditions for admission, years of study, and the vertical and horizontal

---

[1] Yang Mingquan 杨明全, Doctor of Education, Associate Professor, Graduate School of International and Comparative Education, Beijing Normal University.
[2] Gong Pengfei 龚鹏飞, Master's student, Graduate School of International and Comparative Education, Beijing Normal University.

relations between them. At the stage of basic education, different education systems have emerged based on different years of schooling. With the advancement of education reform in China, the education system's reform has become an important topic of concern, and the discussion on the reform of the education system has shown a diversified pattern of discourse.

1   Formulation of the Issue

The education system is the basic system for basic education, which has undergone reform and change as society has developed. During the first three decades of the new China, the education system's reform was very active, with diverse explorations. In recent years, due to the serious problems of examination-oriented education, overburdened students, and the need to cultivate innovative talents, the issue of education system reform has been raised frequently. In the early 1990s, Qian Xuesen, a famous scientist, proposed the idea of "General Wisdom Education," which aimed to shorten the years of schooling, develop the full learning potential of young people, and cultivate highly intelligent and innovative talents. His education system plan was an 8-year continuous system for primary education for students aged 4 to 12 years old and followed by high school and university studies combined for 12- to 17-year-olds. The last year was for "internship" when students were to learn to become an expert in an industry and write a graduation thesis.[3] In recent years, the focus of China's basic education reform has been on curriculum reform, but the issue of reforming the education system has been raised from time to time. In 2011, Gu Mingyuan wrote an article pointing out that the education system established in 1951 is no longer suitable for current societal requirements. And, it is urgent to re-examine and develop a new education system to reflect the concept of lifelong education.[4] Liang Jianzhang, a well-known Chinese demographer, advocated reforming the current education system, proposing shortening secondary education to four years. He believed that this change would inject new vitality into China's innovation

---

3   Qian Xuemin 钱学敏, "Qian Xuesen dacheng zhihui jiaoyu de shexiang, 钱学森大成智慧教育的设想 [Qian Xuesen's Vision of General Wisdom Education]," *Guangming Daily*, October 16, 2008.
4   Gu Mingyuan 顾明远, "Xuexiao zhidu jidai yanjiu gaige, 学校制度亟待研究改革 [The Urgent Need for Research and Reform on Education System]," *Journal of Education*, Issue 3, 2011.

and entrepreneurship by advancing work by two years and adding "golden time" to professional life.[5]

During the 2016 "National People's Congress and Chinese People's Political Consultative Congress," CPPCC National Committee member Mo Yan spoke on the reform of the education system during a group discussion, arguing that the current schooling years from preschool to graduate school education is too long, and basic education accounts for too much. He proposed to shorten the primary and secondary schooling years from 12 years to 10 years, and abolish the secondary school entrance examinations and secondary school examination. As a result, students would be allowed to grow up healthily in a continuous learning environment.[6] This opinion triggered a great debate in the education sector and even the whole society. In March and July 2016, the 21st Century Institute of Education held two seminars on the education system reform, where experts and scholars exchanged different views and formed some consensus.

The education system's reform is an important matter, involving the school life of hundreds of millions of students and the quality of basic education in the country as a whole. Therefore, it requires thorough discussion and scientific decision-making. It is necessary to clarify the concept of the education system and the history of the development of the system, and to learn from the experience of foreign education system reform.

2   International Comparative Perspectives on the Reform of the Basic Education System

2.1   *General Overview of the Education System by Country*

At present, there are two main camps of basic education systems in countries around the world in terms of the division of schooling periods: the "6-3-3" system of education in the United States, which can be called the "U.S. model"; and the "British model," where the education system is based on the division of key stages.

The U.S. model of the 6-3-3 system of education, which comprises six years of elementary school, three years of middle school, and three years of high

---

5   Liang Jianzhang 梁建章, "Zhongxue jiaoyu yinggai jiasu, suoduan, 中学教育应该加速、缩短 [Secondary Education Should be Accelerated and Shortened]," Humanism Economics Society Wechat Official Account: HES2012, June 12, 2016.

6   Mo Yan 莫言, "Jianyi zhongxiaoxue xuezhi cong 12nian gaicheng 10nian, 建议中小学学制从12年改成10年 [Primary and Secondary Schooling Years Proposed to be Changed from 12 to 10 Years]," Legal Evening News, March 4, 2016.

school, is not the mainstream. In the U.S., there are many other education systems, such as 5-4-3, 5-3-4, etc. The situation is similar in other countries, such as France, which has primarily adopted a 5-4-3 system. South Korea and Japan have a predominantly 6-3-3 system, and Australia has a predominantly 6-4-2 system.

Unlike the U.S. model, primary and secondary education in England is divided into five key stages: (1) Key Stage 1 (KS1) is primary education for children aged 5–7 (i.e., Years 1 and 2); (2) Key Stage 2 (KS2) is also primary education for children aged 7–11 (i.e., Years 3, 4, 5 and 6); (3) Key Stage 3 (KS3) is a secondary education stage for students aged 11–14 (i.e., Years 7, 8 and 9); (4) Key Stage 4 (KS4) is also a secondary education stage for students aged 14–16 (i.e., Years 10 and 11); and (5) Key Stage 5 (KS5) is a college preparatory stage for students aged 16–18 and is equivalent to years 12 and 13. Influenced by the British model, many countries around the world have set their own education system on this basis, such as Singapore's primary and secondary schools have a total of 13 years, of which six years for primary school, 4–5 years for secondary school, and 2–3 years for junior college (equivalent to senior high school). In India, the education system is the 8-2-2 system, which consists of 8 years of primary school, two years of junior high school, and two years of senior high school.

In terms of the number of years for primary and secondary schooling, the basic education system varies from country to country around the world. The report of the International Conference on Education (ICE), organized by UNESCO at its forty-first session in 1989, published a survey of the education system in 199 countries. The results of the survey are as follows.

TABLE 2.1   The National Education System Survey at the 41st International Conference on Education

Total schooling years	Total number of countries (%)	Number of developed countries (%)	Number of developing countries (%)
10 years	10 (5.0%)	3 (7.5%)	7 (4.4%)
11 years	28 (14.1%)	4 (10.0%)	24 (15.1%)
12 years	107 (53.8%)	21 (52.5%)	86 (54.1%)
13 years	47 (23.6%)	10 (25.0%)	37 (23.3%)
14 years	7 (3.5%)	2 (5.0%)	5 (3.1%)
Total	199	40	159

Note: Wang Weiya 王维娅, *The Theory and Practice of Basic Education*, Shandong Education Publishing House, 1999.

It can be seen from this result that 77.4% of the countries in the world have adopted 12 or 13 years of education, which is more than three quarters. However, the proportion of countries that have adopted ten years of education is 5.0%, which is a small portion. Therefore, the idea of shortening the primary and secondary education system to 10 years is not supported by the international educational practice.

2.2   The History and Change of the American Education System

The United States was a colony of Great Britain and for a long time had a dual system of schooling following the British. With the end of the Civil War and the completion of the Industrial Revolution, the demand for a better-quality workforce increased, which led to the "public school movement" and the move from a dual-track to a single-track education system. At that time, the public education system formed the 8-4 and 6-6 systems of education. The 8-4 system referred to eight years of primary and four years of secondary school, while the 6-6 system referred to six years of primary schooling and six years of further study in a comprehensive secondary school. The two systems differed only in terms of the division of stages; the curriculum and the form of instruction were the same. At the primary school level, one teacher was responsible for teaching all subjects in a class. At the secondary school level, teaching is divided into subjects.

The problem of the 8-4 system of education was the overly lengthy of primary school. As a result, many students found it challenging to complete eight years of schooling, leading to a high drop-out rate in primary schools. For the 6-6 system of education, the long schooling years of secondary school have led to too many secondary school students and overcrowding in secondary schools. Under these circumstances, American educator Charles W. Eliot proposed shortening the number of years of elementary schooling. With expert opinions and experimental testing, in 1905, most of the United States established the 6-3-3 system of education, where mathematics, science, and foreign languages classes started in elementary schools. The establishment of the 6-3-3 system ensured that many students were exposed to the sciences and laid the foundation for the development of the United States during World War I and World War II periods.

In the 1960s, the "middle school" movement emerged in the United States. Since adolescents' psychological development between the ages of 10 and 14 is very different from that of students in both primary and secondary schools, schools catering to this age group were established. The types of middle schools were divided into two-year schools and three-year schools. Therefore, the original 6-3-3 system of education was divided into 6-2-4 or

5-3-4. Together with the former mentioned 6-3-3 system, 8-4 system, and 6-6 system, the U.S. education system has become very complex.

The coexistence of multiple education systems in the United States has both advantages and disadvantages. On the one hand, the education system can be adjusted according to local conditions. On the other hand, such a highly autonomous education administration has also led to unbalanced quality and uneven development of education in different states, which has long been a problem for educators in the U.S.

2.3   *Japanese Education System and Reform*

After World War II, Japan adopted the 6-3-3 system of education, which was under the influence of the United States. This became the primary education system for elementary and secondary schools in Japan. However, as time goes, the declining birthrate and aging of the population have put great pressure on Japanese society. This new situation has forced Japanese educators to rethink their education system.

Japanese schools are similar to those in the U.S., where one teacher teaches all subjects for a class at the elementary school level, while in junior high school, each teacher is only in charge of one subject. This difference makes it difficult for students to adapt to the transition from elementary school to junior high school. At the same time, Japan is known as a "testing hell" because of the pressure of academic competition. In junior high school, students are under great learning pressure. Teachers emphasize the mastery of knowledge and skills, with classroom study primary focus on listening to teachers and regular examinations. In addition, problems such as school bullying, declining birthrate, and the aging of population resulted in growing calls to change the 6-3-3 system of education in society.

In July 2014, the Council for the Implementation of Educational Renewal proposed to the prime minister to create an "elementary and junior high school continuous schooling system." There are two types of "elementary and junior high school continuous schooling system," the 6-3 system of education and the 4-3-2 system of education. Statistics show that, about 72% of schools use the 6-3 system, while 26% use the 4-3-2 system, and less than 3% of the remaining schools use other systems.

Since 2006, Shinagawa Ward in Tokyo has been a pioneer in exploring a continuous system of elementary and junior high schools. The elementary and junior high schools within the ward have adopted a continuous 4-3-2 system of education. Consistent with the characteristics of children's physical and mental development, the first to fourth grade focus on learning basic knowledge. The fifth to seventh grade focus on ability development. And the main learning objective for the eighth to ninth grade is cultivating independence. Each stage formulates its own teaching plan and curriculum. Starting from the fifth grade, different teachers teach different subjects, so that elementary students can gradually get used to junior high school learning, and the connection between elementary and junior high schools is strengthened. Most subjects in grade one to grade four are basic classes. For example, mathematics classes focus on basic concepts such as "number operations" and "measurement of quantity," while abstract concepts such as "negative numbers" are introduced in grade five. English learning is divided into three main stages, corresponding to each stage of the 4-3-2 system, which are "Get familiar with English," "Mastering English," and "Putting English to Use."[7]

Japan's "elementary and junior high school continuous schooling system," which has been in place for a relatively short period of time, has had some successes as well as some problems. Accompanied with a specially developed curriculum, many students have made academic progress. Since the "elementary and junior high school continuous schooling system" requires teachers to be capable of teaching both elementary and junior high school, the system encourages teachers to consider teaching objectives and students' capacity development over a relatively long period of time, which will be beneficial to the long-term development of children. Currently, only 60% of teachers meet the dual teaching requirement. The "elementary and junior high school continuous schooling system" has several problems. First and foremost, the issue of educational equity. The strong alliance among high-quality primary and junior high schools under the "continuous system" makes it more difficult for children to enter high-quality junior high schools. Students compete for admission to elite schools, leading to worse students' quality and reputation for average schools. As a result, the gap between elite schools and average schools are getting wider. Secondly, while the gradual progression of student learning has improved under the "continuous system" compared to before, many schools are teaching students contents of later grades, which is not a good thing for students. Finally, being in a familiar environment for a long time, interpersonal relationships are solidified, resulting in more school bullying incidents.

---

7   Sun Jinlu 孙晋露 "Riben zhongxiaoxue xinxuezhi gaige tanjiu – yi "chuxiao yiguanzhi" jiaoyu de zhiduhua wei zhongxin, 日本中小学新学制改革探究——以 "初小一贯制" 教育的制度化为中心 [An Investigation of the New Education System Reform in Japanese Elementary and Secondary Schools – Focusing on the Institutionalization of the "Elementary and Junior High School Continuous Schooling System"]," *Comparative Education Research*, Issue 12, 2015.

3 Evolution and Reform of China's Current Basic Education System

The establishment of the modern education system in China began in the late Qing Dynasty with the exploration of the "Gui Mao Education System" as the first formally implemented education system in modern China. In 1912, the Provisional Government of the Republic of China in Nanjing promulgated the "Ren Zi Gui Chou Education System." Under this system, children started school at the age of 6 and graduated from college at the age of 23 or 24. The entire course of study was divided into three stages and four grades. Its most important feature was the shortening of the school year, with junior primary, higher primary, and secondary schools each being shortened by one year compared to the late Qing dynasty's Gui Mao Education System. This shortened the previous 25–26 years of schooling to 17–18 years.

After the May Fourth Movement, a new education system was established in 1922 based on the 6-3-3 system of education of the United States, known in history as the "Ren Xu Education System." This education system highlighted the role of secondary education, changing the duration of secondary education from four years to six years, followed by the division of middle school into two levels, junior high and senior high school. It also introduced a subject selection system and a subject division system in middle schools. The duration of basic education was reduced to 12 years. This education system is still in use today.

Since the founding of New China, the central government has carried out many experiments and reforms of the education system. In 1950, the Ministry of Education implemented the reform of the "five-year continuous education system" in Beijing Experimental Primary School. In 1951, the State Council of the Central Government published the *Decision on Reforming the Education System*, in which it was decided to implement the five-year continuous education system in primary schools. In addition, the distinction between four-year-junior and two-year-senior primary schools was abolished, and the primary schools were no longer divided into two stages. Students entered junior high school at the age of 12, with three years of schooling at this stage. This reform was to a large extent following the former Soviet Union's education system. However, the reform was not complete, and the six-year primary education system was later restored.

From the "Education Revolution" in 1958 until the "Cultural Revolution" started, experiments on many education systems had been implemented in various regions of China, including the five-year continuous system for primary schools, the five-year continuous system for secondary schools, the five-year, nine-year and ten-year continuous system for primary and secondary schools, the 9-2 system of education for primary and secondary schools, the 4-2 system of education for junior and senior high schools. In 1961, an experiment was carried out for the 10-year continuous education system for primary and secondary schools.

After the end of the Cultural Revolution, the ultra-leftist ideology was purged, and the 6-3-3 system of education was reinstated. However, in many areas, the 5-4 system of education continues to be maintained, with five years of primary school and four years of junior high school. After the beginning of the 21st century, with the implementation of the "General Nine Years of Compulsory Education," fewer and fewer places still adopted the 5-4 system of education. Most regions, as well as the railway and petroleum systems, switched to the 6-3 system of education.

At present, most regions in China follow the 6-3-3 system of education, while some regions, such as Shanghai, still implement the 5-4 system. In 2003, Beijing and other cities had begun experimenting with the nine-year continuous education system, whereby primary and secondary schools can choose between the 5-4 and 6-3 systems under the premise of nine-year compulsory education.

4 Proposals for the Reform of the Education System for Basic Education

The formulation and promulgation of a new education system have become the consensus of the academic community on the reform of the education system. The current education system, established in 1951, reflected the economic and social development of the early years of the founding of the People's Republic of China and was no longer suitable for the current modernization of Chinese society and education development. The new education system should adapt to the development of the current society and establish a lifelong education system.

4.1 Shortening the Number of Schooling Years Is Not the Main Objective of the Education System's Reform

In recent decades, from Mao Zedong to Deng Xiaoping and Qian Xuesen, the main demand for reform of the education system has been to shorten the schooling years so that talents can be cultivated in a relatively short time. It is believed that the twelve years of primary and secondary school, plus undergraduate and graduate school (i.e., 16–20 years of study in total), are too long, which can definitely be shortened. The reality of examination-oriented education in primary and secondary schools, where the third years of junior and senior high school are basically devoted to studying and training for exams, adds to the view that too much time is spent on the study that destroys students and wastes their lives.

However, the fact that in most countries around the world, the primary and secondary education last 12 years tells us that a 12-year basic education system is in line with the development of children. Modern physiological and psychological research has shown that human development is a relatively slow process and that schooling needs to follow children's development needs. In contrast to the rapid changes in the world, there is no evidence that children's growth and development stages have been significantly altered, both in terms of their physical, psychological, personality, and cognition development. It may be true that the process of knowledge acquisition alone can indeed be accelerated, with six years of schooling completed in five years or less in primary school. However, we should be aware that the goal of primary and secondary education is not only academic, but also, more importantly, character formation, moral development, and the shaping of socially qualified citizens. All these goals cannot be achieved with "compressed" crash courses. The mismatch between the intellectual and personality development of some "gifted children" is a good example to show that. If the schooling years are shortened, adolescents would graduate from schools and enter society prematurely, which would be inappropriate.

Experts believe that the length of the education system does not cause problems such as academic burden and wasted time, and that shortening the schooling years will not solve these problems. Under the examination-oriented education system, even if the 12 years of basic education were shortened to ten, eight, or even six years, there would still be two years devoted to testing training. This highlights another problem with the education system in China: the division of 12 years of basic education into primary, junior high, and senior high school, with too many stages and selection processes, has intensified competition in education and led to a lack of continuity in talents cultivation.

4.2 *The Key to the Reform of the Education System is How to Segment the Education Stages. Diverse Experiments Are Needed for This Issue*

The consensus of experts is that only shortening schooling years is narrowing the task of educational reform. The education system's reform needs to pay more attention to how the education system is segmented and how to adjust the talent cultivation system coherently and flexibly.

It has been suggested that, ideally, a "12-year continuous education system" would be preferable. At present, it is more feasible to implement the "nine-year continuous education system." One of its advantages is the abolishment of the junior high school entrance exam. In this way, children won't need to spend one year to prepare for the junior high school entrance exam. In addition, children can receive a more coherent education and achieve continuous development. The newly built schools in Haidian District, Beijing, have all adopted the nine-year continuous mode of operation, including the consistent cooperation of the main campus and other campuses. No separate primary or junior high schools are allowed on any of the new campuses.

The reform of the education system need not always follow the same rule. Instead, we should encourage diverse exploration of the reform to try out different systems of continuous education, as well as other ways to divide up the schooling stages. Professor Gu Mingyuan believes that the 5-4 system of education is more reasonable. If junior high school was changed to four years, students could take more comprehensive vocational classes, which will meet the requirement of direct employment of junior high school graduates. Also, with the early onset of puberty and the complex and special educational mission of adolescent years, it would be appropriate to classify sixth-grade students as junior high school students and to change the three-year junior high education system to a four-year one.

Experts believe that the reform of the education system should match the country's development, the overall trend of world science and technology, and the development of world education. The new education system should adapt to the new era of the educational system characterized by inquiry, modernity, digitalization, and selectivity. Diversification of high school education, the selectivity of curricula, modernization of educational content, etc., are all worldwide trends. One of the features of the foreign education system's reform is to increase the number of years in high school. For instance, high schools in the United States are four years. Some countries are implementing a system of two years of college preparation after high school. Because students start thinking independently, begin to form a worldview, and establish independent judgment on various issues, the education system should give strong support for these developments in the third year of junior high and high school. Some scholars suggest that the four years of senior high school can take the form of "3+1", the "+1" can have many flexible ways to increase the richness and selectivity of education. For example, In Hong Kong, the fourth year of senior high school is the college preparatory course. It is also possible for senior high school to remain for three years, but with "2-1 sub-stages", where the final year can be streamed into remain studying in the same school, switch to vocational education, study abroad, etc. Some senior high schools in Shanxi Province are experimenting with this approach. In Beijing, newly approved model high schools have adopted the 6-2-4 system of education for experimental classes, with primary school remaining at six years, two years for junior high school, and four years for senior high school. In this way, students do not have to take the high school entrance exams, reducing the need for competition in middle school exam preparation, and the junior and high school curricula and evaluation systems can be linked.

It was noted that many countries have multiple education systems rather than a single education system. For example, in the United States, 5-4-3, 6-3-3, 4-4-4 systems coexist, of which over 90% of senior high schools adopt the 4-4-4 system. Each state in the United States adopts a unified education system. Therefore, we could also consider the possibility of allowing for different education systems in different provinces of China. Since it is still difficult to determine which education system is better now, it is reasonable to conduct various experiments to compare and evaluate the different systems. Meanwhile, we should also build linkages between the various education systems.

Since changes to the basic education system involve a wide range of factors, including school buildings, teachers, curricula, teaching materials, management systems, etc., the education reform should also include other important aspects, such as the promotion of diversification and flexibility of the education system, the introduction of a credit system and a flexible education system, and allow talented students to skip a grade and graduate early.

4.3 *Reform of the Education System Should Be Oriented towards the Era of Lifelong Education*

Another focus of the education system reform is to respond to the educational streaming and to handle the relationship between general and vocational education. According to the requirement of "mutual communication between vocational education and general education" by the *National Plan for Medium- and Long-term Education Reform and Development* (2010–2020), education reform needs to be effectively integrated with the vocational education system and eventually establish a lifelong education system.

Currently, we see a decline in the number of students in senior high school, and vocational education is not attractive. And it is still difficult for students to attend senior high schools. It is a question of whether it is necessary to adjust the current ratio of 50% for general high schools and 50% for vocational schools. Another main concern for the education system reform is when it is more appropriate to divide the students into either general education or vocational education. The world trend is that the diversion between general education and vocational education is gradually moving to later years. Given the unbalanced economic and social development in different regions of China, the education system should be diverse and flexible. In most regions, the post-junior high school streaming is still appropriate; however, in the economically developed eastern regions, there may be a tendency to upgrade the basic workforce to high school graduates in line with the upgrading of industries and technology.

The number of years of study in vocational schools and the admissions system also need to be adjusted accordingly, with more flexibility. Some majors, such as preschool teaching majors and elementary school teaching majors, can combine secondary vocational education with higher vocational education. For example, the "3+2" and "3+3" training models currently implemented in Hunan, Jiangxi, and other places include three years of high school and two years (or three years) of higher vocational education. Students are graduated with a college or bachelor's degree. These programs are very popular among students and employers. In addition, the duration of vocational high schools is not necessarily three years, but should also be somewhat flexible.

With a future-oriented view, the education system's reform should leave enough room for the formation of a lifelong education system. For example, training institutions, universities for the elderly, and other educational institutions in society can be incorporated into the education system. In this way, educational institutions for people at all life stages can be part of the education system. The future education system will not be an enclosed one, but an open system that embraces all forms of learning in society.

4.4 *Reform of the Education System Requires Scientific Decision-Making*

China's basic education system needs to be improved to keep pace with the social development, and reform of the system needs to be based on current conditions in China. The reform should also draw on foreign experience, and be developmentally appropriate for children and adolescents. We should carry out serious research on this topic, and decisions should be made based on scientific findings.

Therefore, the education system's reform cannot be carried out in a "one-size-fits-all" manner, but must be tailored to local conditions. We should encourage the local government to adopt different education systems in accordance with their own development and cultural and educational needs. Through experimentation, issues such as evaluation criteria, credits, and curricular switch between different education systems should be harmonized. The reform of the education system in rural areas needs to be more careful and prudent. The prerequisite for shortening the primary school learning period is high-quality preschool education. At present, rural preschool education is still facing many problems. Therefore, it is necessary to take opinions from many parties, make prudent decisions, and push forward on the basis of local experiments to reduce the cost of education system reform.

CHAPTER 3

Amendments of Law of the People's Republic of China on the Promotion of Privately-Run Schools and Their Impacts

Wu Hua[1] and Zhang Luhong[2]

Abstract

The revised *Law of the People's Republic of China on the Promotion of Privately-run Schools* has clarified the basic policy framework and reform pathway of the management by categories. Therefore, the policy environment for the development of privately-run schools in China has undergone major changes. The new *Law on the Promotion of Privately-run Schools* has made important revisions in terms of developing CPC organizations in privately-run schools, establishing the legal framework for management by categories, optimizing the governance structure of privately-run schools, improving the pension and benefits system for teachers in privately-run schools, and clarifying the basic approaches for the transform of the existing privately-run schools, etc. It has also made significant institutional changes in terms of clarifying the identity attributes, clarifying the property rights, easing the requirements for running for-profit privately-run schools, and relaxing price regulations. Under the legal framework of categorical management, the adjustment of the private education industry landscape is inevitable. Local policy innovation has great potential, and organizers of privately-run schools need to make prudent decisions. Nevertheless, the ultimate solution for privately-run schools to cope with changes in the external policy environment is to return to the essence of cultivating students and rely on internal development.

Keywords

Law of the People's Republic of China on the Promotion of Privately-run Schools – privately-run schools – tuition schemes – compensation schemes

---

1 Wu Hua 吴华 is a professor and doctoral supervisor, Director of the Center for Private Education Research at Zhejiang University, whose main research interests are education policy and private education.
2 Zhang Luhong 章露红 is a doctor of education at Zhejiang University and a lecturer at Zhejiang Normal University, whose main research interests are education policy and private education.

On November 7, 2016, the 24th Meeting of the Standing Committee of the 12th National People's Congress deliberated and passed the *Decision on Amending the Law of the People's Republic of China on the Promotion of Privately-run Schools*. *Law of the People's Republic of China on the Promotion of Privately-run Schools* (hereinafter referred to as The *Private School Promotion Law*) is a new milestone in the development of privately-run education in China and marks a significant change in the policy and legal environment for the development of privately-run education in China. The *Private School Promotion Law* will also have a substantial and far-reaching impact on the industry landscape, capital markets, private school organizers and principals, teachers, and students, as well as the administration.

1 Background and Main Elements of the Revision

1.1 *Basic Background to the Revision*

Since the reform and opening up of China, private education has developed into an important part of the socialist education system. As of 2015, there were 163,000 private schools nationwide, accounting for 31.8% of the total number of schools. The number of students in private schools reached 45.704 million, accounting for 17.6% of the total number of students nationwide. The number of students in private kindergartens, private primary schools, private junior high schools, private high schools, private junior vocational school (民办中职) and private colleges and universities accounted for 54.0%, 7.3%, 11.6%, 10.8%, 11.0% and 18.7% of the total number of students enrolled in each kind of schools nationwide, respectively. The development of private education has played an important role in increasing educational opportunity, improving education equity, improving education efficiency, stimulating education vitality, and promoting reform and innovations in education and teaching, talent training model, and school running mechanisms. While the scale and quality of private education have been steadily improving, the process of amending the *Private School Promotion Law* has begun. The revision's main objective was to promote the development of private education, and the basic feature of the revision was categorized management. A comprehensive understanding of the background to the revision of the *Private School Promotion Law* can be analyzed at the following three levels.

1.1.1 Several Systematic Issues of Private Education That Need to Be Regulated by National Legislation

From the macro development of policies and regulations on private education, many favorable policy signals have been released at the national level since the promulgation of the *National Plan for Medium- and Long-term Education Reform and Development* (2010–2020) (hereinafter referred to as the *Plan*). For example, the *Plan* gives new recognition to the importance of private education as "an important growth point for the development of education and an important force in promoting education reform." The Third Plenary Session of the 18th Central Committee of the Communist Party of China (CPC) explicitly proposes to encourage social forces to run schools through improvement on five aspects, including "government subsidies, government purchase of services, student loans, rewards funding, encouraging donations." These favorable macro policies have increased the confidence of governments at all levels in the development of private education, and have clarified the direction and path of reform and development of private education. However, at the same time, the vague legal status of privately-run schools, the unclear ownership of property rights, the unrealized system of reasonable profit returns, the chaotic accounting system, the failure to implement tax incentives, and the failure to enforce the equal legal status of privately-run schools and their stakeholder groups have all contributed to the survival and development issues of privately-run schools for a long time. These long-standing systemic problems stem from legal conflicts between the education sector and other sectors, as well as internal legal conflicts within the education sector. They are not only related to the failure of education administrations and organizers to administer and run schools following the law, but also associated with traditional social misconceptions about private education. Indeed, they mainly stem from the inadequacy of China's legal system for private education, and there is, therefore, an urgent need to improve the law on private education. In this way, major policies on private education development can be implemented based on laws.

1.1.2   There Is a Long History of Controversy over "Reasonable Profit Return" and Categorized Management

Categorized management is a major change to the country's roadmap on the development of private education, and is the core content of this amendment. There has been a long history of controversy in the industry over the categorized management of privately-run schools. During the legislative process of the *Private School Promotion Law* in 2002, there were debates on whether to manage privately-run schools by different categories or not. Such debate had continued until the *Private School Promotion Law* was finalized and the "reasonable profit return" system was decided. In 2009, during the formulation of the *Plan*, different views again confronted each other. The *Plan* finally made a compromise of "actively exploring the categorized management of for-profit and non-profit private schools and carrying out pilot projects of categorized management." There were two different views in the academic field regarding whether or not to fully implement the categorized management system. The first view was that "categorized management" has a practical basis around the globe. There is a practical need to use a categorized management system to solve the current systemic problems in China's reform and development of private education. The categorized management system will also allow the implementation of categorized support policies for private education and stimulate social donations to run private schools, and therefore, should be promptly and comprehensively implemented. The second group of voices believed that "categorized management" lacks theoretical preparation and practical basis in China. And that its full-scale implementation is not only inconsistent with the original intent of the *Plan*, but also incompatible with China's national situation of investing in schools. The categorized management system may lead to the withdrawal of a large number of existing privately-run schools and the deterioration of the development environment for for-profit private schools, forcing the vast majority of privately-run schools to be non-profit and thus lose the meaning of categorized management. Therefore, the implementation of the system should move forward gradually based on active exploration and piloting.[34]

The "reasonable profit return" system was considered to be one of the highlights of the old *Private School Promotion Law*, but it has not been effectively implemented in practice due to multiple reasons, such as the lack of policy support, resistance from government departments, conflicting social beliefs, and cumbersome operating procedures. On the one hand, the relevant government departments do not recognize the legal status of privately-run schools that require reasonable returns as non-profit organizations, and the tax benefits have not been offered to these schools, resulting in tensions between privately-run schools and the tax authorities. On the other hand, the vagueness and excessive flexibility of the definition of "reasonable returns" have led to questions on the reasonableness of the profit returns to private school organizers. Therefore, due to the vagueness and controversy over the "reasonable profit return" system, the draft amendment to the *Private School Promotion Law* made a major adjustment to "abolish the reasonable profit return."

3   Wang Wenyuan 王文源 "Minban jiaoyu dingceng zhidu sheji zhizheng, 民办教育顶层制度设计之争 [The Controversy over the Design of the Top System of Private Education]," *Higher Education Development and Evaluation*, Issue 4, 2014.
4   Wu Hua 吴华 "Chongxin renshi minban xuexiao "fenlei guanli" de liyou, 重新认识民办学校"分类管理"的理由 [Reasons for Reacquaintance of the "Categorized Management" of Private Schools]," *Education Economics Review*, Issue 2, 2016.

As to whether or not to abolish reasonable profit returns, the industry has had different views. Those who advocate the abolition pointed out that whether the "reasonable profit return" should be considered for-profit is not clearly defined, leading to failures in implementing many preferential policies and management measures. This actually hindered the enthusiasm of social capital to enter the education industry. The abolition of the "reasonable profit return" system, and the implementation of the categorized management system is not only the international common practice, but also protects the legitimate rights and interests of investors in the education industry. After abolishing the "reasonable profit return" system, the government can still support and promote the development of privately-run schools through tax incentives and public financial support funds. In fact, very few of the existing privately-run schools have chosen to request a "reasonable profit return," so the abolition of reasonable profit return will have little impact on the existing privately-run schools. Defenders of the reasonable profit return system claimed that the original intent of allowing school organizers to obtain reasonable profit returns is a state incentive for private school organizers, which is different from allowing them to make profits by running schools, and there is no contradiction between reasonable profit returns and their non-profit status. The reasonable profit return system has become "empty talk," not because the system itself does not work, but because the relevant departments have not fully implemented the *Private School Promotion Law* and its Implementing Regulations, and the lack of corresponding supporting policies. Given the long cycle of investment in the education industry, the sudden cancellation of reasonable profit return will make private school funders fall into the trap of "zero profit."[5]

1.1.3 Simultaneous Pilot of Local Categorized Management Reform

Following the *Plan*, which proposes "exploring the categorized management of for-profit and non-profit privately-run schools," comprehensive reform of private education and special reform of categorized management have been listed as important elements of the pilot work on the reform of the national education system. Shanghai, Zhejiang, Shenzhen, and Jilin International Studies University are responsible for the pilot reform of categorized management.[6]

5　Wang Wenyuan 王文源 "Minban jiaoyu dingceng zhidu sheji zhizheng, 民办教育顶层制度设计之争 [The Controversy over the Design of the Top System of Private Education]," *Higher Education Development and Evaluation*, Issue 4, 2014.

6　Zhang Luhong 章露红 "Zhongguo difang minban jiaoyuzhidu chuangxin yanjiu 中国地方民办教育制度创新研究 [Research on the Innovation of Local Private Education System in China]," Ph.D. dissertation, Zhejiang University, 2016.

Specifically, Zhejiang Province is responsible for the pilot comprehensive reform of private education, and Ningbo, Wenzhou, and Huzhou's Anji and Deqing counties are further designated as pilot areas. So far, only Wenzhou has made substantial progress in terms of the institutional framework and policy practice of categorized management among these pilot regions. While the various pilot areas have made varying progress on the reform, many non-pilot areas are also making "illegal innovation" – actively exploring categorized management. At present, Shaanxi, Hubei, Fujian, Shandong Weifang, Qingdao, Jinan, Suzhou, and Guiyang have all issued categorized management policies based on the "Wenzhou Program," in addition to the national deployment of "categorized management" pilot programs, forming several regional clusters of reform pilots. In terms of policy content, the localities exploring categorized management reform have basically constructed a differentiated policy system for for-profit and non-profit private schools, which is mainly reflected in the following three aspects. First, the categorized registration procedures for the two types of schools have been clarified. Second, different supporting policies have been introduced on property rights system, accounting system, tuition schemes, financial support from the government, tax incentives, land use, and credit loan support. Third, more public financial support and teacher support have been granted for non-profit privately-run schools. More favorable policies on teachers' social security, taxation, land, and loan are the basic policy guidelines for local categorized management reform.

Unfortunately, there is a lack of efficient communication between the State's good intentions of respecting local exploration and the top-level government. The new law does not incorporate the experience of local pilots on critical issues such as classification criteria. The "pilot program," represented by that implemented in Wenzhou, differs significantly from the "national program" in terms of classification criteria, most notably in terms of how to identify the property rights of non-profit private schools and whether organizers of non-profit private schools should be granted annual incentives while they run schools. According to the current design and practice of the categorized management policies around the country, most regions have established an incentives policy for the property rights of the organizers. Specifically, during the operation of the school, the organizers of private schools will receive incentives calculated based certain rate of the benchmark interest rate of bank loans for cumulative capital. When the school's termination happens, the private school organizers can be compensated with the remaining assets after the legal liquidation procedures, as long as the amount is no more than their capital contribution. In addition, after the organizers receive their cumulative capital contribution, they may also receive certain awards depending on the balance of the assets.[7] The authors have discussed in detail the policy risks of the "national program," such as the dilemma faced by the organizers and the risks of unanticipated withdrawal and institutional transition.[8] In the context of the new law, these pilot areas of categorized management reform will face even greater risks of the institutional transition.

1.2 Main Contents of the Revision

Comparing the legal framework of the old and new *Private School Promotion Law*, the current revision's main contents can be summarized in seven aspects as follows: (1) Developing CPC organizations in privately-run schools (Article 9 of the amendment). (2) Abolition of the provisions on "reasonable profit return" and "administrative measures for running private training institutions" (Articles 51 and 66 of the old *Private School Promotion Law*). (3) Establishing the legal framework for the categorized management of privately-run schools. A differentiated policy system was developed for the two types of privately-run schools, in terms of classification criteria, registration procedures, disposal of surplus assets, market entrance requirements, tuition management, governmental financial support, tax incentives, and land use policies (Articles 19, 38, 46, 47, 51 and 59 of the amendment). (4) Optimizing the governance structure of privately-run schools, requiring private schools to establish supervisory mechanisms; clarifying the right of organizers to participate in management in accordance with their bylaws; and establishing a system of information disclosure and credit files for privately-run schools (Articles 20 and 41 of the Amendment). (5) Improving the pension system for teachers in privately-run schools. Private schools are encouraged to pay supplementary pension insurance for their teaching staff following state regulations (Article 31 of the amendment). (6) Reiterate and refine some of the penalties for government and school violations of the law (Articles 62, 63, and 64 of the Amendment). (7) Clarifying the basic principles for the conversion of the existing privately-run schools, and authoring local government to formulate specific compensation and incentive programs (Amendment Bylaw).

---

7   For example, *the CPC Wenzhou Municipal Party Committee Wenzhou Municipal People's Government Opinions on Further Implementing the National Pilot Comprehensive Reform of Private Education and Accelerating Education Reform and Development* (Wenzhou Municipal Party Committee (2013) No. 63), Articles 20 and 22; *the People's Government of Zhejiang Province Opinions on Promoting the Healthy Development of Private Education* (Zhejiang Provincial Government (2013) No. 47), Article 6.

8   Wu Hua 吴华 and Zhang Luhong 章露红 "Dui minban xuexiao fenleiguanli "guojia fang'an" de zhengcefengxian fenxi, 对民办学校分类管理 "国家方案" 的政策风险分析 [Analysis of the Policy Risk of the "National Program" for the Classification and Management of Private Schools]," *China Higher Education Research*, Issue 11, 2015.

Based on the above analysis, a comparison of the differentiated policies of the two types of privately-run schools, which are at the core content of this amendment and which are of the greatest concern to the school organizers, is as follows.

TABLE 3.1 Comparison of policies related to for-profit and not-for-profit private schools under the legal framework of categorized management

Type of school Policy topics	For-profit	Not-for-profit
Registration	business legal person	Private non-enterprise units or legal persons of public institutions
Allocation of profits from running schools	Treatment under the *Company Law*	Organizers shall not receive proceedings from running schools
Distribution of surplus assets after school closure	Treatment under the *Company Law*	Continue to use for running non-profit schools
Tuition management	Market regulation, self-determination	The provincial government set regulations on tuition
Tax benefits	State-mandated tax benefits	Same tax benefits as public schools
Land use policy	Supply according to national regulations	The government can allocate land
Government support measures	Purchase of services, student loans, scholarships, leasing, transfer of idle state assets, etc.	In addition to what is mentioned above, the government can implement other incentives, including government subsidies, award funds, and donations.
Basic principles for the conversion of the existing privately-run schools	Privately-run schools established before November 7, 2016, to conduct financial liquidation, clarify property ownership in accordance with the law, and pay relevant taxes and fees; the specific measures shall be formulated by the local government of provinces, autonomous regions, and municipalities directly under the Central Government.	When a privately-run school established before November 7, 2016, terminates its operation, it shall, upon the application of the organizer, be given corresponding compensation or reward based on comprehensive consideration of the investment and obtaining a reasonable return. The specific measures shall be formulated by the province, autonomous region, or municipality directly under the Central Government.

2 Major Evolution of the Revision and Important Breakthroughs in the New Law

2.1 *Major Evolution of the Three Review Drafts*

The revision of the *Private School Promotion Law* took nearly five years from the initiation of the revision to the completion of the revision. The following are some of the key timelines and specific events.

In the course of the revision of the *Private School Promotion Law*, the three public review drafts have undergone significant evolution on certain key issues, and were widely debated, which deserves our attention.

TABLE 3.2 History of the amendment of the *Private Education Promotion Act*

Time	Event
July 2010	The *National Plan for Medium- and Long-term Education Reform and Development* (2010–2020) clearly states that "we will actively explore the categorized management of for-profit and non-profit privately-run schools."
September 2012	The Legislative Affairs Office of the State Council sought opinions from relevant parties on the *Package of Revised Proposals for Education Laws* drafted by the Ministry of Education.
September 5, 2013	The Legislative Affairs Office of the State Council released the *Draft Revised Package of Education Laws* (*Draft for Public Comment*) for public comment.
January 7, 2015	At its seventy-seventh executive meeting, the State Council discussed and passed the *Draft Package of Amendments to The Education Law*, which clearly states the management of privately-run schools by categories, and permits the establishment of for-profit private schools. The draft was submitted to the Standing Committee of the National People's Congress for consideration.
August 24, 2015	At the 16th meeting of the 12th National People's Congress Standing Committee, the *Education Law Package Amendment* (*Draft*) was put on the agenda of the National People's Congress Standing Committee meeting for the first time, and the legislative process started formally.

TABLE 3.2 History of the amendment of the *Private Education Promotion Act* (cont.)

Time	Event
December 27, 2015	The 18th meeting of the Standing Committee of the 12th National People's Congress conducted a second review of the *Draft Package of Amendments to Education Laws* and adopted amendments to the *Education Law* and the *Higher Education Law*, but deferred voting on the amendments to the *Law on the Promotion of Private Education*.
January 2016	The Legislative Affairs Commission of the Standing Committee of the National People's Congress publicly solicited comments on the second draft amendment to the *Law on the Promotion of Private Education*.
April 18, 2016	At its 23rd meeting, the Central Leading Group for Comprehensively Deepening Reform deliberated and passed the *Opinions on Developing CPC Organizations in Privately-run Schools (for Trial Implementation)*, the *Details for Implementing the Categorized Registration of Privately-run Schools*, and the *Details for Implementing the Supervision and Management of For-Profit Private Schools*.
November 7, 2016	The 24th meeting of the Standing Committee of the 12th National People's Congress (NPC) deliberated and approved the decision on amending the *Law on the Promotion of Private Education* with 124 votes in favor, seven votes against, and 24 abstentions. The revised *Law on the Promotion of Private Education* came into effect on September 1, 2017.

2.1.1 Definition of Attributes from "Legal Person" to "School"

In the first draft, the types of legal persons and registration procedures for the two types of privately-run schools are as follows: privately-run schools may voluntarily choose to register as non-profit or for-profit legal persons, and enjoy the corresponding preferential policies in accordance with their registered type. Currently, the *General Principles of Civil Law (draft)* has not yet been adopted, and the current *Civil Law* only covers four types of legal persons, including organs, institutions, social organizations, and enterprises; hence it is not appropriate to put forward for-profit and non-profit "legal person" in the *Private School Promotion Law*. Therefore, according to suggestions from some scholars, the relevant expressions in the second and third drafts of the *Private School Promotion Law* have been changed to "the organizers of privately-run schools may voluntarily choose to establish non-profit or for-profit privately-run schools."[9]

2.1.2 From Ambiguity to Clarity in Classification Criteria and Differentiated Supporting Policies

With regard to the criteria for classifying the two types of schools and the policy preferences they enjoy, the first draft is very vague and inadequate, failing to clarify the property rights for the distribution of the school-running profits and surplus assets of the two types of schools, nor to specify the differentiated supporting policies for the two types of schools in terms of tuition, taxation, land use and financial support. Although the second and third drafts still fail to clarify the registration of legal persons and tax benefits for for-profit private schools, they have basically established a categorized management framework for the two types of schools, with clear requirements for their classification criteria and the respective supporting policies they enjoy. This is important for guaranteeing and implementing the legal status and legitimate rights and interests of the two types of private schools.

2.1.3 Setting up Restrictions for Running For-Profit Private Schools

There has been considerable disagreement in the academic community regarding whether or not-for-profit private schools shall be allowed to be established during the compulsory education stage. In the amendment to the new *Education Law* implemented on June 1, 2016, it is only stipulated that "schools and other educational institutions involved with government financial funds or donated assets shall not be established as for-profit organizations" (Article 26, paragraph 4). There is no prohibition on the establishment of for-profit schools in the compulsory education stage. In the second draft, there is no prohibition on establishing for-profit schools in the compulsory education stage either. It is clear that until the publication of the second draft, full permission for the establishment of for-profit private schools was the amendment's mainstream idea. However, in the third draft, there was a provision that "no for-profit private schools for compulsory education shall be established," which caused intense debate among supporters and opponents.

---

9 Wu Hua 吴华 "Dui minbanjiaoyu cujinfa xiudingan zhong yige falvgainian de jiuzheng 对〈民办教育促进法〉修订案中一个法律概念的纠正 [Correction of A Legal Concept in the Revision of the *Private School Promotion Law*]," (amendment proposal to the Law Committee of the National People's Congress).

2.1.4 De-emphasize Transition Period, Clarify Reasonable Compensation

With regard to the "transition period," the second draft set a three-year transition period, while the third draft removed this hard deadline. When answering the media's question, an official from the Ministry of Education explained that a unified transition period is removed, so that local governments and educational department authorities may resolve relevant issues practically based on local situations. Policies will be put-forth according to each school's situation in order to appropriately solve issues related to the reform of categorized management. The revised decision to take effect from September 1, 2017, does not mean that existing private schools are required to make choices before then, but to leave adequate time for localities to develop specific measures to ensure that the reform is carried out in a smooth and orderly manner. Some scholars also believe that the absence of a transition period is to leave room for local governments to be creative, and that they can decide the length of the preparation period according to the local situation, without having to complete the changes within three years.[10] However, we need to be aware that by September 1, 2017, the old law will be repealed and the new *Private School Promotion Law* will come into force, and all privately-run schools will be regulated by the new law. Therefore, although there is no explicit transition period, there is still a time limit, which poses a big challenge for local governments to introduce categorized management supporting policies and specific compensation and incentive schemes.

With regard to "reasonable compensation," the second draft stipulates that schools that make adjustments during the transition period, regardless of for-profit or not-for-profit, may, upon application, receive a one-time reasonable compensation from the balance of the school's financial liquidation of remaining assets. In the third draft, the recipient and principle of reasonable compensation are not clearly regulated. In order to respect history and current national conditions, recognize the social contribution of existing private schools and deal with the complicated property rights of them, we should take a strategy that compensates and rewards all for-profit and non-profit private schools in the same way in accordance with the principles of non-retroactivity and equality of the law. However, the new law only clarifies that private schools that choose to operate on a non-profit basis can receive compensation or rewards upon the termination of their operations. In contrast, the new law

---

10 Wang Feng 王烽 "Renhe xinzheng dou xuyao Shijian qu jianyan 任何新政都需要时间去检验 [Any New Policy Needs Time to Be Tested]," *News of People's Political Consultative Conference (Education Online Weekly)*, November 9, 2016.

provides that private schools that choose to operate on a for-profit basis "shall have clear property rights in accordance with the law," leaving no explanation on whether or not they can receive reasonable compensation. In addition, for private schools that choose to terminate their operation without deciding on for-profit or non-profit, the new law does not make any comments on whether they can receive reasonable compensation. Apart from that, the timeline for non-profit private schools to receive compensation and incentives for termination is unclear in the new law. Private schools can either amend their statutes to continue operating or immediately start the termination process.

2.2　*Major Breakthroughs in the New Law*

Compared to the legal framework of the old law, the new *Private School Promotion Law* has achieved significant institutional changes in at least the four areas, when examined from the strategic perspective of attracting private funds to the education sector and promoting the healthy development of private education.

2.2.1　Clarify the Legal Identity of Privately-Run Schools

Within the framework of the old *Private School Promotion Law*, the issue of legal identity was considered the primary obstacle and source of problems plaguing the development of private education. There are two main aspects: first, all privately-run schools are required to register with the civil affairs department as private non-enterprise units, but the legal status of "private non-enterprise units" fails to dovetail with the supremacy law. As a result, privately-run schools were embarrassingly not recognized under any enterprise categories in terms of related policies and benefits. Secondly, the old *Private School Promotion Law* classified private schools in two different ways. That is, private schools were divided into two categories: non-profit private schools and business training institutions. In addition, they are managed according to two categories: those requiring reasonable returns and those not requiring reasonable returns. However, due to various factors such as the lack of support from the policy, it is common for these two types of schools to carry out profit-making activities and receive returns, even if they claimed themselves to be non-profit and not requiring reasonable returns. The new law clarifies the criteria for classifying for-profit and not-for-profit privately-run schools and the related policies they will enjoy, removing the ambiguity in distinguishing the two types of schools. As the review of the draft *General Principles of Civil Law* proceeds, the legal personality of the two types of privately-run schools will be further clarified, and the work of classification and registration will progress in parallel.

2.2.2   Clarifying the Property Rights System of Privately-Run Schools

The property rights system is a major and practical issue for the long-term development of private education. Within the old *Private School Promotion Law* framework, the property rights of privately-run schools are vague. Specifically, first, during the operation of privately-run schools, it is common for the property rights of legal persons to be left vacant; second, after the termination of a privately-run school, the ownership of the assets invested by the organizer, the accumulation of school running funds and the remaining assets after liquidation are unclear. The lack of clarity in the property rights system had led to improper management of school assets, a setback in the motivation of school operators, and restrictions on the entry of social capital into the education sector. In accordance with the basic principles of categorized management, the new law clearly defines the owner of property rights and the boundaries of property rights for the two types of privately-run schools. In particular, for privately-run schools established after the revision of the law, the property rights system shall set up according to the classification criteria of for-profit and non-profit schools. For privately-run schools established before the revision of the law, the local authorities are responsible for formulating specific implementation measures for the disposal of assets upon their transfer.

2.2.3   Easing Restrictions for For-Profit Privately-Run Schools

Within the old *Private School Promotion Law* framework, there has been a long-standing contradiction between the legal position of private schools as "schools run for the public good" and the general "profit-making intentions" of the organizers. As non-profit organizations, privately-run schools have difficulty obtaining development funds apart from collecting fees for their services. On the one hand, they cannot obtain financing from financial institutions or go public listing following the *Law of Investment Securities* (担保法), the *Company Law* and the *Stock Act* (证券法). On the other hand, private lending is costly and risky. The new law has fully liberalized market access for for-profit private schools, except that for-profit privately-run schools cannot offer services at the compulsory education level. This major institutional change has enriched the provision of educational services and removed legal obstacles to the direct financing of private schools by the capital market.

2.2.4   More Flexibility in Supervision of Tuition for Privately-Run Schools

Within the framework of the old *Private School Promotion Law*, the fees and charges of privately-run schools are subject to the approval of the relevant government departments at the stage of academic education, and to market regulation at the stage of non-academic education. Based on the review of the tuition charged by private schools in various parts of the country, the price-regulatory departments often refer to public schools' operating costs and tuition when approving tuitions of privately-run schools. As a result, in many cases, tuition collected by privately-run schools could not cover the true costs incurred, which include funds set aside for future development, reasonable returns for operators/investors, and special-designed educational services. The organizers, therefore, generally feel the pressure of running schools with tight funds. In some places, the tuition rates set by the local price-regulatory authorities had remained unchanged for more than a decade. And, privately-run schools with different qualities had been set with the same tuition rates, which does not reflect the principle of "price should reflect the quality." The new law has fully liberalized the price regulation of for-profit private schools, and introduced government-guided tuition for non-profit private schools, removing legal obstacles to private schools making full use of the market competition mechanism to provide "quality-price matching" educational services. According to some existing policies and practices, many regions have already fully liberalized their restrictions on the tuitions and fees charged by privately-run schools, allowing private schools to set their own reasonable prices based on their own quality of education services. Those regions include Jiangxi, Shandong, Yunnan, Suqian, and other provinces and municipalities.[11] Provinces such as Tianjin (municipality), Jiangsu, Fujian, Shandong, Hubei, Hunan, Guangxi, Guizhou, Ningxia, and Shaanxi have also liberalized tuition controls on privately-run colleges and universities.[12]

3   Impact and the Way Forward

3.1   *Inevitable Adjustment of the Education Industry Structure*
The major change in the legal system always leads to new opportunities and challenges. Under the legal framework of categorized management, many factors would impact the adjustment of the entire private education industry.

---

[11] *Notice on Matters Relating to the Liberalization of Private Education Fees* (Gan development and reform commission Fee Character [2015] No. 221); Article 4 of the *Opinions of the CPC Suqian Municipal Committee and Suqian Municipal People's Government on Further Deepening the Reform and Development of Private Education* (Su Fa [2015] No. 8); and the *Implementation Plan for Deepening Price Reform in Shandong Province* (Lu Government Office Fa [2014] No. 40).

[12] *Several Provinces and Cities Nationwide have Liberalized Private College Tuition Standards,* GWM.cn, April 2nd, 2016.

Those factors include the local development environment of private education, the development model and operation basis of existing privately-run schools, and the expectations of the private school organizers. It is difficult to make an accurate prediction on the development of different types of privately-run schools at different education stages in the context of the new law, because any kind of prediction has uncertainty and would need time and practice to test. However, based on the new law's relevant provisions, and taking into account the current development of private education in China, we may still make the following basic predictions.

First, the development of different types of privately-run schools will be suppressed at different degrees, considering factors such as legal regulations, operating costs, and policy risks. For example, comparing academic education versus non-academic education, compulsory education versus non-compulsory education, for-profit versus non-profit schools, heavy assets versus light assets schools, high tuition versus regular tuition schools, and large-scale versus small-scale schools, the development of the former types of privately-run schools will be suppressed to a greater extent. Among them, we should pay special attention to the impact on low-tuition privately-run schools in the compulsory education stage, mostly for migrant children, where profit-making is common.

Second, in terms of industry clustering and development focus, privately-run schools in different school segments will also differ in their development direction. For preschool education, the overall industry concentration is low, profit margins are stable, there is still room for growth in scale, and there are no legal and cultural barriers to mergers and reorganization. Therefore, the new law's impact on preschool education is mainly positive, and more impactful preschool education groups are likely to emerge in county-level cities and bigger cities, which will become the preferred focus of industrial capital and venture capital. Privately-run schools in the compulsory education stage have the most substantial overall competitiveness among private education. Although they have less room for natural growth in scale, they have room for product innovation. For instance, the organizers may indirectly gain economic benefits through the schools' internal development, cost control, and brand building. Compared with public schools, privately-run high schools lack a competitive advantage in general. Under the policy framework of categorized management, the prospect is not optimistic. However, if the government opens up the pilot privatization of the secondary level vocational schools, their development could still be promising before the industry recession. Compared with public universities, private higher education is less competitive in the market. However, because of its flexibility and vigorous innovation, it is a potential target for merge and acquisitions in the capital market. However, until a substantial breakthrough is achieved in the education management system's reform, the development of both private universities and independent colleges has uncertainties, and investment decisions need to be made with caution. The industry concentration of non-academic training institutions is low, and the degree of corporatization and marketization of those institutions is high, so the new law supports the development of non-academic education and training as a whole. It is possible to rapidly improve the industry concentration through mergers and reorganization. In addition, there is also significant room for innovation in several emerging areas.

3.2 *Great Potential for Local Policy Innovation*

Since implementing the old *Private School Promotion Law,* two basic facts about privately-run education can be found after reviewing local policies and practices from different regions. First, in contrast to the overall slow progress of the development of law in privately-run education at the national level, local governments have shown a more proactive attitude and a more pronounced vitality in institutional innovation with regard to the development of privately-run education. Since the promulgation of the *Private School Promotion Law* and its Implementing Regulations, 28 provinces across the country have passed local legislation or issued local policies on private education. That legislation and policies actively explore many aspects of private education, including clarifying the attributes of legal persons, clarifying the ownership of property rights, implementing a reward system, exploring categorized management, establishing public financial support, implementing preferential policy support, building a teaching force, expanding the autonomy of school-operation, regulating financial management, deepening reform of the school-operating system, etc. Second, the unequal development of regional private education is related to local economic and cultural factors, but mainly caused by the differences in the local policy environment for private education development. The differentiated policy environment resulting from local institutional innovation directly affects local private education development's scale and quality. This is also supported by evidence from specific private education practices.[13] Therefore, the key to the smooth transformation and sustainable development of the local private education development model under the legal framework of categorized management lies in the ability of local governments. In addition

---

13 Zhang Luhong 章露红 "Zhongguo defang minbanjiaoyu zhidu chuangxin yanjiu 中国地方民办教育制度创新研究 [Research on Innovation of Local Private Education System in China]," Ph.D. dissertation, Zhejiang University, January 7, 2016.

to rebuilding the confidence in the central government's policy in encouraging and developing private education, local government should implement the various support policies specified in the new law, create a positive and flexible policy environment for the development of private education, and attract more private capital to the private education sector.

There are two basic paths to local policy innovations for private education: first, they can take the "first step" to address blind spots, ambiguities, or conflicting policies in the national private education legal system; second, the State's regulations give localities room for policy innovation to refine and operationalize some detailed policies. Therefore, according to the new law's relevant provisions and the overall direction of the national policy on private education, local governments have a lot of room for policy innovation, at least at the following three aspects. First, the new law explicitly authorizes local governments to formulate local policies on privately-run education. Specifically, local governments shall develop policies regarding tuitions and charges of non-profit private schools. As far as the existing policy practice is concerned, there are three basic price regulation models for non-profit private schools: operation cost plus a percentage of surplus, set a maximum price limit, and independent pricing. Given the market attributes of privately-run schools and the state's market-oriented reform direction in terms of price regulation, the preferred option should be independent pricing. In addition, local governments shall also develop compensation and reward measures for the conversion of the existing privately-run schools. In this regard, the recipients and principles of compensation, the basis of calculating compensation, the timeline for obtaining compensation, and how to realize the property rights after it is confirmed are all key issues that local governments should consider. Secondly, local policies need to be developed in accordance with the supporting documents of the amendment law (commonly known as "1+2") promulgated by the State on January 18, 2017. Specifically, local governments should develop detailed implementation policies to speed up the introduction of supporting policies for the local categorized management system. Specific policies should also be formed on the categorized registration, differentiated government support policies, innovative investment and financing system, exploration of multi-party cooperative school operation, regulation and supervision of for-profit private schools, and general information disclosure system. Thirdly, local governments shall actively seek new breakthroughs in local private education policies in accordance with local conditions. For example, pilot areas of the categorized management reform should adjust their support policies, in order to maintain their first-mover advantage and continue to lead the development of local private education. In areas where the proportion of private schools in the compulsory education sector is relatively high, and most of them are schools for children of the migrant population, special attention should be paid to the policy risk management of categorized management reform. In addition to considering the differences in the development models of local private education, attention should also be paid to some common topics that affect the long-term development of private education, such as further deepening the reform of the school-operation system, enriching the organizational forms of private education, further implementing and expanding the autonomy of school-operation, building a modern school system with the guarantee of school-operation autonomy as its core, and stimulating the vitality of private school-operation, and so on.

3.3   Adhere to the Internal Development of Schools

For the school organizers, whether they choose for-profit or non-profit form, there are a lot of things to analyze and consider before and after they make a choice. Firstly, they need to fully understand the relevant state laws and regulations and the local private education support policies. Secondly, they need to unify their thinking. They should inform all the teaching staff of their decision as soon as possible to clarify the principle of guaranteeing teachers' interests, in order to stabilize the teaching team. Thirdly, they should amend the bylaws in accordance with the legal characteristics of the chosen type of school, which include standardizing and improving the supervision mechanism, setting up necessary provisions to protect the legitimate rights and interests of the organizers, and regulating relevant procedures and boundaries for organizers to involve in school activities. Those who choose for-profit private schools must have roughly accurate estimates of conversion costs and future operating costs, as well as a risk assessment of whether society can accept for-profit academic education and develop a risk management plan. Fourthly, the school organizers should have a clear idea of the school's capital contribution (including the additional investment during the continuation of the school), government financial allocation, the donation from society, and assets accumulated by the school operation. They should start the liquidation procedure of assets as soon as possible. This is because if they wait until the termination of the school to carry out the liquidation procedure, they may fail to find the necessary proof of assets when applying for compensation and awards. Fifth, the school operators should rationally face the challenges of the capital market, not only make good use of financing tools for private education, but also enter the capital market cautiously, with adequate risk prevention and control, sticking to the bottom line, and guarantee the interests of teachers and students.

However, under the backdrop of transition from scale expansion to the stage of overall quality improvement for China's private education, when it comes to the essence of education, cultivate students, no matter how the external policy environment changes, regardless of for-profit or non-profit types of schools, private schools shall adhere to the path of internal quality development and run brands and features. Only in this way, can they "respond to all changes with no change," survive with the major institutional changes, and seize the historic opportunity for innovation and development.

CHAPTER 4

Practical Paths, Methods, and Reflections on Precision-Targeted Measures to Alleviate Poverty through Education

Zhang Zhaoqin,[1] Feng Qingyun[2] and Wang Chengde[3]

Abstract

China has set the goal that by 2020 all people must be lifted out of poverty. The foundation status, pilot function, and fundamental role of education in poverty alleviation have been clearly shown. Education has the mission of interrupting the intergenerational transmission of poverty. This paper takes Gansu Province as an example to study the ideas, measures, paths, and methods of precision-targeted poverty alleviation through education in Gansu Province, and provides a reference for promoting precision-targeted poverty alleviation through education nationwide.

Keywords

precision-targeted poverty alleviation (精准扶贫) – poverty alleviation through education (教育扶贫) – rural education – Gansu

In 2015, *Decision of the State Council of the Central Committee of the Communist Party of China on Winning the Battle against Poverty* (中共中央国务院关于打赢脱贫攻坚战的决定) sets the goal that by 2020, all people must be lifted

---

1 Zhang Zhaoqin 张兆勤, Vice President of Lanzhou University of Arts and Science, former Director of the Teacher Education Division of the Gansu Provincial Education Department. His main research interests are in education management, family education, support for rural teachers and principals, school development planning, rural education, language, and literature policy.
2 Feng Qingyun 封清云, cadre of the Gansu Provincial Education Department. He is in charge of poverty alleviation through education and assisting in the work of the Lanzhou New District Vocational Education Park.
3 Wang Chengde 王成德, Professor at Lanzhou University of Arts and Science, Vice President of Gansu Province Counselor Association.

out of poverty. As of August 2015, there were still more than 70 million people under the poverty line in China, and the task of lifting them out of poverty by 2020 is arduous. According to UNESCO's research, the correlation coefficient between the average number of years of education and GDP per capita is 0.562.[4] Education plays a fundamental, pioneering and sustainable role in poverty alleviation and poverty reduction. At present, there is a consensus that education is an effective way to prevent the intergenerational transmission of poverty.

1 Current Status of Precision-Targeted Poverty Alleviation through Education

Poverty alleviation through education refers to investing in education and providing educational support services to people under the poverty line in poor areas, so that they can acquire the knowledge and skills to lift themselves out of poverty and become rich. At the same time, we can promote local economic and cultural development by improving the science and literacy level of the local population, so as to finally get rid of poverty.[5] Poverty is a complex social phenomenon, influenced by both the harshness of the natural environment and the limitations of educational conditions. Poverty is a result of the interplay of many factors, including socio-economic and cultural factors and the subjective initiative of individuals. Therefore, poverty prevention and precise alleviation is a comprehensive and complex systematic project.

The Decision of the State Council of the Central Committee of the Communist Party of China on Winning the Battle against Poverty has made "lifting people out of poverty through education" one of the five important pathways of precision-targeted poverty relief and alleviation. The Ministry of Education has organized and implemented 20 education policies and measures, in the course of implementing the basic strategy of the Central Committee of the Communist Party of China for "precision-targeted poverty relief and alleviation" and the idea of "helping the poor through education" of General Secretary of the CPC, Xi Jinping.

---

4 Chai Wei 柴葳 "Jiaoyu shi zuigenben de jingzhun fupin, 教育是最根本的精准扶贫 [Education is the Most Fundamental Way of Precision-Targeted Poverty Alleviation]," *China Education Daily*, March 3, 2016.
5 Xie Junjun 谢君君 "Jiaoyu fupin yanjiu shuping 教育扶贫研究述评 [Review of Research on Poverty Alleviation through Education]," *Fudan Education Forum*, Issue 3, 2012.

Party committees and governments at all levels have accorded top priority to poverty alleviation through education in the development of social undertakings. Provincial education departments have issued policies on *Implementation Plans for Educational Support Plans for Precision-targeted Poverty Alleviation* (关于精准扶贫教育支持计划的实施方案). In Guizhou Province, eight educational support plans for precision-targeted poverty alleviation are being implemented: a plan to provide precise financial assistance to students, a plan to alleviate poverty through vocational education, a plan to expand school capacity and improve school conditions, a plan to promote information technology in education, a plan to improve the quality of the teaching force, a plan to promote student enrollment in rural and impoverished areas, a plan to provide one-on-one assistance in education, and a plan to care for groups with special difficulties.[6] Hubei Province focuses on the implementation of the "Five Precision Targeting": Precision-targeted Reconstruction, Precision-targeted Enrollment, Precision-targeted Financial Assistance, Precision-targeted Employment, and Precision-targeted Training, and has formulated one action plan and 26 supporting implementation plans. Qinghai Province is implementing six plans, including a plan to upgrade basic education, a plan of action to alleviate poverty through vocational education and higher education, a plan to benefit the people through educational assistance, a plan to care for children with special needs, a plan to improve the quality of education for ethnic minorities, and a plan of action to establish one-on-one pair-up-support in education.[7]

The authors' search in China National Knowledge Infrastructure, or CNKI (中国知网) showed that the precision-targeted poverty alleviation strategy focuses on the study of its content, key milestones, and other contents. The precision-targeted poverty alleviation policy focuses on studying many specific policies, including poverty alleviation through introducing new industry, employment transfer, relocation of poverty population, poverty alleviation through education, relief poverty alleviation, ecological poverty alleviation, poverty alleviation through asset income, etc. In addition, the precision-targeted poverty alleviation policy also studies contradictions, problems, and active support strategies and countermeasures in the implementation of the institutional mechanism of poverty governance.

---

6 Wang Yu 王雨 "Badajihua zuduan pinkun daiji chuandi, 8大计划阻断贫困代际传递 [Eight Plans to Break the Intergenerational Transmission of Poverty]," *Guizhou Daily*, March 2, 2016.

7 Zhao Jing 赵静 "Jiaoyu tuopin: bian "dashui manguan" wei "jingzhun diguan", 教育脱贫：变 "大水漫灌" 为 "精准滴灌" [Poverty Alleviation through Education: Transform General Measures to Precise Policies]," *Qinghai Daily*, April 19, 2016.

2   Dilemma in Practicing Precision-Targeted Poverty Alleviation through Education

Education has the mission of breaking the intergenerational transmission of poverty. The path to achieving poverty alleviation through education is to enable children from low-income families to receive fair and adequate education.

Although the various regions have invested heavily in poverty alleviation in the areas of education, culture, and health and have achieved some success, the imbalanced development between urban and rural areas has yet to be corrected, due to factors such as a weak economic base and harsh natural conditions. We have not yet met the public's expectations on the balanced use of public resources. In particular, with regard to the construction of hardware and software for educational development, the former is mainly due to the arduous task of improving the poor conditions, while the latter is mainly due to the need to strengthen teacher training effectiveness. Detailed analysis is laid out as follows.

2.1   *The Overall Poverty Situation in Poor Areas Remains Grim*

On the one hand, in those impoverished areas, the ecological environment has deteriorated, disasters frequently occur, the ability to rehabilitate the natural environment is limited, and material and human resources are scarce. On the other hand, many poor villages and communities are backward in terms of education, culture, and health facilities. In addition, they suffer from a lack of information and have little awareness of their own development, thus forming a vicious circle that aggravates psychological poverty. With the vigorous advancement of the poverty eradication work, the remaining poor villages and poverty populations are mainly concentrated in these remote villages and communities, which suffer from the harsh natural environment, limited information, and poor economic development. These poverty populations live in scattered settlements, the degree of organization of farmers' associations and professional cooperatives is not high, and most of the farmers are still all by themselves, making it increasingly difficult to deliver skills to help them get rich.

2.2   *Large Infrastructure Debts and Serious Gaps in Matching Funds*

For example, in Dingxi City, Gansu Province, less than 12% of the spending was from the city's own finance. Although nearly two-thirds of the financial funds have been invested in precision-targeted poverty alleviation, there is still a large gap between the requirements of precision-targeted poverty alleviation and the matching funds. In education, the implementation of a comprehensive improvement of school facilities in poverty areas project (全面改薄项目), financial assistance for needy students, teacher training, incorporation of information technology in education, vocational skills training, etc. all need a lot of funds urgently. In terms of cultural aspects of precision-targeted poverty alleviation, although many cultural facilities are being constructed in a wide range of areas, the investment is small. Apart from the special funds allocated by provincial and municipal financial budget on purchasing "village stage" equipment, no special funds are distributed at the county and district level for culture development.

2.3 Slow Progress in the Comprehensive Improvement Project on Facilities for Schools in Poverty Areas in Some Counties, and the Urgent Need to Integrate the Rural Teaching Force

The comprehensive improvement of the basic operating conditions of low-quality compulsory-education schools in poor areas mainly involves two main tasks; one is the renovation of school buildings, the other is the purchase of equipment. At present, the comprehensive improvement projects involve complex procedures during the application and bidding stages, and the project's preliminary procedures are complicated, resulting in some projects failing to start within the expected timeline and the extension of the construction cycle. In some counties and districts, the comprehensive improvement projects cover a wide area and involve a large amount of arduous tasks. In addition, the quality of teachers is the key to the quality of education in poverty areas. Research shows that the following major problems exist in the rural teaching force: insufficient number of teachers, unstable teaching team, serious aging issue of teachers, knowledge is not up-to-date, insufficient teaching capacity, and the general heavy burden and pressure on rural teachers.[8] In most counties and districts' primary schools and teaching centers, teachers of English, music, physical education, and aesthetics were not sufficiently trained in those subjects to have become a prominent problem. With the increasing pace of construction of kindergartens in rural areas, the issue of the shortage of teachers for preschool education is becoming more serious.

---

8 Pang Lijuan 庞丽娟 "Xiangcunjiaoshi duiwu jianshe ying chengwei jingzhun fupin zhongdian, 乡村教师队伍建设应成为精准扶贫重点 [Rural Teacher Team Building Should Become a Focus of Precision-targeted Poverty Alleviation]," *Guangming Daily*, April 19, 2016.

2.4 Lack of Distinctive Features in Vocational Education and Impractical Skills Training for Farmers

Vocational education in many counties is still oriented towards enrollment in higher-education institutions. Many vocational schools are actively organizing a large number of students to take part in the college-entrance examinations, with less than 30% of students getting direct employment after graduation. The short cycle of skills training for farmers and the impracticality of the skills taught, coupled with lack of enthusiasm from the farmers, make it difficult for them to master a truly practical skill.

3 Practical Exploration of Precision-Targeted Poverty Alleviation through Education in Gansu Province

Due to historical, geographical, ecological, and economic constraints, poverty in Gansu is geographically widespread, affects a large proportion of the population, and particularly severe. There are a total of 86 counties in Gansu province, of which 58 counties are part of connected special hardship counties, while 17 counties are stand-alone counties, not belonging to the national poverty-relief zones. Poverty counties account for 87% of the total number of counties in Gansu. According to the data of the State Council's Leading Team Office of Poverty Alleviation and Development, 13% of the total poverty population in Gansu are "poor because of lack of schooling."

In the face of the issue of poverty with complex causes, the Gansu Provincial Party Committee and the provincial government have required that poverty relief measures need to be precision-targeted in six aspects, including recipients of the supportive measures, goal, content, approach, assessment, and guarantee measures. In 2014, Gansu Province issued the *Implementation Opinions on Actively Promoting Poverty Alleviation through Education Project*, promoting poverty alleviation measures such as education to empower the people, skills to enrich the people, and employment to secure the people. Since 2015, the provincial education department has been organizing and implementing a "9+1" special support plan for education for poverty alleviation. The nine special support plans cover preschool education, compulsory education, general high school education, vocational education, rural teachers training, ethnic education, student financial aid, university admissions, and education for left-behind children. The "plus 1" refers to the *Action Plan to Support Expedited Development of Education in the Old Revolutionary Region*. This paper will discuss the practices and experiences in the depth of the four support plans.

3.1 *The Four Plans for Precision-Targeted Poverty Alleviation through Education in Gansu Province*

3.1.1 Special Support Program for the Education of Rural Left-behind Children for Precision-Targeted Poverty Alleviation

The problem of left-behind children is a prominent social problem that requires a timely, equitable, and sustainable solution. The difficulties faced by rural left-behind children include basic living, schooling, and other aspects. Gansu Province took eight initiatives to tackle the problems of left-behind children, in terms of their living, education, and healthy development.

First, improve a mechanism for the dynamic management of basic information on children left behind in rural areas. Municipalities (prefectures) and counties (cities and districts) are to accurately collect the basic information on rural children left behind, such as the location of their parents' workplaces and the financial resources of their families. The "left-behind children" is defined in accordance with the redefined definition of rural left-behind children.

Second, vigorous efforts will be made to improve the educational conditions of rural left-behind children. The coverage of rural preschool education will be expanded, and priority will be given to ensuring that left-behind children in rural areas have access to kindergartens close to their homes. Accelerate the construction of rural boarding schools to basically meet the study and boarding needs of children left behind in rural areas, and priority is given to ensure that meals are provided to left-behind children in rural areas.

Thirdly, strengthening the construction of a team for the care and protection of rural left-behind children. Further establishing and perfecting organizational and leadership structures and working systems to gradually institutionalize, standardize and normalize the education and care of left-behind children in rural areas. More special topic training should be offered to teachers and staff of schools with a relatively high proportion of rural left-behind children.

Fourthly, developing services are offered to left-behind children in rural areas. The construction of after-school activity centers for children and adolescents, youth centers in rural schools, and centers for left-behind children has been strengthened, with an adequate supply of books, communication, and activity equipment to meet left-behind children's emotional and psychological needs.

Fifthly, effectively improve the education quality for left-behind children in rural areas. Attention has been paid to left-behind children's psychological health in rural areas, and individual psychological counseling has been carried out. Also, left-behind children are offered education in the legal system and safety education. Regular cultural and sporting activities have been organized to alleviate feelings of loneliness for left-behind children, to make learning more enjoyable, and to increase their confidence in life.

Sixth, perfecting a long-term mechanism for the education and care of left-behind children in rural areas. A mechanism for mandatory reporting of the special circumstances of rural left-behind children and their guardians has been established, and a system for registering students who have dropped out of school, persuading them to return and resume their studies, and reporting cases in writing has been implemented. Schools regularly conduct surveys of rural left-behind children on their studies, lives, physical development, and health conditions.

Seventh, improving the educational level of guardians of left-behind children in rural areas. Schools are required to establish a communication system with the parents of left-behind children in rural areas. Schools should support the development of close emotional connections between children and their parents through various activities and programs. Parents' committees and schools for parents are to be brought into full play, and special service activities are to be carried out extensively.

Eighthly, actively establishing a care and assistance network for rural left-behind children. Local education departments should strengthen communication with the Communist Youth League, Women's Federation, and the Caring for the Next Generation Working Committee to form a working network to work on common concerns, education, and care for rural left-behind children.

3.1.2 Special Support Programs for Rural Teachers for Precision-Targeted Poverty Alleviation

The quantity and quality of teachers in rural areas are key factors that impact the development of education and teachers force in China, in the efforts to precision-targeted poverty alleviation through education. In Gansu province, the aim is to expand the sources of quality teachers for schools in poor counties (cities and districts) through various channels, so that they are willing to teach in those schools, willing to stay in those schools, and offering high-quality teaching.

First, understand the current situation of schools and teachers in poverty areas. We have registered and kept documentation of schools where students from poverty households enrolled, and teachers who teach them, in order to manage their basic situations promptly. We also formulated precise plans on teacher supplementation, training, promotion, and other programs to attract more talented people to help education in impoverished areas.

Second, promote the professional capability of teachers in poverty areas. Through various forms of teacher education, a long-term mechanism for building teacher moral character has been formed. The national and provincial training programs are integrated, planned, and designed as a whole, focusing on improving the professional capability of teachers in primary and secondary schools and preschools in impoverished areas.

Third, the recruitment of talented people to teach in rural areas. Efforts have been made to resolve structural conflicts, and strictly supervise the recruitment process to ensure that teachers are recruited according to their posts. We implemented the Special Post Plan for Kindergarten Teachers, which focuses on supporting rural teachers' recruitment in impoverished areas, old revolutionary areas, and ethnic minority areas. From 2012 to 2016, a total of 34,313 teachers were recruited for primary, secondary, and kindergarten in the province, of whom 32,230 were rural teachers, accounting for 93.9% of the total number of teachers recruited.

Fourth, enhance the capability of teachers to serve poverty villages. In rural areas, the Government has launched a provincial-level program to cultivate, train and select backbone teachers in rural towns and villages. It has built a platform and channel for the professional growth and development of teachers in rural towns and villages. In addition, it has implemented the "three plans and two projects" to enhance the capability of rural teachers, training 600 kindergarten principals and 3,000 teachers in impoverished areas each year. It is also implementing the "3,000 Rural Teachers Visiting Famous Schools" and "Itinerant Teaching Support" projects and strengthening teachers' training in disciplines where teachers are in short supply and of bilingual teachers in ethnic minority areas.

Fifth, improve the remuneration of teachers in impoverished areas. When selecting teachers for the Gardener Award and other awards for outstanding teachers at all levels, preferences are given to teachers in impoverished areas, and conditions are appropriately relaxed. Honors are given to teachers in poverty areas who have long been rooted in rural areas and have served as exemplary teachers. From 2013 to 2016, a total of 1.059 billion yuan in subsistence allowances were granted to teachers in remote rural areas, ensuring that rural teachers are generally treated more favorably than their counterparts in counties and cities.

Sixth, implement the "Talents for Three Districts" support program for teachers' special plan. Each year 1,400 outstanding teachers were selected and sent to the "three districts" for one-year teaching support. This program has effectively enhanced the quality of teaching staff in schools in "the three districts", and provided human resources to support educational reform and development.

TABLE 4.1 List of annual tasks for teacher training, exchange, and support programs for precision-targeted poverty alleviation

Year Region		2015	2016	2017	2018	2019	2020	Totals
Pre-school teacher training	national	520	600	690	760	660	600	3830
	provincial	130	150	170	190	160	150	950
Primary and secondary school teacher training	national	12,800	14,400	16,000	17,600	16,000	15,600	92,400
	provincial	3,200	3,600	4,000	4,400	4,000	3,900	23,100
Teachers in ethnic areas training (bilingual)		1,340 (290)	1,340 (290)	1,340 (290)	1,340 (290)	1,340 (290)	1,340 (290)	8,040 (1,740)
Secondary vocational school teacher training		2,000	2,000	2,000	2,000	2,000	2,000	12,000
"Dual type teacher" in secondary vocational school teacher training		4,000	4,500	5,000	5,500	6,000	6,500	
Teacher support in the "three districts"		1,400	1,200	1,200	1,200	1,200	1,200	7,400
Tibetan "internship" support teacher		300	400	400	400	400	400	2,300
Urban primary and secondary school principals to serve primary and secondary schools in poverty areas		200	200	200	200	200	200	1,200

SOURCE: "GANSU PROVINCE PRECISION-TARGETED POVERTY ALLEVIATION RURAL TEACHERS SPECIAL SUPPORT PLAN (2015–2020)" (甘肃省精准扶贫乡村教师队伍专项支持计划 (2015～2020年)) IN THE NOTICE OF GANSU PROVINCIAL EDUCATION DEPARTMENT ON THE ISSUANCE OF "GANSU PROVINCE PRECISION-TARGETED POVERTY ALLEVIATION PRE-SCHOOL EDUCATION SPECIAL SUPPORT PLAN (2015–2020)" (甘肃省精准扶贫学前教育专项支持计划 (2015～2020年)) AND OTHER SEVEN PRECISION-TARGETED POVERTY ALLEVIATION THROUGH EDUCATION SPECIAL SUPPORT PLANS (GAN EDUCATION DEPARTMENT) ([2015] NO. 94). THE SAME SOURCE APPLIED TO THE FOLLOWING TABLES.

3.1.3 Special Support Program for Preschool Education for Poverty Alleviation

Preschool education is an important component of the national education system. In order to ensure that children at preschool age in poverty areas and families in difficulty can receive preschool education, Gansu Province has formulated eight measures.

First, efforts are being made to increase preschool education resources in impoverished rural areas. A plan for the construction of rural kindergartens in impoverished areas has been scientifically prepared and incorporated into the Government's program of practical work for the people to receive special attention. Emphasis is placed on the renovation and construction of a number of kindergartens using idle rural primary and secondary school buildings. New kindergartens will be established in multiple ways, such as the expansion and renovation of existing kindergartens, the establishment of branches of kindergartens in towns and villages, the joint operation of kindergartens, and the establishment of roving teaching stations for poverty areas.

Second, efforts are being made to establish a team of high-quality early childhood teachers. More rural kindergarten teachers are gradually being recruited. Favorable policies have been offered to rural kindergarten teachers in impoverished areas in such areas as job title evaluation, training and advanced training, and promotion. Beginning in 2016, rural kindergarten teachers' temporary housing has been listed as a project of the provincial government for serving the people.

Third, vigorous efforts have been made to improve the teaching conditions of rural kindergartens. Special funds have been set up to enhance rural kindergartens' teaching conditions in phases and equip rural kindergartens with safe, green, and environmentally-friendly facilities, toys, teaching aids, and books. Social forces are actively guided and encouraged to help kindergartens improve their conditions through donations and assistance.

Fourth, the focus has been put on supporting the accelerated development of rural preschool education in old revolutionary and Tibetan areas. The Government coordinates the implementation of practical projects related to people's life, bilingual kindergarten projects in Tibetan areas, and the Development and Reform Commission's project to promote rural preschool education. In addition, the Government announces more favorable policies for old revolutionary areas and Tibetan areas in such areas as project implementation, capital investment, teacher resources, and teacher training.

Fifth, the development of private preschool education is being supported in a standardized manner. Social forces are encouraged to run private preschools through various policies and measures, including the guarantee of reasonable land use, tax exemptions and reductions, the provision of awards in lieu of subsidies, the assignment of public teachers, and the government purchase of services.

Sixth, the preschool education financial support system has been improved and perfected. Plans are being drawn up to gradually implement the free preschool education policy in phases and batches. Beginning in 2016, the province's kindergarten children will be exempted (subsidized) from tuitions and charges at a standard rate of 1,000 yuan per student per year. The 65,700 registered households under the poverty line in 58 poor counties will receive an additional 1,000 yuan in the form of preschool education voucher subsidies for three years for their kindergarten children, taking the lead in the country.

Seventh, a partnership and support mechanism has been established for urban and rural kindergartens. Guidance has been provided to encourage provincial and municipal model kindergartens and category 1 kindergartens to establish one-to-one support program with rural kindergartens. Fifteen provincial-level preschool education research and training bases have been established to provide teacher training and teaching and research services.

Eighth, the quality of standardized management and scientific teaching has been improved. Efforts are being made to standardize the operation of kindergarten. Guidance for rural kindergartens on childcare and education has been strengthened, with play as the basic activity, and parental training has been initiated to encourage scientific childcare.

TABLE 4.2   Number of kindergartens in villages under the Gansu Provincial Precision-Targeted Poverty Alleviation through Pre-school Education Support Program

region / annual	Total	2015	2016	2017	2018	2019	2020
Entire province	10,003	1,346	1,855	2,656	1,447	1,434	1,265
Lanzhou	202	10	64	74	22	22	10
Jinchang	2	1	1				
Baiyin	434	183	121	79	22	21	8
Tianshui	1,902	178	261	611	357	355	140
Wuwei	350	62	86	129	22	22	29
Zhangye	28	3	2	5	6	5	7
Pingliang	518	279	197	42			
Jiuquan	15	3	4	2	3	2	1
Qingyang	1,063	275	443	345			

TABLE 4.2 Number of kindergartens in villages under the Gansu Provincial (cont.)

region \ annual	Total	2015	2016	2017	2018	2019	2020
Dingxi	1,491	148	250	555	256	253	29
Longnan	2,815	36	102	379	658	656	984
Linxia	902	165	208	273	101	98	57
Gannan	281	3	116	162			

3.1.4 Special Support Program for Compulsory Education for Precision-Targeted Poverty Alleviation

The compulsory education stage is a critical period in a child's life, a crucial period for the formation of moral and character traits, as well as physical development, psychological development, knowledge, and skills training.

First, increase governmental financial investment. From 2015 to 2018, a total of 14.63 billion yuan has been invested at all levels of government. Financial investment in compulsory education has been increasing continuously, ensuring the "one ratio" and "three increases" in education funding.

Second, overall scientific planning. Related government departments analyze and determine the gaps in each school's operating conditions, list them one by one, and formulates specific programs based on special plans for the infrastructure of compulsory-education schools. The work on improving compulsory-education-level schools is comprehensively promoted, and various types of educational projects are scientifically integrated.

Third, an assessment system has been established. The progress, quality, and effectiveness of the implementation of compulsory education for precision-targeted poverty alleviation will be assessed. The assessment results are the focus of the performance appraisal of municipal (provincial) governments. Key projects will be monitored and supervised closely, and administrative accountability will be enforced.

Fourth, publicity efforts will be stepped up. The government is doing a good job of publicizing compulsory education for precision-targeted poverty alleviation project, so that the general public, teachers, and students will understand the policies of the central and provincial governments that benefit the people. In addition, the general public gets information on the project content, implementation progress, and achievements of the compulsory education for precision-targeted poverty alleviation project, so as to ensure that the project advances steadily and orderly.

TABLE 4.3   List of annual construction tasks for the "comprehensive improvement of school facilities in poverty areas project" for precision-targeted poverty alleviation

unit: million yuan

	Project Budget Funds					
	Central government funds	Provincial funds	Municipal funds	County funds	Total
Total Gansu Province	6,778.3479	3,177.8916	747.2127	3,915.9032	1,4629.7512
2015	1,738.1282	832.2692	219.5449	1,063.9008	3,752.9357
2016	1,680.4657	773.2906	179.6129	973.1920	3,606.5618
2017	1,679.3456	791.1802	185.2064	964.8186	3,676.0208
2018	1,680.4083	781.1516	162.8485	913.9917	3,594.2328
Subtotal 58 poverty counties	5,422.0610	2,807.4652	490.8468	2,899.1939	11,730.8702
2015	1,388.4559	689.5930	117.6709	784.2209	2,979.9407
2016	1,344.9453	700.6813	113.7935	722.8096	2,882.2303
2017	1,343.7987	698.5843	126.7739	722.6787	2,947.3056
2018	1,344.8611	718.6066	132.6085	669.4846	2,921.3935
Total 17 isolated poverty counties	1,356.2869	370.4264	256.3659	1,016.7093	2,898.8810
2015	349.6724	142.6762	101.8740	279.6799	772.9950
2016	335.5204	72.6093	65.8194	250.3824	724.3315
2017	335.5469	92.5959	58.4325	242.1399	728.7152
2018	335.5472	62.5450	30.2400	244.5071	672.8393

Note: Information on "infrastructure construction (square meters)" and "living facilities, teaching instruments, and equipment" has been omitted from the table.

In order to ensure the smooth implementation of the various special support plans, education departments at all levels have clarified the main responsibilities, the division of labor, and the time frame for the completion of the tasks, and have established relevant systems for inspection and supervision, as well as incentive and accountability mechanisms.

3.2 Achievements of Precision-Targeted Poverty Alleviation through Education Projects in Gansu Province

Gansu Province, focusing on the strategic goal of building a moderately prosperous society simultaneously with the rest of the country, has implemented the "9+1" special support plan for precision-targeted poverty alleviation through education. Gansu province has achieved the goal of no students dropping out of school because of poverty. From 2012 to 2015, a total of 785,200 students from economically disadvantaged families were granted student loans totaled 4.33 billion yuan. The information on poverty alleviation targets, the status of poverty alleviation, support measures, and progress of poverty alleviation at each stage of education is collected. Based on that information, the policy measures are quantified into specific indicators embedded in the modules to accurately reflect poverty alleviation projects' progress and effect and efficiently serve the precise implementation of education policies for poverty alleviation. In 2015, Gansu Province's Precision-targeted Poverty Alleviation through Education project won the "National Education Reform and Innovation Special Award." In February 2016, the Ministry of Education's press conference gave a special introduction to the achievements of precision-targeted poverty alleviation through education in Gansu. In recent years, education in Gansu Province has shown a rapid development trend.

3.2.1 Rapid Expansion of Resources for Inclusive Preschool Education

Projects on preschool education have been consistently considered major projects that relate to people's livelihood and important reform initiatives to ensure the projects' progression. Since 2011, a cumulative total of 5.795 billion yuan has been invested in providing financial and policy guarantees in such areas as the construction of kindergartens, the provision of facilities, awards and subsidies for privately-run schools, teacher training, and childcare subsidies. As a result, the total number of kindergartens built, the number of children in kindergartens, the number of kindergarten teachers, and the gross enrolment rate in preschool education have all doubled. There are now 6,436 independent kindergartens and kindergartens affiliated to primary schools in Gansu, with an increase of 4,029 over 2010. There are now 701,100 children enrolled in kindergartens, 311,700 more than in 2010. With the development of rural preschool education as an essential measure to liberate the rural labor force, a "three-step, full-coverage" strategy has been implemented. By 2014, Gansu aimed to achieve full coverage of preschool education for the 58 poverty towns, and counties. By 2015, the goal was to achieve full coverage of kindergartens for the villages with more than 2,000 inhabitants in the 58 poverty towns. By 2016, the goal was to achieve full coverage of kindergartens for the villages with more than 1,500 inhabitants in the poverty towns, isolated poverty counties, needy administrative villages in old revolutionary and Tibetan areas. The gross kindergarten enrolment rate for the three years of the preschool stage has increased from 39% in 2011 to 82% in autumn 2016. Social forces are encouraged to participate in running kindergartens in a variety of forms, such as privately-run kindergartens built by the government. All rural kindergarten teachers in impoverished counties will be included in the scope of the subsistence allowance for rural teachers.

3.2.2 Comprehensive Improvement in the Conditions of Compulsory Education Schools

The Government will adhere to the ideas of balanced development and quality improvement, and accelerate the integrated development of urban and rural education. The establishment of "three thousand model schools in three areas" has been promoted. Since 2014, 600 model schools for moral education, 600 model schools for happy campuses, and 600 model schools for standardization of language and writing in primary and middle schools have been established in the province. In recent years, through the implementation of educational construction projects such as the Primary and Middle School Building Safety Project and the Central and Western Rural Junior High School Building Renovation Project, the conditions of disadvantaged schools in compulsory education have been continuously improved. A total of 14.53 billion yuan has been invested over the past three years, representing 68% of the five-year plan's total investment budget (21.4 billion yuan). A total of 15,821 civil construction projects and 54,790 equipment purchase projects have been implemented. The average floor area of school buildings per student at the compulsory education stage increased by 1.34 square meters, with 78% of schools reached the standard. The number of new student desks and chairs has reached 1,317,000 sets, achieving the goal of one desk and one chair per student. Promoting the exchange and rotation of principals and teachers in compulsory education schools within the counties. The construction of the "three connections and two platforms" project has been vigorously promoted, with 47,600 sets of equipment have been installed in the past three years to connect high-quality teaching resources in different classrooms. In 2015, the proportion of primary and secondary schools with broadband internet connections reached 84.1%, and the proportion of classrooms with high-quality resources connected reached 73.3%. The number of special education schools in the province has reached 37, and 38 counties and districts have established resource centers where children with disabilities can attend classes.

3.2.3 Year-on-Year Improvement in the Level of Educational Funding

A mechanism for steady growth in education investment has been established. Public spending on education increased from 23.334 billion yuan in 2010 to 49.72 billion yuan in 2015, with an average annual increase of 18.8%. In 2015, public spending on education amounted to 49.719 billion yuan, accounting for 7.32% of the province's GDP, making it the province's largest public expenditure for five consecutive years. The per-student public funding standards for senior vocational, middle vocational, preschool education, and special education have been set, realizing an institutional increase in education investment and a historic breakthrough in the province's education funding level. Innovate the teacher recruitment system in rural primary and secondary schools, insisting on setting up job openings according to needs and targeted recruitment. Through the provincial government's projects such as livelihood projects and the Ministry of Education's "Special Post Plan," more than 16,000 rural primary and middle school teachers, 9,221 kindergarten teachers, and 1,357 tuition-free regular school students have been recruited in the past three years. The government also works on improving the benefits of rural teachers. The province is the first in China to introduce measures to implement the Rural Teacher Support Program, which stipulates that rural teachers in poor counties should receive a monthly living allowance of not less than 500 yuan. In the past three years, the province has invested 534 million yuan in subsidies, benefiting 166,900 rural teachers. Efforts have also been made to create a professional teaching force. In the past three years, a cumulative total of 440,000 teachers in primary, secondary, and kindergarten schools have been trained.

3.2.4 Steady Progress Has Been Made in the Comprehensive Reform of Education. Education Quality Has Been Improving Every Year

By deepening reforms, we will continue to meet the public's new demands for "high-quality education." The first is to promote comprehensive education reform. Gansu has completed 14 pilot projects in the national education system's reform, including the "Outdoor Sports" campaign and the running of schools by vocational education groups. Gansu has also introduced an implementation plan for deepening the reform of the examination and admission system. It has also implemented the policy of direct enrollment to nearby schools without taking enrollment exams at the compulsory education stage. For general high schools, it has promoted the reform of academic level examination. For the college entrance examination, extra points opportunities were reduced and standardized, and the enrollment procedures were improved. The reform of vocational education admission examinations has been accelerated. Specifically, the scale of enrollment in targeted secondary vocational schools and provincial separate enrollment examinations has been expanded, and pilot programs for the examination-free-admission of fresh high school graduates and secondary vocational graduates have been implemented. Second, the reform of basic education curricula and teaching will be deepened. A plan to promote the reform of the compulsory education curriculum has been formulated, as have guidelines for the reform of the compulsory education curriculum. The reform of vocational education has been intensified, and implementation plans have been drawn up to comprehensively improve the quality of students' training, as well as curriculum reform plans for secondary vocational education.

4 Reflections on Education for Precision-Targeted Poverty Alleviation

The policies and measures to alleviate poverty through education have benefited many students from poverty families. However, difficulties and problems still exist in education development in the less developed western provinces, such as outdated infrastructure, lack of high-quality teachers, insufficient quality educational resources, and weak school running vitality and research and innovation capacity. The 13th Five-Year Plan period is the decisive stage of winning the battle of precise poverty eradication and achieving the goal of constructing a moderately prosperous society together with the rest of the country. Education development should be oriented to serve economic and social development, improve the teaching team's overall quality, and focus on mitigating the main conflicts and outstanding problems that plague education reform and development. The development of rural education in impoverished areas is a comprehensive and systematic project that cannot be achieved through any one initiative. Instead, it must be promoted as a whole with a systematic mindset.

4.1 *Implementing Pay Raise and Better Benefits to Retain Rural Teachers*

Due to non-wage factors such as housing, allowances, subsidies, and transport subsidies, rural teachers' standard of living is in general lower than that of their urban counterparts. Also, the overall ratio of the number of teachers getting promoted and receiving awards for rural teachers is also relatively low. In particular, in the past decade, the majority of primary and secondary school teachers in rural areas have been recent college and university graduates. Once they become key teachers or teaching experts, their desire to transfer to urban schools is growing stronger. The next step is to continue to improve the remuneration of rural teachers and to expand the construction of temporary housing for rural teachers at the provincial level, so that rural teachers are willing to stay and work in rural areas.

4.2   Address the Quantity and Quality of Pre-school Education Teachers

Many issues related to preschool teachers need to be carefully studied and resolved as soon as possible. Those include how to focus on recruiting the teaching staff for kindergartens in villages in impoverished areas, how to recruit full-time teachers and caregivers for rural kindergartens from among university graduates, college-graduates appointed as village officials, surplus primary school teachers in rural areas, and unemployed university graduates, and how to include rural kindergarten teachers in the scope of the subsidy and allowance plan for rural teachers.

4.3   Improve the Nutritional Status of Children in Rural Kindergartens in Impoverished Areas

Early childhood is known as an important period for children's physical and mental development and a crucial stage in their socialization from a human development perspective. A large proportion of newly built, expanded, and renovated kindergartens are attached to rural primary schools. However, primary school children are provided with nutritious meals every day, while kindergarten children on the same campus are not. The inclusion of rural preschool education stage in poverty areas in the "nutrition improvement plan" and solving the problem of the physical and mental development of young children in rural areas are worth considering.

4.4   Further Expand the Enrollment Plans of Key Universities in Poverty Areas

In the long run, precision-targeted poverty alleviation requires substantial human resources. In order to increase the opportunities for students in poor areas to receive quality higher education, support should be increased through the "Central and Western Regional Cooperation Plan," "Special Enrolment Plan for Impoverished Areas," and "Local Special Rural Enrolment Plan." In particular, it is especially important to train teachers for impoverished areas who are willing to serve the poverty areas and to stay there and are capable of high-quality teaching.

4.5   Continue to Strengthen the Construction and Oversight of Compulsory Education Boarding Schools

We need to consider how to provide special support in terms of funds and projects to improve boarding conditions for students in remote areas, complete the provision of relevant living and sports facilities in accordance with standards, and strictly supervise the construction of kindergarten and compulsory education school projects in impoverished areas. It is recommended that regular and random inspections be adopted to ensure building high quality and reliable projects, and to improve the overall conditions of schooling. This is a matter of concern to the entire nation.

CHAPTER 5

"School Education in the Eyes of Parents" Survey Report

Qin Hongyu[1]

Abstract

This survey was conducted from the perspective of parents to understand their satisfaction level with school education, their evaluation of the tendency of examination-oriented education, and their demands for improvement of school education. The results show that parental satisfaction with school education is not optimistic, ranging between "neutral" and "slightly satisfied." In addition, parental satisfaction with schools in most provinces is below the average. Parents' feelings towards privately-run schools are better than those towards public schools. More than half of parents believe that their children's school has a "severe" tendency to teach to the test. Parents strongly expect schools to make changes to "focus on the all-round development of the children."

Keywords

parent education – satisfaction level – examination-oriented education

From November 23 to December 9, 2016, the 21st Century Education Research Institute and Tencent Education Channel jointly launched a survey on "School Education in the Eyes of Parents" to understand parents' satisfaction level with school education, their evaluation of and thoughts on the tendency of examination-oriented education, and their demands for improvement of school education. A total of 13,561 parents participated in the survey.

---

1 Qin Hongyu 秦红宇, Associate Fellow, 21st Century Education Research Institute.

1 Basic Information

1.1 Basic Information on Parents Who Participated in the Survey

Parents who participated in the survey were mainly those with bachelor's and college degrees, with a combined total of about 61.75%, followed by parents with high school or junior college degrees, with 18.62%. The largest group of parents who participated in the survey was parents of primary school students (42.76%), followed by parents of junior high school students (20.02%) (see Table 5.1). Overall, 75.92% of parents who participated in the survey had children studying in public schools, whereas 16.59% were parents of children studying in privately-run schools, and very few parents had children from government-subsidized-privately-run schools (2.06%), public schools with private support (1.53%) and other types of schools (3.89%).

1.2 Geographical Distribution of Schools Attended by Children Reported by Parents

Participating parents reported that their children attended schools in 31 provinces. As shown in Figure 5.1, ranked in descending order by the proportion of schools, the highest proportion of schools was in Guangdong (11.65%), followed by Sichuan (7.62%) and Jiangsu (7.40%), Zhejiang (5.93%), and Hubei (5.47%), with a relatively balanced distribution in the middle, east and west regions. Ningxia, Hainan, Qinghai, and Tibet had the lowest proportion of schools participating in the survey.

TABLE 5.1 Parents education level and status

unit: %

Parental education level		Status of Parents	
Ph.D. and above	1.32		
Master's or double degree	4.69	Parents of Kindergarten students	12.80
undergraduate	36.16	Parents of primary school students	42.76
post-secondary	25.59	Parents of junior high school students	20.02
High school or junior college	18.62	Parents of high school students	13.78
junior high school	10.91	other	10.63
Primary school and below	2.72		

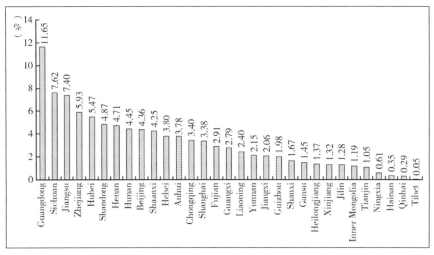

FIGURE 5.1   Provincial distribution of schools attended by children reported by parents (%)

For the urban versus the rural location of the schools in which participating parents reported their children attending, the majority of parents reported that their children attended schools in large and medium-sized cities (provincial or prefecture-level cities), followed by schools in county towns, and lastly schools in townships and villages[2] (See Table 5.2).

TABLE 5.2   Urban-rural distribution of schools attended by children reported by parents

	Counts	Percentage (%)
Provincial city schools	5,194	38.30
City schools	3,567	26.30
County schools	3,025	22.31
Township schools	1,436	10.59
Village schools	339	2.50

2   The question in the survey is: "Where does your child go to school currently?" Five options are offered, including: provincial city, prefectural city, county, township and village. Parents are assumed to choose the location of school that one of their children currently attends.

TABLE 5.3 Indicators for parents' evaluation of their satisfaction with school education

	Indicators	Average score	Overall mean
Parental satisfaction level to school education	The extent to which the child likes school	3.61	3.54
	The extent to which parents are satisfied	3.57	
	The extent to which parents are satisfied with classroom teachers	3.43	

2 Evaluation of Parental Satisfaction with School Education

2.1 *Parents' Satisfaction Level with School Education*

The current parental satisfaction survey mainly reflects the subjective feelings of parents towards their children's current schooling. The survey covers the parental evaluations of three indicators: first, how much parents think their children like the school; second, how much parents are satisfied with the school education their children are currently receiving; and third, how satisfied they are with their children's classroom teachers in general. Taking the average of total scores of each indicator,[3] we got an overall mean score of 3.54 for parental satisfaction of school education from parents who participated in this survey. Meanwhile, we also calculated the mean parental satisfaction score for each province. Results show that the mean scores of parental satisfaction for each province ranged from 3.00 to 3.66. In general, the overall parental satisfaction with school education in the survey was between "neutral" and "slightly satisfied."

2.2 *Ranking of Parental Satisfaction with School Education*

Participating parents reported that their children attended schools in 31 provinces, among which 11 provinces had higher-than-average parental satisfaction, while 18 had lower-than-average parental satisfaction. Results indicate that school education is not that satisfactory from the parents' perspective.

---

[3] The satisfaction scores were reverse coded, with the score ranging from 1 to 5, out of 5. The higher the value indicates the more satisfied the parents are.

The top five provinces, central government-controlled municipalities, and autonomous region in terms of average parental satisfaction with school education were Jilin, Guangdong, Chongqing, Hunan, and Fujian; the bottom five were Gansu, Guizhou, Liaoning, Shanxi, and Tibet. For schools in Beijing and Anhui, parental satisfaction was comparable to the national average (see Table 5.4). Of particular concern are the schools in Jiangsu and Shanghai, where the mean parental satisfaction levels are lower than the national average (3.52 for Jiangsu, ranked 17th, and 3.48 for Shanghai, ranked 21st).

TABLE 5.4   Ranking of parental satisfaction with school education

Province where the school is located	Mean parental satisfaction with school education	Rank
Jilin	3.66	1
Guangdong	3.61	2
Chongqing	3.61	3
Hunan	3.61	4
Fujian	3.60	5
Guangxi	3.57	6
Sichuan	3.57	7
Shandong	3.56	8
Inner Mongolia	3.56	9
Shaanxi	3.56	10
Zhejiang	3.56	11
Beijing	3.54	12
Anhui	3.54	13
Ningxia	3.53	14
Xinjiang	3.52	15
Qinghai	3.52	16
Jiangsu	3.52	17
Jiangxi	3.51	18
Hainan	3.50	19
Hubei	3.49	20
Shanghai	3.48	21
Tianjin	3.47	22
Henan	3.46	23
Yunnan	3.46	24
Hebei	3.45	25

"SCHOOL EDUCATION IN THE EYES OF PARENTS" SURVEY REPORT

TABLE 5.4 Ranking of parental satisfaction with school education (*cont.*)

Province where the school is located	Mean parental satisfaction with school education	Rank
Heilongjiang	3.44	26
Gansu	3.44	27
Guizhou	3.44	28
Liaoning	3.41	29
Shanxi	3.36	30
Xizang	3.00	31

Note: The average satisfaction score for each province was calculated using Excel. Scores were rounded so that only two decimal places were presented in this table. For provinces with equal scores shown in this table, the ranking was decided based on the actual average score before rounding.

2.3 *Regional Distribution of Parental Satisfaction with School Education*

Parental satisfaction with school education was higher in the eastern regions than that in the western regions. In general, parents in the western provinces were less satisfied than parents in the central and eastern provinces.[4]

The average satisfaction score of the nine eastern provinces was 3.53, of which four provinces (Jiangsu, Shanghai, Tianjin, and Liaoning) were below the overall national average (overall average is 3.54). The mean score for the ten central provinces was 3.50, with half of the provinces (Hebei, Henan, Heilongjiang, Hubei, and Shanxi) having schools with parental satisfaction scores below the overall average. For the 12 western provinces, central government-control municipalities and autonomous regions, the mean value was 3.48, with parental satisfaction higher than the overall average in

---

4 Ministry of Finance: *Opinions on the Clarification of the Regional Classification of the Eastern, Central and Western Regions*. The document pointed out that since the implementation of proactive fiscal policy in 1999, the central government first clearly defined the eastern region with 9 provinces, including Beijing, Tianjin, Liaoning, Shanghai, Jiangsu, Zhejiang, Fujian, Shandong, and Guangdong. The western region has 12 provinces, including Inner Mongolia, Guangxi, Chongqing, Sichuan, Yunnan, Guizhou, Tibet, Shaanxi, Gansu, Qinghai, Ningxia, and Xinjiang. The central region, although not specifically defined, includes 10 provinces: Hebei, Shanxi, Jilin, Heilongjiang, Anhui, Jiangxi, Henan, Hubei, Hunan, and Hainan. The classification of Central, East, and West regions in this paper follows this document, taking into consideration of economic geography and regional policy.

Chongqing, Shaanxi, Guangxi, Sichuan, and Inner Mongolia, and lower than the overall average in the remaining seven provinces, centrally-controlled municipalities and autonomous regions (Ningxia, Xinjiang, Yunnan, Guizhou, Gansu, Qinghai, and Tibet).

2.4 Comparison of Parental Satisfaction with School Education by Geographical Location

Figure 5.2 shows the mean values of parental satisfaction of schools in different geographical areas. The comparison of the mean values shows that the highest mean value of parental satisfaction was found in urban schools and the lowest in schools at the village level.

One-factor ANOVA results showed that parental satisfaction of schools in different geographic locations differed significantly.[5] Multiple comparison results showed that parental satisfaction of provincial city schools and city schools were significantly higher than the county, township, and village schools, but there was no statistically significant difference in parental satisfaction between provincial city schools and city schools. Parental satisfaction scores for county schools were significantly higher than township schools, and parental satisfaction scores were significantly higher in township schools than in village schools.

In general, parental satisfaction was higher in urban schools than in rural areas. Parents' satisfaction level in provincial and prefectural cities, counties, towns, and villages showed a decreasing trend, in line with the pattern of urban-rural structural differences.

2.5 Parental Satisfaction with School Education by Different Parents' Education Background

Figure 5.3 shows the comparison of the mean values of parental satisfaction with school education by parents' educational background. It can be seen from the figure that parents with bachelor's degrees had the highest mean satisfaction score, and parents with high school/junior college degrees had the lowest mean satisfaction score.

One-way ANOVA results showed that parents with different education backgrounds differed significantly in their satisfaction with school education. Multiple comparisons results showed that parents with bachelor's degrees were significantly more satisfied than parents with college degrees and high school/junior college degrees. This may occur due to the fact that the higher proportion of parents in urban schools had bachelor's degrees. There was no

---

5 Statistical significant level: p=0.05.

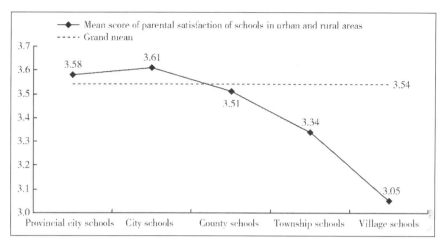

FIGURE 5.2 Comparison of mean values of parental satisfaction in schools of different geographical areas

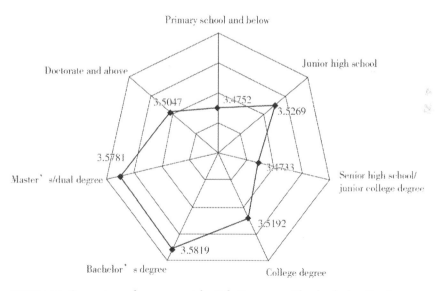

FIGURE 5.3 Comparison of mean parental satisfaction score with school education by parents' education background

significant difference in satisfaction level between parents with a college education and parents with high school/junior college education, nor was there a significant difference between parents with other education backgrounds (doctorate and above, master's/dual degree, bachelor's degree, junior high school, primary school and below) when pair-wise comparisons were performed.

In other words, in terms of statistically significant differences, parents with bachelor's degrees were more satisfied with school education than parents with college and high school/junior college degrees. However, there was no statistically significant difference in satisfaction between parents with bachelor's degrees and other degrees.

3   Parental Evaluation of Schools by Detailed Categories

In a further survey on aspects that parents were satisfied with schools, "proximity to home" was the aspect that parents were most satisfied with, with 61.99% of parents chose this aspect. Especially for township and village schools, over 75% of parents reported satisfaction in this aspect. This showed the importance and achievements of the policy that students shall enter schools close to their homes. In addition, parents were most concerned about schools' facilities (33.57%), teachers' quality (26.80%), school management (26.19%), as well as the schools' enrollment rates to further education and school ranking (25.64%), but only about 30% of parents were satisfied with each of these four aspects. Regarding schools' extracurricular activities and curriculum system, only over 10% of parents reported satisfaction.

Further comparing the specific aspects that parents were satisfied with schools in provincial city schools, city schools, county schools, township schools, and village schools, it can be seen that the proportion of parents satisfied with the provision of educational resources (facilities, teachers, curriculum system, extracurricular activities) and the school management was lower in township schools and village schools than in urban schools in counties, cities and provincial cities.

TABLE 5.5   Proportion of parents that were satisfied with schools by detailed categories in urban and rural schools (%)

	Provincial city schools	City schools	County schools	Township schools	Village schools
Enrollment rates to further education and school rankings	25.66	31.06	28.00	11.35	7.67
Close to home	62.32	57.44	58.88	75.21	76.40
Facilities for learning and living	36.58	36.16	32.79	21.94	16.22

TABLE 5.5   Proportion of parents that were satisfied with schools (cont.)

	Provincial city schools	City schools	County schools	Township schools	Village schools
Curriculum	16.65	12.59	9.19	6.82	7.08
Extracurricular activity	15.40	12.78	10.15	9.05	7.67
Teaching staff quality	27.09	30.59	29.26	14.90	10.91
School management	27.36	29.32	26.58	16.36	13.57
Others	9.30	9.14	10.05	12.95	16.22

4   Parents' Evaluation on the Tendency of Examination-Oriented Education in Schools

4.1   Overall Evaluation

Overall, 31.30% of the participating parents considered that the tendency of examination-oriented education was "very serious," and 29.74% thought it was "quite serious," adding up to roughly 60% of parents considered schools had a serious issue of examination-oriented education. For the rest of the parents, 25.43% of them thought that the tendency was "neutral," and 4.89% thought that it was "not serious." Only 8.62% of parents thought that the tendency of their child's school to teach to the test was not serious at all.[6]

4.2   Comparison of the Severity of the Tendency of Examination-Oriented Education in Schools by Province

Participating parents reported that their children attended schools in 31 provinces. Figure 5.4 showed the mean severity level of the tendency of examination-oriented education for schools in those 31 provinces. The overall average severity of the tendency of schools to teach to the test was 3.70, with 11 provinces, centrally-controlled municipalities and autonomous regions had schools with the severity of the tendency to teach to the test below the overall average value, namely Tianjin, Guangdong, Beijing, Zhejiang, Fujian, Guangxi, Shanghai, Hainan, Jiangxi, Henan, and Hunan. Around two-thirds of the provinces in the country had the examination-oriented education

---

[6] Effective sample size is 13157. A total of 404 invalid samples were not included in the summary statistics. The scores were reverse coded, with 1 representing not serious at all and 5 for very serious. Higher scores mean more serious.

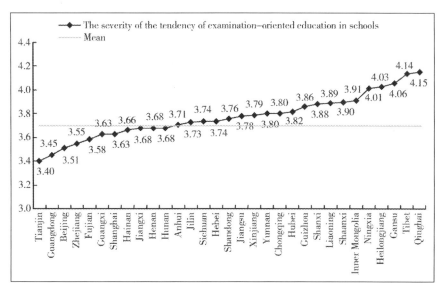

FIGURE 5.4 Comparison of the mean values of the severity of schools' tendency to teach to the test in 31 provinces

tendency severity score higher than the overall average. Most of those schools were located in the central and western regions where education was relatively under-developed, namely, Qinghai, Tibet, Gansu, Heilongjiang, Ningxia, Inner Mongolia, Shaanxi, Liaoning, Shanxi, Guizhou, Hubei, Chongqing, Yunnan, Xinjiang, Jiangsu, Shandong, Hebei, Sichuan, Jilin, and Anhui, adding up to a total of 20 provinces.

In parents' opinion, the tendency of schools to teach to the test was the least serious in Tianjin (mean = 3.40), followed by Guangdong (mean = 3.45) and Beijing (mean = 3.51). In parents' eyes, schools' tendency to teach to the test was not serious in Shanghai, with a mean of 3.63, which was slightly higher than that in Beijing. The five provinces and autonomous regions where parents reported the most serious tendency of schools to teach to the test were Qinghai (mean = 4.15), Tibet (mean = 4.14), Gansu (mean = 4.06), Heilongjiang (mean = 4.03), and Ningxia (mean = 4.01).

4.3   Comparison of the Severity of the Examination-Oriented Education Tendency in Schools in the Central, East and West Regions

In general, the western provinces had the highest number of schools with a higher tendency to teach to the test than the overall average, followed by the central provinces and finally the eastern provinces. Figure 5.4 showed that schools in the west regions reported by parents in this survey had the highest severity level for examination-oriented education tendency.

TABLE 5.6   Comparison of the mean severity of the tendency to teach to the test in urban and rural schools

Provincial city schools	City schools	County schools	Township schools	Village schools	Overall mean value
3.61	3.74	3.87	3.61	3.52	3.70

4.4   Urban-Rural Comparison of the Severity of the Tendency of Schools to Teach to the Test

In the parents' view, the tendency to teach to the test was most severe in county schools, followed by prefecture-level city schools. The severity of the tendency to teach to the test for these two types of urban schools was statistically significantly higher than in provincial-level city schools, township schools, and village schools (see Table 5.6).

One-way ANOVA results showed that the severity of the propensity to teach to the test was significantly different for schools in different urban and rural areas. Multiple comparisons showed that the severity of the propensity to teach to the test was higher in county schools than in prefecture-level city schools, and both types were significantly higher than in schools at other levels. City schools were significantly higher than provincial city schools; however, there was no significant difference between provincial city schools and township and village schools; nor was there a significant difference between township schools and village schools.

4.5   Evaluation of the Severity of the Tendency to Teach to the Test in Schools by Parents of Children at Different Grades

It can be seen from Figure 5.5 that parents of junior and senior high school students reported the highest severity of examination-oriented education tendencies in their children's schools, which was consistent with our common sense that middle schools continued to suffer most from examination-oriented education.

One-way ANOVA results showed a significant difference in the severity of the propensity to teach to the test in schools as reported by parents of children at different age groups. Multiple comparisons showed that the severity of the propensity to teach to the test was significantly lower in primary schools than in junior and senior high schools, and significantly lower in kindergarten than in all other age groups. The difference in the severity of the propensity to teach to the test was not significant between kindergarten and primary schools, nor was the difference significant between junior high and senior high schools.

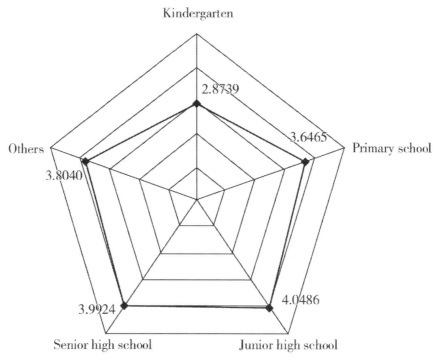

FIGURE 5.5   Mean severity of examination-oriented education tendencies in schools as reported by parents of children at different grades

4.6   *Parents' Evaluation of Reasons for the High Tendency of Examination-Oriented Education in Schools*

Parents considered five major reasons for the serious tendency of examination-oriented education in schools. First, "the single evaluation system for the middle and college entrance examinations"; second, "the pursuit of high rates of students entering further education by principals and teachers"; third, "the government's pursuit of achievement in the education sector"; fourth, "parents attaching too much importance to test scores," and fifth, "training institutions fueling the problem." It can be said that a score-based test evaluation system plays a central role in examination-oriented education.

Comparing the feelings of parents with children at different school years, it can be seen that parents of children in junior and senior high schools had the most "painful feeling" about the single evaluation system by examinations and the pursuit of higher rates of students entering further education by principals and teachers (See Table 5.7).

TABLE 5.7   Attribution of reasons for examination-oriented education in schools by parents with children at different school-age groups (%)

	Principals, teachers pursuing high rates of students entering further education	Parents place too much emphasis on test scores	Training institutions contribute to the problem	Government pursues achievements in the education sector	Single assessment system for middle school and college entrance examinations	Others
Parents of primary school students	44.56	37.97	27.16	43.30	49.73	13.88
Parents of junior high school students	52.49	32.68	22.71	40.75	72.92	6.57
Parents of high school students	51.02	31.99	17.72	39.86	72.03	7.42
Others	52.27	37.23	22.10	47.26	56.11	17.95

5   Parents' Perceptions of the Education Quality of Their Children's Schools

The question "What do you think are the main focuses of the school's education for your child?" was designed to measure parents' views on the emphasis of school's education. Overall, the highest percentage of parents (57.27%) thought that schools focused on "test scores and academic achievements," which to some extent indicates that "teach to tests" was still the most apparent educational goal of schools in the eyes of parents. Only less than 30% of parents thought schools emphasized areas such as "moral and character development," "development of personality, interests, and potential," "physical fitness

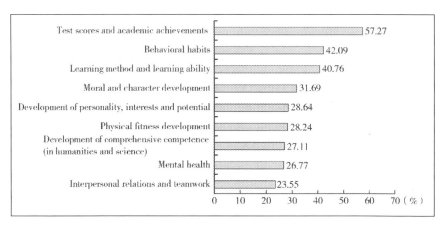

FIGURE 5.6 Percentage of parents that reported their perception of the focused areas of their child's school's education

development," "development of comprehensive competence (in humanities and science)," and "mental health" (See Figure 5.6).

Further comparing parents' views on the focuses of school education in urban and rural schools (See Table 5.8), we can see that the highest proportion of parents (63.11%) who believed that schools focused on "test scores and academic achievements" were parents of students in county schools. To some extent, this result echoes the aforementioned findings that county schools had the most serious tendency to examination-oriented education. The lower proportion of parents of students in village schools than in other kinds of schools chose areas including "learning method and learning ability," "behavioral habits," "development of personality, interests, and potential," "development of comprehensive competence (in humanities and science)," "physical fitness development," and "interpersonal relations and teamwork." This shows that, under the backdrop of examination-oriented education, education quality was lowest in village schools.

TABLE 5.8 Parents' evaluation of school education focuses in urban and rural schools, % of parents

	Provincial city schools	City schools	County schools	Township schools	Village schools
Test scores, academic achievements	54.49	58.48	63.11	54.11	48.67
Learning methods, learning capabilities	41.84	43.45	38.71	36.07	33.92

TABLE 5.8 Parents' evaluation of school education focuses in urban and rural schools (*cont.*)

	Provincial city schools	City schools	County schools	Township schools	Village schools
Behavioral habit	45.53	42.44	38.81	37.95	32.45
Comprehensive competence (in humanities and science)	31.04	28.37	22.18	22.28	17.99
Physical fitness	30.55	28.43	25.72	25.42	25.07
Mental health	28.15	27.50	24.93	24.30	24.78
Interpersonal relations, teamwork	25.51	24.84	20.50	20.61	19.47
Development of personality, interests and potential	30.69	29.04	25.36	28.06	24.78
Moral character	31.84	33.64	29.65	30.99	30.09
Others	6.03	6.11	5.69	9.33	13.86

6   Parental Satisfaction of Public and Privately-Run Schools

Of the parents surveyed, 75.92% and 16.59% were parents of students in public schools and private schools, respectively.[7] The independent sample t-test showed that private schoolers' parents were more satisfied with school education than parents of public schools, and the difference was statistically significant. Further analysis of how much children liked schools and the parents' satisfaction with their children's classroom teachers revealed that private schools were more popular than public schools for children, and parents of private-school students were more satisfied with their children's classroom teachers than parents of public schools' students. Those differences were both statistically significant. This reflects the better education quality of private schools.

---

[7] Some other parents were of students in private-support public schools (1.53%) and government-support private schools (2.06%). Given the low percentage, those data were not included in the analysis.

TABLE 5.9 Comparison of mean parental satisfaction for public and private schools

Public school	Private school	Grand mean
3.53	3.58	3.54

Specifically, the proportions of students that continued to further education were comparable in public and private schools. Parents of public-school students were more satisfied with the fact that schools were close to their homes. However, compared with public-school parents, parents of private-school students were more satisfied with areas including facilities, curriculum system, extracurricular activities, school management, etc. (See Figure 5.7). This difference in schools' education quality can be explained by the contents of school education and the tendency to teach to the test. Figure 5.8 shows the parental evaluation of the contents of their children's schooling in public and private schools. With the exception of "test scores and academic achievements," a higher proportion of parents of private-school students than of public-school students believed that their children's school education focused on areas such as students' behavior and habits, comprehensive competence (in humanities

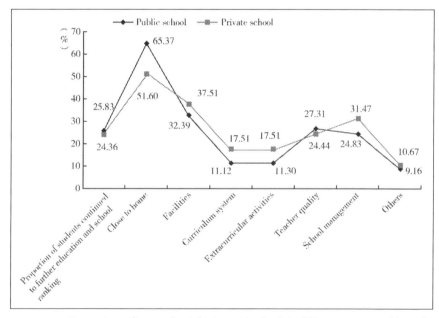

FIGURE 5.7 Comparison of parental satisfaction with schools in different areas in public and private schools

and science), physical fitness, mental health, interpersonal relations and teamwork, development of personality, interests, and potential, and character and personality development.

In parents' opinion, the tendency to teach to the test was more severe in public schools. Analysis of variance shows a statistically significant difference in parents' perceptions of the level of severity of examination-oriented education in different types of schools. The results of multiple comparisons show that public schools were statistically significantly more likely to teach to the test than private schools.

TABLE 5.10 Comparison of mean parental evaluation of the severity of the tendency to examination-oriented education in their child's current school

Public school	Private school	Grand mean
3.79	3.39	3.70

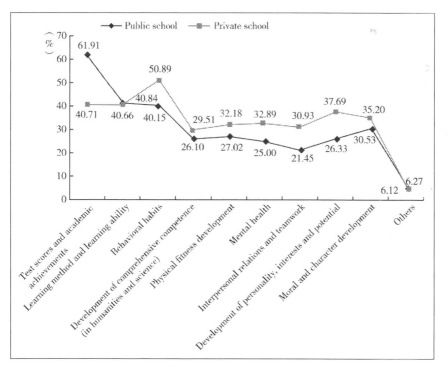

FIGURE 5.8 Comparison of parental perception of focuses of school education in different areas in public schools and private schools

TABLE 5.11 Parental evaluation of their child's classroom teachers (%)

	Parents of public schools	Parents of private schools	Other
Too lax in student management	18.31	15.02	21.02
Discrimination or differential treatment against students	21.73	19.33	26.33
Physical punishment or disguised physical punishment of students	11.41	10.36	15.72
Arbitrary evaluation of children	26.48	23.6	31.63
Making student test results public	32.44	20.58	34.47
Ranking students	31.79	23.07	38.83
Disrespecting parents	9.72	6.89	11.55
Requesting gifts or personal favor from parents	5.54	4.76	12.69
Fewer assignments for students, but more tasks for parents	14.95	11.73	13.45
Paid to make up classes	13.91	10.62	20.45
Others	28.21	36.67	33.71

Parents' evaluations of their child's classroom teacher provided a more in-depth reflection of their evaluation of the school education. Further investigation found that a much higher proportion of parents of public-school students than parents of private-school students reported issues of teachers such as "too lax in student management," "too arbitrary in student evaluation," "made public students' test scores," "ranking students according to test scores," "disrespecting parents," "assigning less homework to students but more tasks to parents," "paid to make up classes" etc. This result is very surprising (See Table 5.11).

7   Parents' Expectations of School Education

Parents' expectations of school education can be seen through the question, "What changes would you most like to see in your child's current school?" The ranking of parents' choices in descending order is shown in Figure 5.9. The most popular one was "fostering all-round development of students" (68.84%),

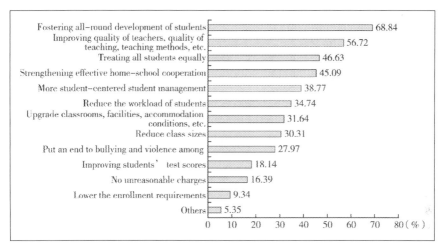

FIGURE 5.9 Parents' expectations of school education

followed by "improving quality of teachers, quality of teaching, teaching methods, etc." with more than half (56.72%) of parents choosing this option. "Treating all students equally" (46.63%) came in third place. More than 40% (45.09%) of parents chose "strengthening effective home-school cooperation." Over 30% of parents chose areas including "more student-centered student management," "reduce the workload of students," "upgrade classrooms, facilities, accommodation conditions, etc.," and "reduce class sizes."

We compared results for parents of students in different school age groups and parents of students in schools in different locations. Results indicate that kindergarten students' parents were most likely to call for schools to "lower the enrollment requirements" and "stop unreasonable charges." Parents of primary school students, parents of prefecture-level city schools and county schools were the strongest in calling for "reducing class sizes." Parents of primary and junior high school students, parents of students in city schools, and county schools were the most in choosing "reducing the students' workload in schoolwork." The call to "put an end to bullying and violence in schools" was the strongest among parents of students in town schools and village schools. In terms of improving the quality of education, treating students equally, focusing on all-around development, implementing student-centered management, and strengthening home-school cooperation, parents' demands in all school ages and in urban and rural schools were relatively consistent (see Table 5.12).

TABLE 5.12 Changes that parents expected from schools (%)

	Lowering the enrollment requirements	No unreasonable charges	Reduction of class size	Improvement of school hardware	Improving teaching quality	Treating all students equally
Parents of kindergarten students	12.79	25.46	28.05	39.29	56.91	49.25
Parents of primary school students	7.52	11.62	33.01	30.16	59.46	49.53
Parents of junior high school students	7.99	14.14	28.88	29.21	53.11	42.87
Parents of high school students	9.26	17.44	26.59	29.59	55.91	40.50
Others	15.12	27.53	29.68	35.64	53.33	46.81
Parents of provincial city school students	9.32	13.80	25.09	28.28	56.20	47.57
Parents of prefecture-city school students	9.53	15.56	31.37	29.89	55.96	47.94
Parents of county school students	9.16	18.88	40.36	35.74	57.12	45.45
Parents of town school students	9.26	21.24	27.72	36.91	59.19	43.73
Parents of village school students	9.44	22.12	20.35	42.77	58.70	41.00

ucing olwork kload	Improving student test scores	Focusing on students' overall development	Student-centered management	Ending bullying and violence	Strengthening home-school cooperation	Others
1	6.57	55.13	36.23	30.76	43.55	8.29
2	13.92	71.86	40.11	28.64	47.44	4.38
2	24.83	73.11	39.19	26.81	44.24	3.83
0	31.73	69.02	35.74	20.71	46.07	4.49
2	18.86	64.98	39.53	33.50	37.79	9.71
4	17.00	66.71	40.35	24.99	43.86	5.70
7	18.59	69.89	39.33	27.45	46.76	4.99
9	18.58	70.98	37.39	30.15	46.05	4.73
2	20.47	70.68	35.93	33.50	44.36	5.50
9	17.11	63.72	32.74	36.28	40.71	8.85

8 Discussion and Conclusion

Parents are an essential force in educational reform. Understanding parental evaluation and opinions on school education from their own reports offers an important perspective in school education evaluation. For a long time, our evaluation of school education has been mainly through the administrative system, and has focused on the aspects such as school running conditions, teachers' quality, academic achievements, etc., lacking the participation of students and parents. As an experiment, the current survey had some new findings, some of which matched our experience and some of which were unexpected. The parents' evaluations of school education presented in the survey not only provided parental aspirations and opinions for improving school education, but also reflected their attitudes toward education reform and provided a public opinion for deepening education reform.

8.1 Overall Low Satisfaction Level of Students' Parents with School Education

Overall, most parents who participated in the survey reported "neutral" or "slightly satisfied" with school education, with the mean score of parental satisfaction for schools in the 31 provinces, centrally-controlled municipalities and autonomous regions ranged from 3.00 to 3.66 (out of 5). About two-thirds of the country's provinces had parental satisfaction level with school education lower than the nation's average. Parental evaluations reflected the reality of high levels of satisfaction with school education in east regions and low levels in the west, with parental satisfaction being lower in the western provinces, where educational resources were relatively fewer. It is worth pointing out that parental satisfaction was not fully correlated with the level of educational development. Some provinces that received high ratings, were not advanced regions in terms of academic quality evaluations. However, in some provinces and centrally-controlled municipalities with relatively rich educational resources, parental satisfaction with school education was lower than the national average, such as Jiangsu and Shanghai, ranked 17th and 21st, respectively. The reasons for this disparity deserve further study. It may indicate that parents' subjective feelings about school education come more from aspects such as teacher-student and home-school relations, rather than from indicators such as academic achievement.

8.2 Significant Differences in Parental Satisfaction with School Education among Parents of Students in Urban and Rural Schools

The differences in parental satisfaction with school education in schools in urban and rural areas were consistent with our expectations. Parental satisfaction was statistically significantly higher in provincial cities, prefecture-level cities, and counties than in town and village schools. In terms of the supply of educational resources (school conditions, teachers, curriculum system, extracurricular activities) and the school management levels, town schools and village schools were far worse than schools in counties and cities. This is the main reason for the lower parental satisfaction level in town and village schools.

8.3 Parents' Evaluation of School Education in Private Schools Was Higher than in Public Schools

The current parents' survey revealed that private schools scored significantly higher than public schools in terms of overall satisfaction, the content of school education, teachers' evaluation, and the tendency to teach to the test. This result was unexpected. We usually think of public schools as more representative of "quality educational resources," while private schools are often associated with "stigmas" such as profit-making, examination-oriented, and not following education principles. The current survey overturned this stereotype, showing that private schools did a better job than public schools in many areas, including student behavioral habits development, comprehensive competence, physical fitness, mental health, interpersonal relations and teamwork, development of personality, interest, and potential, character and moral development.

8.4 More than Half of the Parents Believed That Schools Had a Serious Tendency to Teach to the Test

Survey results showed that in around two-thirds of the provinces, the severity of the tendency to teach to the test in schools was higher than the national average. The tendency to teach to the test in schools in the western regions was more severe than those in the eastern regions. In terms of urban-rural comparisons, county schools had the most serious tendency to teach to the test. As for different school stages, middle schools had the most serious tendency to teach to the test.

What deserves attention is parents' perspectives on the reasons for the tendency of schools to teach to the test. Parents believed that the two main reasons for the series issue of examination-oriented education in schools were "a single test evaluation system for the high school and college entrance examinations" and "principals and teachers pursuing higher rates of students advancing to further education." In fact, these two reasons pointed to the same issue: the decisive role of evaluation by examination. Relevant factors, as ordered by their importance, were: a single test evaluation system for the high school and college entrance examinations, principals and teachers pursuing higher rates of students advancing to further education, government pursuing achievements in the education sector, parents' overly emphasis on test scores, and training institutions' push for fuel. This showed that parents had a quite clear and rational understanding of the issue. Government plays a major role in changing the examination and evaluation standards. Parents' view on this issue showed an effective path to stop examination-oriented education.

8.5 Parents Had the Strongest Expectation for Schools to Focus on the "All-Round Development of Children"

Parents' expectations of changes in education varied by their children's age and school types. Parents of kindergarten students were most likely to expect that schools would "lower enrollment requirements" and "stop unreasonable charges." Parents of middle school students were most likely to expect that schools would "reduce students' workload." Parents of county school students were most likely to expect that schools would "reduce class sizes." Village school students' parents were most likely to call for "school facilities upgrade" and "cracking down on bullying and violence in schools."

However, in terms of improving the quality of education, treating students equally, focusing on all-round development, implementing student-centered management, and strengthening home-school cooperation, the demands of students' parents were relatively consistent across all school stages and in both urban and rural schools. In particular, the demand to focus on the all-round development of students was the strongest in primary schools, junior high schools, senior high schools, and urban and rural schools. Parents' concern for the distance between home and school, and for students' moral and character development, personality, and interest development has, to a certain extent, overturned the stereotype that parents were only concerned with scores and the rate for students to advance to further education, and that they were supporting the examination-oriented education. This helps us to correctly recognize the role of parents.

CHAPTER 6

Report on the Learning and Development of First-Generation College Students in China

Zhang Huafeng,[1] Guo Fei[2] and Shi Jinghuan[3]

Abstract

The popularization of higher education in China has led to an increasing number of families with first-generation college students. Promoting the learning and development of first-generation college students requires a comprehensive understanding of this group's characteristics and the challenges they face. This study analyzes the pre-college experience of first-generation college students, their college experience, their evaluation of colleges, and their educational gains, using data from the 2015 Tsinghua University "Chinese College Students Survey on their Learning and Development" (CCSS). The results show that first-generation college students' families had lower economic status and cultural capital. They enjoyed fewer high-quality educational resources in high school, rarely got guaranteed admission or independent recruitment opportunities for college enrollment, and most of them went to local ordinary colleges and universities. During their college years, first-generation college students were less likely to be active learners and less likely to have active social interactions. They were less likely to participate in extracurricular activities, but spent more time on part-time jobs. In addition, they were less likely to participate in two types of high-impact educational activities: extension of existing work and research-related work. In terms of evaluating colleges and educational achievement, first-generation college students had low ratings of support for social interactions provided by colleges and low perceived gains in communication and leadership skills. First-generation college students had preexisting disadvantages that were difficult to change. They experienced a lack of

---

[1] Zhang Huafeng 张华峰, is a doctoral student at the Graduate School of Education, Tsinghua University, with research interests in college student learning and development and higher education.
[2] Guo Fei 郭菲, Ph.D. in Educational Economics, is a postdoctoral scholar at the Graduate School of Education, Tsinghua University, with research interests in college student learning and development and higher education economics.
[3] Shi Jinghuan 史静寰, Ph.D. in Education, is a professor of education and executive vice president of the Graduate School of Education, Tsinghua University, with research interests in higher education.

support both academically and financially during their study in colleges. They require colleges and universities to promote their better development through improved resource allocation and support measures.

Keywords

first-generation college students (第一代大学生) – learning and development – pre-college characteristics – schooling experiences – educational gains

With the rapid development of higher education in China, the country's gross enrollment rate in higher education institutions has reached 40% in 2015, beginning the transition from the late stage of mass into the early stage of universal higher education. The rapid expansion of higher education has led to an increase in the number of first-generation college students (college students whose parents did not receive higher education, hereinafter referred to as first-generation college students). As a result, first-generation college students are becoming the majority of college students. According to the 2011 to 2015 data from the China College Students Survey (CCSS) project, which was conducted by Professor Shi Jinghuan of Tsinghua University, 70%–75% of undergraduate students in China were first-generation college students. This, to some extent, reflected equal opportunity to receive higher education. However, to promote the growth and success of first-generation college students and to promote the transformation of China's human resources from large scale to high quality, it is necessary not only to expand the number of first-generation college students, but also to focus on improving the quality of their learning process. Therefore, the CCSS project team has been focusing on the first-generation college students since 2014, and has conducted a comprehensive analysis of their basic characteristics, college experience, and the challenges they face, so as to provide a useful reference for promoting their learning and development.

1 Survey Instruments and Data Sources

The CCSS project team surveyed college students' learning experience during their time in school using a questionnaire called "China College Student Survey on their Learning and Development (general undergraduate version)." The questionnaire had two parts: Part A and Part B. Part A mainly reflected students' learning experience during their time in school, including their learning behaviors and attitudes, their participation in educational activities both inside and outside the classroom, their self-perceived learning gains, their evaluation of the educational support from college and university, and their satisfaction level with the school experience. Part B was on students' background information, which mainly reflected students' demographic characteristics, family situation, and pre-college education experience.

Since 2009, a cumulative total of about 147 colleges and universities have participated in the CCSS project. In 2015, the project team distributed 121,140 questionnaires within the 38 general undergraduate colleges and universities that participated in the study and received 71,969 completed questionnaires, a 59.41% response rate. Then, among the stratified random sample from 37 institutions, invalid questionnaires (1.1%) with a proportion of missing responses greater than two-thirds and polygraph question scores greater than two were removed, leaving a valid random sample of 60703. The participating institutions were located in the eastern municipalities, eastern non-municipalities, northeast, central and western regions of China, involving seven 985 institutions (sample size 9664), eight 211 institutions (sample size 10,723), 14 local undergraduate universities (sample size 25,481), and eight local undergraduate colleges (sample size 14,835), reflecting a good nationwide representation.

2   Findings and Conclusions

2.1   *Pre-College Characteristics of First-Generation College Students*

Pre-college characteristics of first-generation college students refer to the basic characteristics and educational experiences of first-generation college students before they enter college, including their family background, high school educational experiences, and college entrance exams and college choices. Key findings from the data analysis are as follows.

2.1.1   Low Socioeconomic Status of the Family, Low Cultural Capital

The results of the analysis of the family background of first-generation college students are shown in Table 6.1. It is found that, firstly, compared with non-first-generation college students, more first-generation college students were from rural areas (69.74%), more were from families with multiple children (70%), and their parents were more likely to be engaged in ordinary occupations[4] (76.89%). This reflected the lower socioeconomic status of

---

[4]   In this study, occupational status was classified into three levels: ordinary, middle and high level. Among them, ordinary occupations included junior professional technicians, clerks,

first-generation college students' families and their difficulty in obtaining sufficient financial support in education and other areas from their families. It also reflected that the origin of first-generation college students was clearly related to China's urban-rural dual structure. Secondly, a further breakdown of the educational background of the parents of first-generation college students revealed that not only had their parents never attended college, but also that most of them only received junior high school and less education (69.76% for fathers and 79.80% for mothers), which indicated that the families of first-generation college students had low cultural capital, making it difficult for them to provide adequate and effective academic guidance in the educational experiences.

TABLE 6.1   Background information and family situations (in %)

Categories	First-generation college students	Non-first-generation college students
Male students	53.18	53.53
Students from rural areas	69.74	16.83
Ethnic minority students	9.99	11.9
Only child	30.00	75.32
Parental occupation: ordinary occupation	76.89	31.13
Parental education: junior high school or less	69.76 (fathers) 79.80 (mothers)	–

2.1.2   Less Access to Quality Educational Resources in Senior High School and More Science Students

An analysis of the senior high school education experiences of first-generation college students was conducted, and the results are shown in Table 6.2. The analysis found that, first, compared with non-first-generation college students, a smaller proportion of first-generation college students (45.16%) attended key senior high schools at the city level or municipal city level, and a larger

self-employed, itinerant vendors, skilled workers/maintenance workers/craftsmen, manual workers/handymen/carriers, and those who earn their living by speculating in stocks/rent, etc.; middle-level occupations included middle-level management, middle-level technicians, foremen/team leaders, head of village or neighborhood committee, freelancers, military/police; and high-level occupations included senior management, senior technician, private business owners.

proportion (52.05%) never attended after-class tutoring classes. However, in the last semester of senior high school, more first-generation college students (64.37%) ranked in the top 20% of their class in terms of academic performance. The above results indicated that first-generation college students had less access to quality educational resources during their senior high school years and less opportunity to improve themselves through after-class tutoring, which required them to study hard and become the "top students" in order to enter colleges and universities.

Second, only 30.25% of first-generation college students served as school-level student leaders during senior high school, slightly lower than non-first-generation college students (36.16%). This result could be due to the lack of ability of first-generation college students or their choice to devote more time to their academic studies.

Third, during senior high school, first-generation college students were more likely to choose science (62.95%) and less likely to choose to be art students (5.82%) than non-first-generation college students. This may be influenced by the common belief that "science students have more employment opportunities," which partly reflected their more pragmatic motivation for choosing a major. In contrast, the growth and development of art students required support from a family that was aware of the need to actively accumulate cultural capital and had the ability to provide adequate financial support, while the family situation of first-generation college students limited their options in this field.

TABLE 6.2   Characteristics of subject choices in senior high schools and college-entrance examinations (in %)

Categories	First-generation college students	Non-first-generation college students
Type of senior high school: key schools at the city and municipal level	45.16	68.19
Senior high school classes: key classes	43.23	43.21
The senior high school student leader at the school level	30.25	36.16
Top 20% of the class in senior high school	64.37	57.53
Never received tutoring outside of class in senior high school	52.05	32.49

TABLE 6.2 Characteristics of subject choices in senior high schools (*cont.*)

Categories	First-generation college students	Non-first-generation college students
Type of college-entrance examination: liberal arts students	26.30	26.29
Type of college-entrance examination: science students	62.95	59.39
Type of college-entrance examination: art and performance students	5.82	8.08

2.1.3   Very Few Got the Opportunity of Guaranteed Admission or Independent Undergraduate Recruitment, Most of Them Attended Local Undergraduate Colleges and Universities, Less Likely to Choose Humanities Majors

The analysis results of how first-generation college students were admitted to colleges, types of universities, and types of majors are shown in Table 6.3. The analysis found that, in terms of college entry paths, first-generation college students basically all took the normal college-entrance examination, and a tiny proportion (1.94%) were admitted to colleges through guaranteed admission or independent recruitment procedures. Moreover, more first-generation college students than non-first-generation college students had taken the college-entrance examination several times (19.91%), i.e., they had one more year in senior high school to study for the examination. This was consistent with the fact that their average age of college-admission was 0.4 years higher than that of non-first-generation college students.

The vast majority of first-generation college students were enrolled in local undergraduate colleges and universities, with no more than 10% enrolled in "211" or "985" universities. Although higher education has been seen as an important way to move up socially, whether entering local undergraduate universities or colleges could help first-generation college students move to a higher position in society require further research and discussion. In terms of choice of major, first-generation college students were more likely to study science, engineering, management, or education majors (74.58%), while a smaller proportion chose humanities (literature, history, philosophy, or art) as their major, which was consistent with their choice of senior high school subjects.

TABLE 6.3 Information on college-entrance examination and college/university admissions (in %)

Categories	First-generation college students	Non-first-generation college students
Admission through guaranteed admission or independent recruitment	1.94	4.54
Have taken college-entrance examination multiple times	19.91	11.76
Average college-admission age	18.83 (years)	18.43 (years)
Admission to "211" or "985" universities	9.98	17.96
Majors in college/university		
Literary	7.9	9.23
History	0.16	0.17
Philosophy	0.03	0.06
Education	2.76	1.38
Economics	4.77	5.72
Law	3.58	5.00
Science	6.38	5.68
Engineering	43.06	41.02
Agriculture	1.41	1.3
Medical science	1.69	2.33
Management	22.38	19.46
Art	5.88	8.66

2.2   *Experience of First-Generation College Students during Their College Studies*

Focusing on first-generation college students' experiences and the issues that arise during their college years provides the basis for targeted efforts to improve the quality of the learning process for first-generation college students. This report provides a detailed analysis of first-generation college students' in-class and out-of-class learning behaviors, interpersonal interaction behaviors, extracurricular time allocation, and participation in high-impact educational activities, and draws the following preliminary findings.

TABLE 6.4   Performance in terms of different learning styles

Learning styles	First-generation college students		Non-first-generation college students		Difference (significant)	Cohen's d
	Mean	Standard deviation	Mean	Standard deviation		
Receptive learning	57.55	19.19	59.23	21.03	−1.16***	−0.06
Active learning	42.03	20.06	46.99	23.34	−4.27***	−0.20
Reflective and integrated learning	57.00	17.14	60.05	18.92	−2.55***	−0.14

Note: The difference here was derived from comparisons made after controlling for social acceptability, and was slightly different from the direct difference between the scores of the two groups. The same applied below.

2.2.1 Acceptable Performance in Receptive Learning and Inadequate Performance in Active Learning

Individuals tend to adopt multiple, rather than a single, learning style when they have diverse learning objects and complex learning processes. This report considered three learning styles: receptive learning, active learning, and reflective and integrative learning. Receptive learning refers to the basic learning behaviors such as attentive listening required for course-content learning. Four questions measured this aspect, Cronbach's α = 0.78. Active learning was measured by five questions (Cronbach's α = 0.82), referring to students actively participating in learning activities such as discussions outside of the mandatory course requirements. Nine questions measured reflective and integrative learning (Cronbach's α = 0.88), which involves multi-perspective thinking, reflection, and integration to obtain a more profound understanding and application of knowledge.

An analysis of first-generation college students' course-learning behavior in terms of their learning styles was conducted, and the results are shown in Table 6.4. The analysis found that the performance of first-generation college students was significantly worse than that of non-first-generation college students in all three learning styles. The gap was the smallest with receptive learning, followed by reflective and integrative learning, and the largest gap was with active learning (absolute value of Cohen's d greater than 0.20). Receptive learning is the basic learning behavior required by the course. Active learning emphasizes proactive learning and outward expression. Reflective and integrated learning places more emphasis on implicit knowledge processing and construction. The poor performance of first-generation college students in active learning reflected the fact that they may not be good at actively expressing their opinions or actively seeking discussion and assistance in their coursework.

2.2.2 Overall Underperformance in Interpersonal Interactions, with the Worst Performance in Social Student-Student Interactions

We defined four types of interpersonal interactions at school for college students, including: academic student-student interactions, social student-student interactions, academic student-teacher interactions, and social student-teacher interactions. Academic student-student interactions refer to interactions with peers on course learning topics, and were measured by four questions, Cronbach's $\alpha = 0.73$. Social student-student interactions refer to interactions with peers for the purpose of enriching interpersonal life, etc., and were measured by four questions, Cronbach's $\alpha = 0.75$. Academic student-teacher interactions refer to interactions with teachers around course learning, and were measured by five items with Cronbach's $\alpha = 0.83$. Social student-teacher interactions refer to teacher-student interactions aimed at enriching interpersonal life and developing students' view of life, values, and future plans. It was measured by five items with an internal consistency coefficient of 0.92.

Results of the analysis on the four types of interactions were summarized in Table 6.5. The analysis found that first-generation college students performed significantly worse than non-first-generation college students on all four types of interactions. Specifically, the gap between first-generation college students and non-first-generation college students was smaller for academic interactions, but larger for social interactions, especially for social student-student interactions. In part, this suggests that first-generation college students were more focused on academic interactions on course content than on social interactions outside the classroom, suggesting that they valued course work the most. However, in contrast to senior high school, "learning" in higher education institutions extends beyond the confines of the curriculum and classroom to include interactions with peers and other resources. This requires first-generation college students to go beyond classroom learning to enhance their knowledge and skills development and to obtain non-academic advice and assistance to improve their college readiness and academic development, through social interactions with students and faculty.

TABLE 6.5 Interpersonal interactions of first-generation college students

Interpersonal Interaction on Campus	First-generation college students		Non-first-generation college students		Difference (significant)	Cohen's d
	Average value	Standard deviation	Average value	Standard deviation		
Social student-teacher interactions	34.79	26.32	40.92	29.06	−5.14***	−0.19
Academic student-teacher interactions	41.29	19.90	45.49	23.18	−3.52***	−0.17
Social student-student interactions	45.55	19.70	51.42	21.72	−5.45***	−0.27
Academic student-student interactions	58.50	18.54	61.84	20.45	−2.87***	−0.15

2.2.3 Less Time Spent on Participation in Extracurricular Activities and More Time Spent on Part-Time Jobs

Students have more free time outside of the classroom when they study at college than they do in senior high school. This makes it important for the college education to consider not only the traditional classroom, but also students' extracurricular time allocation and activities. This report analyzes the extracurricular time allocation and activities of first-generation college students. The results are shown in Table 6.6.

The results show that while the time spent on academic studies outside of the classroom was significantly lower for first-generation college students than for non-first-generation college students, the actual difference was small (only 0.365 hours/week). In terms of the time spent on extracurricular activities, there was a statistically significant difference (0.838 hours/week) between first-generation and non-first-generation college students, and the difference was relatively large in magnitude. The biggest difference between the two groups was in the number of hours spent on part-time jobs, with first-generation college students spent about one more hour/week than non-first-generation college students, and the difference was statistically significant.

TABLE 6.6 Allocation of time for different extracurricular activities

Allocation of extracurricular time	First-generation college students		Non-first-generation college students		Difference (significant)	Cohen's d
	Mean	Standard deviation	Mean	Standard deviation		
Academic study outside of classroom hours/week	13.52	8.94	13.91	9.08	−0.37***	−0.04
Part-time job hours/week	6.26	8.07	5.27	7.66	1.10***	0.14
Extracurricular activity hours/week	7.44	7.27	8.38	7.76	−0.84***	−0.11

This reflects that first-generation college students were more likely to spend their free time on part-time jobs rather than devoting their time to studying and participating in campus activities. Involvement in campus activities is a necessary part of integrating into campus life and improving adaptability and social skills. First-generation college students need to improve their social interactions with students and faculty, but the lack of active involvement in campus activities can have a negative impact on them. This also suggests that schools should further increase financial support for first-generation college students, in order to reduce their financial need for taking part-time jobs, and encourage them to spend more time on-campus activities and academic studies.

2.2.4 Performance of First-Generation College Students at High-Impact Educational Practices

Given the importance of participation in extracurricular activities, this report selects the more representative high-impact educational practices to analyze the performance of first-generation college students in such activities. High-impact educational practices are autonomous extracurricular activities that require students to invest considerable time and effort, actively interact with students and faculty, reflect on learning processes, and experience real-world applications of knowledge. Research has shown that participation in such activities can positively impact students' academic and overall development.[5,6] Based on the relevant literature and the actual educational practice in China, this report constructs a total of nine high-impact educational practices in three categories: extended learning activities, research-related activities, and social practice/internship activities.

In particular, extended learning activities refer to advanced or multidisciplinary learning beyond the regular requirements of the curriculum and major, including language study beyond the curriculum requirements, study abroad, and a second-degree minor. Research-related activities refer to research exploration based on in-depth study, which requires a strong research intention and more academic guidance from faculty, including doing research with faculty, submitting articles to professional journals/conferences, and participating in various academic, professional, entrepreneurial, or design competitions. The social practice/internship category refers to activities that take place off-campus in real-life situations that increase students' social experience and promote the application of knowledge in real-life situations, including three types of activities: internships, social practice or research, and community service or volunteering. The results and findings of the analysis are shown below[7] (see Table 6.7).

2.2.4.1 *First-Generation College Students Were Engaged in Social Practice Activities, but Significantly Under-Engaged in Extended Learning and Research-Related Activities*

Overall, a smaller proportion of first-generation college students participated in all high-impact educational practices than non-first-generation college students. Specifically, first-generation college students differed most from non-first-generation college students in their participation in extended learning activities, followed by research-related activities. There was almost no difference between first-generation and non-first-generation college students in terms of participation in social practice activities.

---

5 Kuh, G. (2008). High-impact educational practices: What they are, who has access to them, and why they matter. Washington, DC: American Association of Colleges & Universities (AAC&U).
6 McMahan, S. (2015). Creating a model for high impact practices at a large, regional, comprehensive university: A case study. *Contemporary Issues in Education Research*, 2:111–116.
7 In the process of analysis, in order to reduce the impact of special students such as repeaters and students on suspension on the data analysis, such special samples were excluded. We included 60,181 valid samples in the analysis.

Participation in extended learning activities requires not only students' own willingness, but often some external supports, such as financial investment from parents or academic help from faculty. As the parents of first-generation college students were not highly educated, their socio-professional status was relatively low: only 17.57% of first-generation college students had at least one parent who was a senior executive or professional in an enterprise or institution (according to data from CCSS 2015, same applied to rest of the article), compared to 71.44% of non-first-generation college students. This makes it difficult for first-generation students to understand from their parents the importance of participating in extended learning activities and obtain sufficient financial support to participate in such activities.

Participation in research-relevant activities requires not only solid basic knowledge and research skills, but also a strong desire and motivation to engage in scientific research. The survey found that students who plan to attend graduate schools after graduation were more likely to engage in such activities. Only 17.79% of first-generation college students chose to continue their education after graduation, compared to 33.47% of non-first-generation college students who chose to pursue graduate education. The smaller proportion of students interested in graduate school may be related to the fact that first-generation college students participated less in research-related activities. This is a phenomenon that deserves our attention and discussion. College should seriously consider and do their best to find ways to stimulate the interest, create the environment, and provide support for first-generation college students to encourage them to participate more in research-related activities. In this way, we can further develop their research potential and enhance their research interest, and also enable those who really have the willingness and ability to conduct research to continue their study.

There was essentially no difference between first-generation and non-first-generation college students in terms of participation in social practice activities. This is probably because, in most colleges, internships, social practice, and community service have become compulsory modules in students' training. The colleges already have institutional requirements and supportive conditions in place that promote student participation in these activities. As a result, both groups had high rates of participation in such activities, with little difference.

The above analysis suggests that in order to improve the process quality of education for first-generation college students, schools and faculty should take measures that focus on promoting their participation in extended learning activities and research-relevant activities.

TABLE 6.7 Proportion of first-generation and non-first-generation college students participating in each high-impact educational practices (in %)

High impact educational practices category	Specific high-impact educational practices	First-generation college students	Non-first-generation college students
Extended learning activities	Language learning in addition to course requirements (e.g., attending New Oriental, studying a second foreign language, etc.)	15.16	27.12
	Study abroad (short or long term)	5.45	10.15
	Minor in the second degree	6.64	12.09
Research-related activities	Do research with faculty	20.20	25.56
	Submission of manuscripts to professional journals/conferences, etc.	12.46	16.58
	Participation in various academic, professional, entrepreneurial, or design competitions	23.80	27.29
Social practice activities	Internship	37.56	38.96
	Social practice or research	53.32	54.07
	Community service or volunteer	46.29	47.54

2.2.4.2 *First-Generation College Students with Less Economic and Cultural Capital and Worse Pre-College Academic Performance Were Less Likely to Participate Actively in High-Impact Educational Practices*

Further analysis of first-generation college students' participation in high-impact educational activities using logistic regression (See Table 6.8) found that first-generation college students differed in their participation in high-impact educational practices. Overall, students with less economic and cultural capital (e.g., ethnic minority students, students with parents of lower socio-occupational status), students with worse pre-college academic performance (e.g., from non-key senior high schools, lower college-entrance examination scores), male students, and more junior students were less likely to participate in high-impact educational practices, especially extended high-impact educational practices. This reflects, on the one hand, gender and grade level disparities in high-impact educational practices participation among first-generation college students and, on the other hand, the fact that the primary focus of attention and support should be given to students with less economic and cultural capital and worse pre-college performance, given a large number of first-generation college students and the limited resources available to colleges and universities.

TABLE 6.8 Performance of different types of first-generation college students in their engagement in high-impact educational practices

	Extended learning activities	Research-related activities
	Odds ratio/(se)	Odds ratio/(se)
Female students	1.272*	1.079
	(0.150)	(0.0806)
Ethnic minority students	0.917	0.801**
	(0.0711)	(0.0542)
Only child	1.132**	1.026
	(0.0500)	(0.0545)
Highest occupational status of parents (with agricultural work as the control group)		
General workers/business services staff	1.015	0.851***
	(0.0661)	(0.0418)
Skilled workers/self-employed	1.228**	0.968
	(0.0832)	(0.0436)
Elementary technician/general clerical staff	1.250**	0.959
	(0.0952)	(0.0739)
Middle and senior professional technicians	1.731**	1.177*
	(0.313)	(0.0889)

TABLE 6.8 Performance of different types of first-generation college students (*cont.*)

	Extended learning activities	Research-related activities
	Odds ratio/(se)	Odds ratio/(se)
Heads of enterprises and institutions of party and government agencies	1.574***	1.095
	(0.133)	(0.0588)
Others	1.242***	1.096
	(0.0612)	(0.0630)
Students from the rural area, of agricultural hukou families or farming families	1.012	1.067
	(0.0599)	(0.0577)
Key senior high schools (above prefectural city level)	1.272***	1.100***
	(0.0567)	(0.0335)
College-entrance examination score	1.046	1.051
	(0.0289)	(0.0445)
Type of university (with "985" universities as the control group)		
"211" universities	0.988	0.964
	(0.158)	(0.154)
Local undergraduate universities	0.802	0.905
	(0.111)	(0.151)
Local undergraduate colleges	0.823	0.986
	(0.120)	(0.158)
Grade level (using freshman as the control group)		
Sophomore year	1.636***	1.795***
	(0.164)	(0.136)
Junior year	2.120***	1.988***
	(0.109)	(0.197)
Senior year	2.930***	3.891***
	(0.310)	(0.722)

TABLE 6.8 Performance of different types of first-generation college students (*cont.*)

	Extended learning activities	Research-related activities
	Odds ratio/(se)	Odds ratio/(se)
Major (using humanities as the control group)		
Social sciences	0.497***	0.930
	(0.0447)	(0.112)
Natural sciences	0.406***	0.944
	(0.0347)	(0.139)
Engineering disciplines	0.442***	0.951
	(0.0263)	(0.151)
Missing college-entrance examination scores (dummy coded)	1.150*	0.881*
	(0.0820)	(0.0459)
constant term	0.200***	0.325***
	(0.0347)	(0.0946)
N	36017.000	36004.000
Pseudo R^2	0.0476	0.0415

2.3 Evaluation of Support from School and Their Educational Gains

2.3.1 High Ratings for School Hardware and Financial Support, Low Ratings for Social Support

Students' perceptions and evaluations of the campus environment and support reflect, on the one hand, the support and services provided to students in different aspects of the schools and, on the other hand, students' access to and use of campus-related resources. Based on the differences in the content of campus environment support, we defined six areas: learning hardware facilities, learning software, living hardware facilities, living software, development guidance, and financial support. Specifically, learning hardware facilities refers to the school's facilities, including classrooms, libraries, laboratories, the internet, etc. It was measured with one question. Learning software refers to the quality of the learning environment, curriculum, quality of teaching, and faculty. Three questions were included on this aspect, with Cronbach's α = 0.61. Living hardware facilities referred to the school's facilities related to living conditions (e.g., canteens, dormitories, sports facilities, etc.) and was measured by one question. Life software refers specifically to social support, which refers to the variety of social activities provided and encouraged by the school. It was measured by four questions, Cronbach's α = 0.75. Development guidance refers to the school's support to students on their studies, physical and mental health, and employment. Three questions were included to evaluate this aspect, Cronbach's α = 0.76. Financial support refers to the financial support and assistance (e.g., scholarships, grants, and student loans) that the school provided to students and was measured with one question.

The results are shown in Table 6.9. The analysis reveals that, firstly, first-generation college students rated significantly higher than non-first-generation college students in terms of their perception and evaluation of learning and living hardware facilities. This is likely because first-generation college students mostly came from families with lower socioeconomic status, which made them not have high expectations of school facilities. Thus, they were more satisfied with learning and living facilities on campus.

Second, first-generation college students perceived and rated financial support significantly higher than non-first-generation college students. This may be due to the fact that, compared to non-first-generation students, first-generation students needed more financial support. In addition, they were more aware of the policies and resources available and were more likely to apply and receive them. Therefore, they were more satisfied with the financial support they received from their schools.

TABLE 6.9   First-generation college students' evaluation of supportive campus environment

Support type	First-generation college students		Non-first-generation college students		Difference (significant)	Cohen's d
	Mean	Standard deviation	Mean	Standard deviation		
Learning hardware	62.56	27.50	60.65	29.08	2.57***	0.09
Learning software	60.99	18.53	62.00	20.04	0.09	0.00
Living hardware	55.24	27.10	54.61	28.88	1.18***	0.04
Living software	61.20	19.50	62.41	20.29	−1.01***	−0.05
Developmental guidance	60.88	18.84	61.16	20.06	−0.07	0.00
Financial support	62.56	20.25	61.03	20.87	1.73***	0.08

Third, first-generation college students perceived and rated social support significantly lower than non-first-generation college students. Participation in social activities was not necessary and mandatory, nor was it strength for first-generation college students. With the lack of emphasis on social interactions on campus, together with their lack of social skills, they rarely participated in social activities. As a result, they didn't feel supported and rated low for the school's social support. This suggests that schools, while providing social opportunities and platforms, also need to focus on developing and enhancing first-generation college students' social skills.

Finally, there were no significant differences between first-generation and non-first-generation college students in their perceptions and evaluations of learning software and developmental guidance.

2.3.2 Self-Reported Educational Gains Were Less than Non-First-Generation College Students, with the Least Perceived Improvement in Communication and Leadership Skills

We defined four categories for the self-reported educational gains, including: knowledge acquired, communication and leadership skills development, problem-solving skills development, and self-awareness development. Knowledge acquired refers to students' acquisition of general and specialized areas of knowledge. It was measured by two items, Cronbach's α = 0.73. Communication and leadership skills development refers to students' improvement in presentation and organizational leadership skills. Three items were included, Cronbach's α = 0.85. Problem-solving skills development refers to students' improvement in analyzing and solving complex problems using various approaches. It was measured with seven items, Cronbach's α = 0.89. Self-awareness development refers to the student's improvement in self-awareness (e.g., life view, values, future development plans), measured by two items, Cronbach's α = 0.81.

An analysis of the self-reported educational gains of first-generation college students was conducted, and the results are shown in Table 6.10. Results show that first-generation college students scored significantly lower than non-first-generation college students in all types of educational gains, with the largest gaps in communication and leadership skills, followed by problem-solving skills and knowledge acquired. In contrast, students had smaller gaps in self-awareness development (clarifying their life view, values, and plans for future development in life).

TABLE 6.10 Self-reported educational gains of first-generation college students

Self-reported educational gains	First-generation college students Mean	First-generation college students Standard deviation	Non-first-generation college students Mean	Non-first-generation college students Standard deviation	Difference (significant)	Cohen's d
Knowledge acquired	62.79	22.06	65.21	22.98	−1.76***	−0.08
Self-awareness development	63.48	23.54	64.83	25.17	−0.713*	−0.03
Problem-solving skills	61.19	19.56	63.63	21.14	−1.79***	−0.09
Communication and leadership	56.67	23.66	60.37	24.41	−2.91***	−0.12

Communication, leadership, and problem-solving skills are not developed through specific courses, but rather through social interaction and extracurricular activities provided by the school and family. Compared with non-first-generation college students, first-generation college students had fewer economic and cultural resources, and lack the platform and resources needed to support their ability development. As a result, they were unable to effectively practice and improve their oral expression, written expression, organizational skills, and problem-solving skills. In contrast, students' self-awareness development was usually uncovered by the university curriculum and was often neglected by family education. It depended more on students' natural growth and development. Thus, the difference between the two groups was smaller.

3   Conclusions and Recommendations

Martin Trow has pointed out that higher education will go through three stages of development: elite, mass, and universal, as the number of students enrolled in higher education increases. As the stage of mass higher education progresses, learners' family backgrounds, learning objectives, and future plans will become more diverse.[8] With the deepening of the popularization of

---

[8] Trow, M. (1973). *Problems in the Transition from Elite to Mass Higher Education.* Carnegie Commission on Higher Education, Berkeley, Calif.

higher education in China, many research projects on educational situations in China were carried out, responding to the concerns for diverse groups and educational equity. Consequently, the number of research projects on first-generation college students in China also increases. The CCSS project team's preliminary findings can provide a useful reference for more targeted educational practices in colleges and universities.

We found that first-generation college students' lower family economic status and less cultural capital had a cumulative negative impact on their academic performance. The analysis shows that due to their lower family socioeconomic status and less cultural capital, first-generation college students were more likely to attend ordinary senior high schools. In addition, they seldom received outside-of-class tutoring; they were less prepared for college studies; and they seldom attended "985" and "211" universities. This reflects the fact that the families of first-generation college students were unable to provide their children with sufficient academic guidance and financial support, nor were they able to help them develop good learning habits, which had a long-term and cumulative impact. Moreover, such predispositions were largely unchangeable and could only be ameliorated by education through targeted support and assistance.

First-generation college students were at an overall disadvantage place in their performance in college. Colleges and universities need to promote their academic development through better resource allocation and support measures. The analysis results show that first-generation college students were less engaged in active learning and social activities. First-generation college students, especially those with lower economic status and less cultural capital, and worse pre-college academic performance, were less engaged in high-impact educational practices, such as extended learning activities and research-relevant. They had relatively lower evaluations on the social support provided by schools. They also felt less development in communication and leadership skills. While the total amount of educational resources in colleges and universities is increasing, it is important for colleges and universities to consider how to promote the development of disadvantaged groups in schools through better allocation of resources and targeted support measures. According to the findings of the current study, we have several recommendations. First, colleges and universities can develop orientation programs for newly admitted students to help first-generation college students improve their knowledge base and understand the characteristics of college coursework. This will improve their academic readiness for college. Second, help first-generation college students develop interpersonal skills while in college to facilitate good interpersonal relationships in their new environment. Third, faculty members should provide more guidance and assistance to first-generation college students on life development and academics to help them clarify their future direction. Lastly, financial support for first-generation college students should continue to be increased to promote their participation in high-impact educational practices that require more financial resources, especially for first-generation students whose families have less economic and cultural capital or who have worse academic performance before college.

Based on this report's findings, the CCSS project team has further explored topics including the academic performance of rural first-generation college students, how to promote academic outcomes, and their engagement in high-impact educational practices among first-generation college students. Related results will continue to be published. In future research, the project team will go beyond education theory to analyze the issues related to first-generation college students from psychological and sociological perspectives. We will go beyond exogenous learning experiences to explore the college adjustment and value conflicts faced by first-generation college students. We will also go beyond quantitative research to interpret the difficulties encountered by first-generation college students with a qualitative approach. Finally, we will go beyond general research to focus on the within-group differences of first-generation college students, thus pushing the more in-depth study of first-generation college students.

CHAPTER 7

Studying China's "Super Secondary School" Phenomenon through the "Hengzhong Model"

Wang Shuai[1]

Abstract

Over the years, Hengshui High School has developed a popular "Hengzhong Model" that has been copied and expanded on a large scale across the country, because of the high admission rate to top Chinese universities, such as Peking University and Tsinghua University, of graduates of Hengshui High School. As a model for "Super Secondary School," the "Hengzhong Model" is an extreme form of examination-oriented education, with problems such as only accepting only top-performing students to gather excellent students, not distinguishing between public and private operations, running mixed schools, and harsh education management and training. In this article, through analyzing the "Hengzhong Model," we advocate the value of well-rounded education, the need to breakthrough from examination-oriented education, and cultivate talents for the future.

Keywords

Hengshui High School – "Hengzhong Model" – "Super Secondary School"

In April 2017, Hengshui No. 1 High School, affiliated with Hengshui High School, opened a new branch in Zhejiang Jiaxing Pinghu City. It raised public concern because of the suspected illegal early enrollment of students. Hengshui High School, famous for its high admission rate to higher education institutions and fast-expanding speed throughout the country, was once again caught in the whirlpool of public opinion. On May 5, the private education research organization, 21st Century Education Research Institute, urged the Ministry of Education to investigate and punish Hengshui High School and other super secondary schools for their illegal operations. Under the Ministry

---

[1] Wang Shuai 王帅, Ph.D., Graduate School of Education, Beijing Institute of Technology.

of Education's charge, the Hebei Provincial Education Department conducted a special inspection on this issue and ordered rectification. Later, the education departments of Shijiazhuang, Langfang, Chengde, and many other places issued documents restricting the illegal enrollment of students in local Hengshui No. 1 High Schools.

In recent years, Hengshui High School and the phenomenon of "super secondary schools" represented by Hengshui High School have aroused widespread concern in society. We should be on the alert and cautious about the trend of the increasing number of "super secondary schools." The analysis of Hengshui High School, a representative example of the "super secondary school," will help understand the problem, clarify issues, and rectify the direction of the reform and development of basic education.

1   The Rise of Super Secondary Schools with the "Hengzhong Model"

Huang Xiaoting, an education scholar at Peking University, defined a "super secondary school" as a school with a large student body located in a prefecture-level city or a provincial capital city, which monopolizes local sources of excellent students and teachers, with a relatively large proportion of students admitted to Peking University and Tsinghua University.[2] Hengshui High School is a typical example of such a "super middle school." It is a remarkable superstar that is sought after by some local governments and parents. But it has also been repeatedly criticized, investigated, and punished by the government. There has been an ongoing heated debate on the "Hengzhong Model," where the two sides totally disagree with each other. We need to step back and focus on the facts to better understand all aspects of the "Hengzhong Model."

The "Hengzhong Model" was characterized by the development model of accepting only top-performing students to gather the best students, the school operation model that does not distinguish between public and private operations, and the extremely harsh examination-oriented education model. These three aspects support each other, creating the myth of the "super secondary school." In fact, this is also the typical model of other "super secondary schools."

---

2   Huang Xiaoting and Lu Xiaodong 黄晓婷、卢晓东 "Chaojizhongxue weibi chaoji, "超级中学"未必"超级" ["Super Secondary School" may not be "Super"]," *China Youth Daily*, January 4, 2016.

1.1 *Enrolling Only the Top-Performing Students to Gather the Best Students*

According to many years of investigation reports, the high college-admission rate and super secondary school under the "Hengzhong Model" were highly related to the fact that those schools have adopted some measures to enroll only top-performing students.

Over the years, in the shadow of several super secondary schools such as Hengshui High School, Hebei has waged a fierce competition for good students. As a result, the normal ecology of secondary school examination and high school admissions has been severely impacted, deeply felt by the education community in Hebei. The *Phoenix Weekly* has reported that Hengshui High School is mighty in getting the best students. It has agents in junior high schools in many counties and cities, who will be heavily rewarded for recommending the best students. This cross-district recruitment of good students has made other cities in Hebei, especially nearby cities, suffer a lot and are forced to fight back in various ways. For example, in order to retain local students, a county in Xingtai City used to prohibit the children of the communist party and government organs and institutions from attending high schools in other cities such as Hengshui. Those who work for the government would risk losing their jobs if they sent their children to high schools in Hengshui.[3] Many counties and cities "hide" the high scorers after the high-school-entrance examination. Examination results were not announced or deliberately changed to a lower score, in order to prevent the best students from being recruited by the "Super Secondary Schools." However, these measures cannot retain the excellent students. The *People's Daily* reported that in 2013, a student of Hengshui High School, who just finished the college-entrance exam, revealed that he was from Cangzhou, claiming that over 70 students in his class, out of over 110 students, were not from Hengshui city.[4]

According to educators in Hebei, if the Hengshui High School only recruited local students, it would have, at most, a dozen students who get into Tsinghua and Peking University each year. Over recent years, the data that over 100 students of Hengshui High School got admitted by Tsinghua and Peking University each year, was actually combining the data from Hengshui No. 1 High School, which was misleading advertising. With Hengshui No. 1 High School's

---

3 Guo Tianli 郭天力 "Hengshuizhongxue yinyingxia Hebei shengyuan zhengduozhan, 衡水中学阴影下河北生源争夺战 [The Battle for Good Students in Hebei under the Shadow of Hengshui High School]," *Phoenix Weekly*, Issue 5, 2015.

4 Yang Liu 杨柳 "Hengshuizhongxue: meiduishou youyinyou, 衡水中学：没对手，有隐忧 [Hengshui High School: No Competitors, but Hidden Concerns]," *People's Daily*, July 18, 2013.

establishment in 2014, the "Hengzhong Model" made use of the legal cross-region recruitment policy for privately-run schools to recruit many excellent students from other cities in Hebei province under legal disguise, circumventing the policies and regulations of public-school recruitment. Hou Shujun, principal of Zanhuang County Middle School in Shijiazhuang, commented that the "excellent-student-only recruitment" activity of Hengshui High School and other Super Secondary Schools has made the situation of most of the middle schools in counties get worse and worse. "Success of one school, failure of many others."[5]

1.2 Failure to Distinguish between Public and Private Schools, and the Mixed Operation of Schools

One of the key approaches for the rise and expansion of the "Hengzhong Model" was the mixed operation of private and public schools by establishing privately-run schools. In 1999, Fuyang Middle School was established as a private-supported public school based on Hengshui High School. The school adopted the same teaching and management model as Hengshui High School. In February 2013, Hengshui No. 1 High School, a privately-run school, was founded, with investment from the Hebei Taihua Jinye Real Estate Company. According to its official website, "the school's management, teachers, enrollment, education, and teaching are all based on Hengshui High School."

In the late 1990s, against the backdrop of the reform of the school-running system, it became a trend for "elite schools to set up private schools" in the name of expanding quality educational resources. However, from the very beginning, those schools have problems such as "one school, two systems" and "school within a school," which have made it impossible to distinguish between public and private schools. Some public schools opened some "transitional type schools," such as public-supported private schools and private-supported public schools. Those schools were, in fact, "fake private schools," with issues such as illegal charges and high tuitions, which seriously undermined educational equality. Those schools have been banned since around 2005. According to the *Implementing Regulations of the Law of the People's Republic of China on the Promotion of Privately-run Schools* implemented in 2004, privately-run schools with public schools' involvement in establishment and operation should have "five independents," including independent legal personality, independent

---

5   Lei Lei and Zang Jin 雷磊、藏瑾 "Hengshuizhongxue de 'fengshen' zhilu – chaoji gaokao gongchang, 衡水中学的 "封神" 之路 – 超级高考工厂 [The Path to the Myth of Hengshui High School: Super Factory for College-entrance Examination]," *Southern Weekend*, October 10, 2013.

school operation, independent finance, independent enrollment system, and independent issuance of degree. However, many of these schools, including the "Hengzhong Model" schools, are still stepping on and even crossing the policy boundaries and adopting a public-private-mixed way of operation, taking up public education resources and enjoying the benefits of private education at the same time.

Over the years, the relationship between Hengshui High School and the privately-run Hengshui No. 1 High School has been "ambiguous." They advertise themselves with a unified image and announce combined statistics of the two schools' college-entrance examination results on Hengshui High School's official website. The locals refer to Hengshui No. 1 High School as the "Hengshui High School South Campus," while the earlier-established Fuyang Middle School was referred to as "Hengshui High School East Campus." On June 1, 2017, the *Notice of Rectification* issued by the Hebei Provincial Department of Education ordered several rectification requirements, including that Hengshui High School's legal representative should not act as the legal representative of Hengshui No. 1 High School.[6] On June 16, the Hebei Provincial Department of Education made further explanations on the "issues related to the school operations of Hengshui High School and Hengshui No. 1 High School". It pointed out that the two schools' operation problems include: the school corporate governance structure was not complete, Hengshui High School performed school operations on behalf of Hengshui No. 1 High School; in the admissions publicity process, the two schools names were used interchangeably; enrolled more students than planned resulting in oversize classes; teachers teach in both schools, etc.[7] On the same day, the Hebei Taihua Jinye Real Estate Company announced a "Hengshui No. 1 High School Board of Directors Statement," declaring that "since September 19, 2014, at 23:40, the official seal of the privately-run Hengshui No. 1 High School was forcibly taken by a person from Hebei Hengshui High School," and stating that "From then to now, the board of directors of Hengshui No. 1 High School has never authorized any individuals or groups to cooperate on matters such as the establishment of a

---

6 Wang Yu 王煜 "Hengshuizhongxue yu Hengshuiyizhong weigui banxue bei ling 'qiege' 衡水中学与衡水一中违规办学被令"切割" [Hengshui High School and Hengshui No. 1 High School Illegally Operate Schools and was Ordered to be Separated]," *Beijing News*, June 17, 2017.

7 Wang Ge and Zhong Yuhao 王哿、钟煜豪 "Hebeisheng jiaoyuting: jiang jiaqiang dui gongbanxuexiao canyu minbanxuexiao banxue gongzuo de guanli, 河北省教育厅：将加强对公办学校参与民办学校办学工作的管理 [Hebei Provincial Education Department: Strengthen the Regulation of Public Schools' Involvement in the Operation of Private Schools]," *The Paper*, June 19, 2017.

branch school, nor has it received sponsorship money or franchise fees from any of the schools."[8] This has further brought to the surface the inside stories of Hengshui High School's interference in Hengshui No. 1 High School's operation.

To date, Hengshui High School has not made any serious efforts to rectify the problem of illegal school operations. Although the Hebei Provincial Education Department issued notices and requirements for the rectification of the operations of Hengshui High School and Hengshui No. 1 High School, there are indications that Hengshui High School has not carried out the required rectification and still bundled the two schools for publicity and advisement. For example, on October 15, 2017, when the seventh annual Hengshui High School Campus Tour for the nation's leading universities opened, Zhang Wenmao, principal of Hengshui High School, said on the opening ceremony that 174 students were admitted to Tsinghua University and Peking University and 41 students were admitted to Hong Kong University and other universities in Hong Kong in the most recent year. The headcount of "174" students was apparently the combined number of Hengshui No. 1 High School and Hengshui High School. In 2016, for example, a total of 139 students from Hengshui High School were admitted to Tsinghua University and Peking University, but only 23 of them were actually students of Hengshui High School.

The "Hengzhong Model" is intended to create a "Super Secondary School" of a much larger scale. In June 2017, the privately-run boarding junior middle school "Hengshui Middle School Experimental School" was established. The school was invested by Hengshui Chengbo Real Estate Company and managed by Hengshui High School. Its enrollment brochure advertises that "the school will have full access to Hengshui High School's various educational resources. The school's excellent graduates can enter Hengshui High School or Hengshui No. 1 High School".[9] This kind of enrollment propaganda obviously violated the policy requirement of independent operation and enrollment of privately-run schools. In addition, the school plans to enroll students for all three grades at the same time, including 600 students for the seventh grade, and 360 students for each of the eighth and ninth grades. This would inevitably end up recruiting many students from other junior middle schools, impacting the normal and stable junior middle school education order in the region.

---

8   Xiong Bingqi 熊丙奇 "Hengshuiyizhong buren de 'fenxiao' shi 'jia minban', 衡水一中不认的"分校"是"假民办" [The Hengshui No. 1 High School Disowned 'Branches' were 'Fake Privately-run Schools']," *Beijing News*, June 24, 2017.
9   Hengshui High School Experimental School, *Hengshui High School Experimental School 2017 Admissions Guide*, http://www.hbhz.net/Article_Print.asp?ArticleID=19635, June 11, 2017.

Since the late 1990s, in order to promote the balanced development of compulsory education, the Ministry of Education has explicitly required model high schools to separate junior and senior high schools. However, many high schools have set up privately-run junior high schools for their own benefit in order to select and recruit excellent students to the senior high schools. The Hengshui Middle School Experimental School can use the cross-regional students recruitment rights of privately-run schools to recruit junior high students from all over Hebei province, consolidating the privilege of the Super Secondary School under the "Hengzhong Model." Of course, it will take time to find out whether this is the case or not. In any case, this means that the "Hengzhong" schools have been involved in the compulsory education stage, which may have a more complicated impact on the regional education ecology.

1.3   *Implementation of Military-Style Management and Rigorous Test-Taking Training*

The alienation of school education by examination-oriented education exists on a spectrum of varying intensities of school, training center, military-style boot camp-"model prison." Hengshui High School, initially known for its super-intense test-taking training and strict education management, has achieved the ultimate degree in this regard. The school strictly monitors students' working hours and even their every move in class, and implements meticulous, military-style teaching management. Graduates from the school revealed that the students wake up every morning at 5:30 and go to bed at 10:10 at night, with five classes in the morning and five classes in the afternoon every day. Timetables are precise to the minute.

Students' time on campus is occupied by various tests and exercises. Since the first year of high school, Hengshui High School has implemented a training pattern of numerous practice exercises and frequent exams, including weekly tests, monthly tests, "research exams" (for class and subject placement), midterm and final exams, and so on. The *Southern Weekend* reported that a girl who graduated from Hengshui High School in 2011 had a stack of papers as high as 2.41 meters from her first to the third year of high school.[10] Besides "devil training" for students, Hengshui High School also associates students and teachers to test scores and rankings for high-pressure management.

---

10   Lei Lei and Zang Jin 雷磊、藏瑾 "Hengshuizhongxue de 'fengshen' zhilu – chaoji gaokao gongchang, 衡水中学的 "封神" 之路——超级高考工厂 [The Path to the Myth of Hengshui High School: Super Factory for College-entrance Examination]," *Southern Weekend*, October 10, 2013

Guided by the idea that college-entrance rate is above all else, the "Hengzhong Model" has created an assembly-line operation and harsh test-taking training "factory" for the college-entrance exams, and the strict control of students has reached the degree of disregarding human nature, controlling every minute and every behavior of students. For example, the student's sitting posture, looking around, pencil turning, leg shaking, leaning against the wall, etc., were all included in the strict quantitative assessment and disciplinary report. One graduate recalled that "staring blankly, snacking, and tearing paper were all recorded. One night, she went to the bathroom in a hurry to pee, and the staff recorded it, and the next day she was publicly criticized on Blackboard.[11] Another female student recounted her "disciplinary history" during her three years in high school: "In my first year of high school, when I fell asleep at night and rolled over, the teacher saw me and deducted points for 'tossing and turning in bed without sleeping.' In my senior year in high school, one night, my feet cramped. And I sat up just in time to get a flashlight from the bed check teacher, with points deducted. Senior year, after the lunch break, I was walking towards the classroom with a half-eaten apple, caught by the teacher. I was asked to take a photo with the apple for proof, and later wrote an inspection report to reflect on my wrongdoings in the office of the faculty". So much so that she lamented, "The most intimidating thing about Hengshui High School was that every little action could be tied to something very important, such as a moral issue. So much so that your secretly drinking milk in class would affect your parents' well-being; and your rolling over while sleep would affect your roommate's life."[12] Under the harsh management, students become a "standardized" commodity of the school, and the "quality goods" will eventually become a number in the school's outreach.

High-intensity test training and military-style management measures are used to control students' consciousness and minds, which is, in fact, a kind of "brainwashing." From the imposing pledge ceremony to the slogans all over the campus, the misuse of the stimulant of success studies all reflects this characteristic. There are many "popular" sayings, such as "Raise one point, beat a thousand"; "Today's crazy, tomorrow's brilliant"; "If you won't die from learning, learn to death," and so on.

---

11   Lei Lei and Zang Jin 雷磊、藏瑾 "Hengshuizhongxue de 'fengshen' zhilu – chaoji gaokao gongchang, 衡水中学的 "封神" 之路——超级高考工厂 [The Path to the Myth of Hengshui High School: Super Factory for College-entrance Examination]," *Southern Weekend*, October 10, 2013

12   Wang Luxiao and Zhang Zixuan 王露晓、张紫璇, "Hengshuizhongxue de fanpanzhe 衡水中学的反叛者 [Rebels at Hengshui High School]," http://news.ifeng.com/a/2017 0928/52208007_0.shtml, September 28, 2017.

In early 2017, commenting on the scandal of Hengshui No. 1 High School Pinghu Branch, Fang Hongfeng, director of the Basic Education Department of Zhejiang Provincial Education Department, openly questioned the schooling model of Hengshui High School, arguing that "this school is a typical example of examination-oriented education, with only scores and no people in its eyes." Through the harsh test-taking training, the Hengzhong Model has created the myth of the high college-entrance rate. Further through the Matthew effect and siphon effect, it has become a monopoly of quality educational resources and expanded into the current Super Secondary School.

2   Nationwide Expansion of the "Hengzhong Model"

Since the establishment of Hengshui No. 1 Middle School in 2014, the "Hengzhong model" has expanded significantly in Hebei and across the country, with the construction of the "Hengzhong system" schools in many places through the local introduction and enterprise funding. According to incomplete online statistics, 22 branch schools have been opened in the name of Hengshui High School or Hengshui No. 1 High School, as shown in Table 7.1.

TABLE 7.1   Branch schools exported to the whole country under the "Hengzhong Model"

Provinces	School name	Date established	Opening method	Fact sheet
Hebei (5 schools)	Hengshui No. 1 High School Handan Branch	September 2017	Opening of new schools	A privately-run full-day boarding school funded by the Hebei Hongda Group and co-cooperated with Hengshui No. 1 High School
	Baoding Heyang Hengshui No. 1 High School (Hengshui No. 1 High School Baoding Branch)	September 2017	Opening of new schools	A high school jointly operated by Hengshui No. 1 High School and Baoding Heyang Education Investment Co.
	Zhangjiakou Dongfang High School (Hengshui High School Zhangjiakou Branch)	August 2014	Additional School License Plate	Hengshui High School and Zhangjiakou Oriental Middle School established in cooperation

TABLE 7.1   Branch schools exported to the whole country under the "Hengzhong Model" (cont.)

Provinces	School name	Date established	Opening method	Fact sheet
	Hengshui No. 1 High School Kangbao Branch (Zhangjiakou)	August 2016	Additional School License Plate	Cooperated by Hengshui No. 1 High School and Kangbao No. 1 High School
	Hengshui No. 1 High School Fuping Campus (Baoding)	August 2016	Additional School License Plate	Hengshui High School and Baoding Fuping County Government Sign Cooperation Agreement
Henan (1 school)	Qinyang Yongwei School (Hengshui High School Henan Branch)	April 2016	Change of school name	As of the fall 2016 semester, the Yongwei High School has been renamed the Henan Branch of Hengshui High School
Yunnan (5 schools)	Yunnan Hengshui Experimental Middle School Chenggong Campus	December 2014	Opening of new schools	Co-founded by Yunnan Changshui Education Group and Hebei Hengshui High School
	Yunnan Hengshui Experimental Middle School Yiliang Campus	April 2016	Opening of new schools	Same as above
	Yunnan Hengshui Experimental Middle School Xishan Campus	May 2016	Opening of new schools	Same as above
	Yunnan Qujing Hengshui Experimental Middle School (Hebei Hengshui High School Qujing Branch)	December 2016	Opening of new schools	Co-funded by the government of Malong County, Qujing City, and Yunnan Changshui Education Group. Zhang Wenmao was appointed as honorary principal of Hebei Hengshui High School Qujing Branch and Yunnan Qujing Hengshui Experimental Middle School.

TABLE 7.1 Branch schools exported to the whole country under the "Hengzhong Model" (*cont.*)

Provinces	School name	Date established	Opening method	Fact sheet
	Yunnan Yuxi Hengshui Experimental High School	April 2017	Opening of new schools	Co-operated by the government of Hongta District of Yuxi City and Changshui Education Group.
Sichuan (1 school)	Suining Middle School Foreign Language Experimental School (Hengshui High School Sichuan Branch)	August 2014	Additional School License Plate	Co-operated by Hengshui High School and Suining Jingcheng Education Investment Co.
Anhui (3 schools)	Hengshui High School Chuzhou Branch (formerly Dingyuan Yinghua Middle School)	December 2016	Additional School License Plate	Co-operated by Hengshui High School and Dingyuan Yinghua Middle School
	Hengan School (Hengshui High School Anhui School, in Hefei)	September 2017	Opening of new schools	Privately-run middle school co-established by Hengshui High School and Anhui Sanhuan Group
	Hengshui No. 1 High School Pengcheng Branch (Xiao County)	October 2016	Additional School License Plate	Co-operated by Xiaoxian Pengcheng Middle School (private) and Hengshui No. 1 High School
Zhejiang (1 school)	Hengshui No. 1 High School Pinghu School	September 2017	Opening of new schools	Co-established by Hengshui No. 1 High School, Jiaxing Port Development and Construction Management Committee, and Guangzhou High-Tech Group
Hunan (2 schools)	Xiangyin Zhiyuan School (Hunan Zhiyuan Branch of Hengshui No. 1 Middle School)	December 2016	Additional School License Plate	Cooperated by Xiangyin Zhiyuan School and Hengshui No. 1 High School

TABLE 7.1 Branch schools exported to the whole country under the "Hengzhong Model" (cont.)

Provinces	School name	Date established	Opening method	Fact sheet
	Shaodong Innovative Experimental School Branch	September 2017	Opening of new schools	Cooperated by Shaodong Innovative Experimental School and Hengshui High School
Jiangxi (1 school)	Jiangxi Sanghai Middle School (Hengshui High School Jiangxi Branch, in Nanchang)	May 2016	Additional School License Plate	Cooperated by Hengshui High School and Sanghai Middle School
Gansu (1 school)	Lanzhou Foreign Language School of Science and Technology (Hengshui No. 1 High School Lanzhou Branch)	May 2017	Additional School License Plate	With the Lanzhou Education Department's approval, "Hengshui No. 1 High School Lanzhou Branch" was added to Lanzhou Foreign Language School of Science and Technology.
Xinjiang (1 school)	Shihezi Hengshui Experimental High School	October 2016	Opening of new schools	Public-supported privately-run school
Guizhou 1 school)	Guizhou Puding County First High School (Hengshui High School Puding Branch)	January 2015	Additional School License Plate	Cooperated by Puding County First Middle School and Hebei Hengshui High School

SOURCE: SUMMARIZED FROM ONLINE INFORMATION

The 22 schools listed in Table 7.1 were all opened in and after 2014. Among these, 11 are new schools, and the other 11 are schools with additional licenses or were renamed. They were established by either Hengshui High School or Hengshui No. 1 High School.

The process of brand expansion under the "Hengzhong Model" involves three parties: schools, the government, and enterprises. With regard to the establishment and management of branch schools, Hengshui High School and Hengshui No. 1 High School mainly provided their educational management brands or some of their teachers, while local governments provided policy support and school premises, and enterprises provided funding for the schools. In order to open a new school under the brand name, or to add the school brand to the original school name, or change the name of a school, the schools need to obtain the "license" of Hengshui High School or Hengshui No. 1 Middle School, and pay a certain amount of joining fee, which has a hidden chain of business interests.

This expansion model of opening branch schools and super secondary schools is often synchronized with the construction of new local developmental areas and closely linked to the real estate market and financial industry. For example, Jiaxing Pinghu School is located in the Jiaxing harbor district, Hengshui High School Chuzhou Branch is located in the Su-Chu Modern Industrial Park, and Yunnan Hengshui Experimental High School Chenggong Campus is located in Chenggong New District, Kunming. School size is usually relatively large, with the intention of driving the surrounding real estate, food, and other consumer industries to obtain considerable economic and social gains, through the "famous school" brand of Hengshui High School.

3 Analysis and Evaluation of the Hengzhong Model

Over the years, there has been a lot of controversy and debate over the achievements and mode of operation of Hengshui High School. Some people think it is great and show full support, whereas others are very concerned and say "no" to the "Hengzhong Model." Shall we consider the "Hengzhong Model" as an innovative approach in educational reform, or a "barbarian" and a "black sheep" in the education sector? Is the "Hengzhong Model" stigmatized?

Generally speaking, as opposed to a well-rounded education (素质教育), examination-oriented education can also be called cramming education (填鸭式教育). It takes the advancement rate to higher education as its primary goal, aims to improve students' test scores, and advocates rote memorization and training in question-based tactics. China's education administration, the education sector, and the public have already formed a consensus on this. Overcoming the shortcomings of examination-oriented education and promoting well-rounded education are the basic requirements of the educational policies and guidelines of the Party and the Center Government.

It is evident that the practice of recruiting only top students by the super secondary school has caused deterioration of regional educational ecology. Also, the fact that super secondary schools, represented by the "Hengzhong model," do not distinguish between public and private school operations and run schools in a mixed manner has been demanded by the authorities for rectification. The more deceptive, confusing, and in fact, fundamental questions are: first, are the "super secondary schools" conducive to promoting educational equity and increasing educational opportunities for rural students? Second, is the examination-oriented education approach, which focuses on test scores, reasonable or not, and is it really the way out and the gospel for children from low-income families?

3.1 Have "Super Secondary Schools" Increased Educational Opportunities for Rural Students?

Supporters of the "Hengzhong Model" often claim that, as a high school in an economically underdeveloped area, Hengshui High School provides a pathway for rural students and children from low-income families to go on to higher education and change their lives. This claim is highly misleading. What is the truth? We need to make a judgment based on facts.

Researchers analyzed data on students from the country's top university, K University, for five consecutive years, 2005–2009, and found that "Super Secondary Schools" accounted for an average of 14.4% or even higher of the province's K University admission plan. However, the proportion of students from super secondary schools from rural households was way much lower than that of ordinary high schools, at only one-eighth of ordinary high schools.[13] This is not difficult to understand. "Super Secondary Schools" are often located in prefecture-level cities or provincial capitals, which implies higher enrollment standards. Rural students' opportunity to access them is inevitably much lower due to their lack of economic, social, and cultural capital. Moreover, through their monopoly of quality educational resources, "Super Secondary Schools" have given rise to the phenomenon of school selection and a variety of under-the-table admission methods, such as admission based on connections and the payment of high school selection fees, which magnify the differences in students' backgrounds and make it more difficult for rural students to attend those schools.[14]

---

13 Huang Xiaoting, Guan Kexin, Xiong Guanghui, Chen Hu, and Lu Xiaodong 黄晓婷、关可心、熊光辉、陈虎、卢晓东 "Chaojizhongxue' gongping yu xiaolv de shizheng yanjiu – yi K daxue xuesheng xueye biaoxian weili "超级中学"公平与效率的实证研究 – 以 K 大学学生学业表现为例 [An Empirical Study of Equity and Efficiency in 'Super Secondary Schools' – Taking K University Students' Academic Performance as an Example]," *Education Research Monthly*, Issue 5, 2016.

14 Feng Bang and Li Ziling 冯帮、李紫玲 "Cong 'chaojizhongxue' xianxiang kan chengxiang zinv jiaoyu gongping wenti, 《从"超级中学"现象看城乡子女教育公平问题–以湖北省 D 市为例》,《教育发展研究》2014年第2期。[Reflecting on Educational Equity

Take the example of Hengshui No. 1 High School Pinghu School, a controversial school established in Zhejiang province in early 2017. It was reported that the annual tuition is 35,000 yuan, and the annual accommodation charge is 2,000 yuan, adding up to 37,000 yuan per school year per student, not including living expenses. The Hengan School in Hefei, Anhui Province, is a school under the brand name of Hengshui High School. Its high school annual tuition is 18,000 yuan. Fuyang High School and Hengshui No. 1 High School also have very pricey tuitions. Such a high tuition standard far exceeds the general charges of public high schools and universities, and is unaffordable for ordinary rural families. How many of the students in the "Hengshui High School System" schools are local Hengshui students, and how many of them are rural students are the key information of the schools' actual operating situation. However, those information has always been kept as "secrets" by the schools.

Due to its location in an economically underdeveloped area, the "Hengzhong Model" has gained a particular "moral crown" for running schools for rural students. However, the inevitable consequence is that county and township high schools are becoming increasingly challenging to run, with quality students and quality teachers being attracted to the Super Secondary Schools.[15] On the whole, the Super Secondary School model, as represented by the "Hengzhong system" of schools, is not a blessing for the students of low-income families, but rather an aggravation of the educational inequality between urban and rural areas, narrowing the path of upward mobility for rural students.

3.2 *Should We Destigmatize Examination-Oriented Education?*

On April 19, 2017, Lu Jianguo, Director of Education Bureau of Gangyu District, Lianyungang City, Jiangsu Province, made a speech on *"Fully Understanding the Political Correctness Of Test-Oriented Education"* at the Party School Theme Class. He argued that it has now become politically correct to criticize and oppose test-oriented education; in fact, should education is the philosophy and practice of the basic education stage with a focus on students' entrance exams as the orientation, and it is the most useful and effective way of education. Accordingly, he believes that Hengshui High School should not be demonized, nor should test education be stigmatized. On May 15, 2017, *China Youth Daily* published Chen Zhiwen's article *We Need More Education Officials*

---

        for Children in Urban and Rural Areas through Studying the Phenomenon of 'Super Secondary Schools' – Taking City D of Hubei Province as an Example]," *Research in Educational Development*, Issue 2, 2014.

15 "Pinglun: bubi yi 'qiongren de mingyi' cheng Hengshuizhongxue moshi, 评论：不必以 "穷人的名义" 撑衡水中学模式 [Commentary: Don't Support the Hengshui High School Model in the Name of the Poor People]," *Beijing News*, April 16, 2017.

Like Director Lu, echoing Lu Jianguo's remarks that the mainstream viewpoint's criticism of test selection and test education is divorced from the reality and China's unique national culture, resulting in the effectiveness of education governance. It is not good, and therefore should not be criticized for Hengshui High School and teaching to the test, and should not be held hostage to educational reform by political correctness.

The defense of the "Hengzhong Model" is usually justified by the reality of competition in college-entrance examinations. However, examinations should not be equated with examination-oriented education. Examinations are a kind of educational evaluation, and well-rounded education cannot be achieved without examinations and selection. The difference lies in whether examinations and test scores are the sole purposes of education, or whether it is used as a tool, with the overall development of students as the more important pursuit. The goals and values of these two types of education are completely different and are clearly differentiated.

Examination-oriented education is still the dominant model of education, and the most popular teaching model in many county secondary schools. However, there is a big difference between the super secondary schools and county secondary school models. The core of the "Hengzhong Model" (or super secondary school) is to bring together high-quality students from all over the province into one school or a few schools, so as to carry out examination-oriented education with higher intensity and more fierce competition, which is a "qualitative change" to the alienation of education. As long as examination-oriented education is still education, it must follow the minimum rules and principles, just as competitive sports should not use doping, restaurants should not use gutter oil. However, as mentioned above, the "Hengzhong Model" does break the bottom line in many aspects, becoming a kind of "anti-education."

Today, the defense of well-rounded education and the vigorous modernization of education are based not only on the fundamental values of humanitarian conscience and humanism, but also on the practical need to cultivate talents for the future. In the age of the Internet and artificial intelligence, the need to cultivate talents for the future goes far beyond the narrow goals of examinations and test scores. As some online article says: "Knowledge has developed tremendously, you're still foolishly chasing housing in good school districts; knowledge has developed tremendously, you're still foolishly focusing on the college-entrance exam score rankings; robots are capable of taking the college-entrance exam, you're still cultivating exam machines!" China's education is in the midst of the tug and pulls of two forces. Although examination-oriented education has not yet been fundamentally changed, changes are emerging, and there are more and more options. As educators, educational institutions, and newcomers of the times, if we cannot embrace and promote innovation in education, can we at least refrain from eulogizing examination-oriented education and advocating it?

3.3 Cultivating Talents for the Future and Saying Goodbye to "Super Secondary Schools"

Today, if we want to continue to promote well-rounded education, we must keep resisting examination-oriented education. Promoting people-centered education reform requires breaking away from examination-oriented education, and this is not a pipe dream. Many resource-poor rural schools, such as Du Langkou Middle School in Shandong Province and Xin Jiang Middle School in Shanxi Province, have realized student-centered class through implementing classroom teaching reform. Their shared experience is to allow students to master studying techniques and have a joyful experience in independent and cooperative learning, thus improving academic achievement. These innovative practices demonstrate that using the harsh monitor of students, excessive time and effort to improve test scores is a reflection of rigidity, unthinkingness, and incompetence.

In the course of the modernization of education, there are some distinctive features of education for cultivating talents for the future, such as the emphasis on comprehensive competence and the cultivation of core skills rather than examinations and test scores, the emphasis on personality formation, and the development of characters, and the emphasis on imagination and creativity. All of these features point in the opposite direction to that of examination-oriented education. In addition, there is another crucial aspect, that is, the focus on personalized, exploratory, cooperative modern education inevitably requires the implementation of "small classes and small schools," which is the most basic indicator of education modernization and the basic reality of basic education in developed countries. At present, the sizes of primary schools in China easily reach 3,000 to 5,000 students, and that of secondary schools can be as large as 10,000 to 20,000 students. Such an "education factory" model in the era of industrialization will certainly step off the stage of history. Thus, the current popularity and proliferation of "Super Secondary Schools" is just a flashback and final performance before their demise.

CHAPTER 8

The New Policy on "Burden Reduction" for Shanghai Primary and Secondary School Students: Reflections and Recommendations

Liu Hong[1] and Zhang Duanhong[2]

Abstract

Through interviews and research with primary and secondary school teachers and parents, this paper reflects on Shanghai's recent fifteen years of "burden reduction" policy, and the new round of policy in Shanghai on "burden reduction" in 2017. It is argued that the reason why "burden reduction" policies of primary and secondary school students have not been effective for many years, and the academic pressure of students has been increasing instead of decreasing is due to the competition in secondary school enrollment and the disorderly development of education and training market. These two factors have been forcing parents to voluntarily increase the burden for their children. Therefore, it is necessary to have a more rational understanding of the causes of and strategies for "burden reduction." Merely rectifying and standardizing the education and training market is to work from the "demand side," but the key to successful "burden reduction" is to change the "supply side."

Keywords

primary and secondary schools – overburdened with schoolwork – education and training

---

1 Liu Hong 刘虹, Ph.D. in Public Policy, Associate Professor, Department of Public Administration, School of Management, Shanghai Institute of Technology, and Deputy Director of the IDM Research
2 Zhang Duanhong 张端鸿, Ph.D. in Management, Executive Director of Well-rounded Education Research Center, Tongji University, and Executive Director of the IDM Research.

In 2017, Shanghai launched a high-profile work to reduce the education burden, set the focus on rectifying and regulating the education and training market, and launched a number of initiatives to try to "treat both the symptoms and the root causes." In other cities across the country, a new wave of reducing students' schoolwork burden has also been launched. In order to get out of the strange circle of repeated failure of policies on the reduction of students' workload for more than a decade, it is necessary to understand the underlying causes of students' excessive workload from different angles, including parents, schools, training institutions, and the government, and to improve the overall educational ecology of primary and secondary schools.

1   Policy Concerns on the New Round of "Burden Reduction" of Basic Education in Shanghai

At the beginning of 2017, "reducing the burden" of primary and secondary school students and purifying the education and training market became the hot topics of Shanghai's "two sessions" (the National People's Congress and Chinese People's Political Consultative Congress).

In response to a speech by a delegate to the National People's Congress, Shanghai Party Secretary Han Zheng attended the delegation meeting and pointed out that "education should never be influenced by capital, never be kidnapped by capital. If the training institutions are purely for profit, the Party and the government should certainly take measures to regulate such training market. Or, it will be a dereliction of the government's duty." "Is it okay for a third-grader to be trained with junior high school content? That's going against the education principles and disrupting the education system." "We should really reduce the workload of students, and improve the benefits of teachers who actually stay in the classrooms."[3]

This round of work in Shanghai to further regulate the order of compulsory education targets three areas: the education and training market, privately-run schools in the compulsory education stage, and compulsory education schools. A leading group for regulating the order of compulsory education was set up, led by the municipal government head in charge, with the participation

---

3 "Shanghai Rendaihui jujiao xuesheng jianfu, jiaowei cheng jiang tui yilanzi jucuo, 上海人代会聚焦学生减负　教委称将推一揽子举措 [Shanghai People's Congress Focuses on Reducing Student Workload, Education Commission Says It will Push a Package of Initiatives]," http://www.chinanews.com/gn/2017/01-16/8125770.shtml, January 16, 2017.

of departments of propaganda, education, industry and commerce, civil affairs, human society, finance, public security, fire-fighting, auditing, culture and broadcasting, housing management, press and publishing, and women's federations, forming a synergy. A long-term mechanism will be established on the basis of collecting data, clarifying laws and regulations, in-depth discussions, and extensive consultation.

After a comprehensive investigation of education and training institutions in Shanghai, there are currently around 7,000 training institutions in Shanghai, of which only 2,000 are fully licensed, 3,200 have business licenses, but no education and training qualifications, and more than 1,300 operate without licenses. The focuses of rectifying and managing the training institutions were on the institutions that have potential fire and safety hazards, teach subjects related to enrollment examinations and extended academic subjects for students in compulsory education stage and younger, and charge fees but without valid education and business licenses. The government also worked on guiding "institutions without valid qualification on education and training" that basically meet the conditions for running schools to apply for "school operation permits" following the law and regulating school operation behavior. In addition, the government also further regulated "education and training-qualified" institutions in terms of fees and charges, fire and school safety, qualifications of personnel, advertising, education, and teaching content, and the establishment of centers and branches of the institutions, etc. Training institutions were required to carry out self-inspection and self-rectification.

After the start of the school year in February, Shanghai introduced a "package" of new policies to reduce the burden of primary and secondary school students, in the hope that through the "combination fist" that address both the symptoms and the root causes, the academic burden of primary and secondary school students will be effectively reduced.

First of all, schools should be made to "not dare to increase the burden." In public schools, stricter regulations on systems have been implemented in such areas as curriculum and teaching arrangements, homework-load management, examinations, and tests. First, "burden reduction" in curriculum and teaching arrangements. It is strictly forbidden to arrange any exercises, tests, and examinations for students within two weeks of the school semester. It is strictly forbidden to rank students' grades. It is also strictly forbidden to start any teaching activity before 8:15 a.m. in primary schools and 8:00 a.m. in junior high school. It is strictly forbidden to exceed the total number of class hours. Students are guaranteed with the "three classes, two exercises, and two activities" arrangement and "one hour of physical exercise at school every day." Second, "burden reduction" with homework and examinations. Keep a record of the homework assigned, examinations organized, and quizzes in various forms. Third, regulate the behavior of principals and teachers. Principals and teachers' violations of regulations will be monitored and recorded, such as "keeping true and fake class schedules," organizing examinations and quizzes that violates the regulations, conducting cross-school joint examinations, teachers engaging in paid tutoring activities, and transferring interests with external training institutions. Such violations will be recorded in the responsible persons' credibility files, and will affect issues such as the promotion of positions, evaluation of job titles, job recruitment, merit assessment, selection for further training, and performance appraisal. Fourth, ensure "burden reduction" from teaching and evaluation aspects. Comprehensively implement and improve the "zero starting point" teaching. Primary schools should increase the intensity of intensive Hanyu pinyin teaching, and alleviate parents' excessive anxiety. All primary schools should implement the "zero starting point" teaching and "letter grade system." Continue to optimize the curriculum system for a better transition from kindergarten to primary school. Strengthen home-school collaborative education and the management of classroom WeChat groups.

Second, to make families "not want to increase their burden." The first is to deepen the reform of the school admissions system. Further standardize the teaching and examination management of primary and secondary schools. Gradually increase the proportion of admission quotas allocated to junior middle schools for quality senior middle schools. Regulate the operation and admission of privately-run schools, such as formulating new policies on the admission of privately-run schools, and promoting the featured operation of private schools. Adjust the composition of the plan for allocating quotas to public and private junior middle schools. Secondly, further implementing grouping of school districts to run schools and cluster development of new high-quality schools, and expanding the coverage of high-quality educational resources. Third, promote the balanced development of quality compulsory education within the city. Fourth, strengthen the support for public education services, achieve full coverage of evening care classes in primary schools. We should formulate policies and supporting measures to further extend after-school care service hours in primary schools and improve teachers' corresponding performance incentive policies. All public primary schools in the city implemented the "Happy 30 Minutes" comprehensive activity from September. After school hours between 16:00 and 17:00 every day, schools provide student care services for families in need. In addition, winter camps and summer camps focusing on sports, art, and science are being held to meet students' parents' needs.

Lastly, it is necessary to make the market "not able to increase the burden." A cross-sectoral mechanism will be set up to regulate the education and training market in a comprehensive and integrated manner. Measures were implemented to purify the education and training market, to shut down training institutions that violate the law, to resolutely fight against damage to the education ecosystem, and to severely punish collusion of interests and misleading advertising. By strengthening during-event and post-event supervision and comprehensive law enforcement, and enhancing the disclosure of information about education and training institutions, the achievements of the rectification measures will be further consolidated, and training institutions will be guided to run schools in accordance with the law.

In order to consolidate the achievements of the work on education and training market regulation, to address the outstanding problems in the current education and training market, and to further promote the standardized and orderly development of the city's education and training market, in December 2017, the General Office of the Shanghai Municipal People's Government issued a statement on forwarding the *Shanghai Private Training Institution Setting Standards*, *Measures on the Management of For-Profit Private Training Institutions in Shanghai*, and *Measures on the Management of Not-For-Profit Private Training Institutions in Shanghai* jointly formulated by the Municipal Education Commission and four other departments. The Notice was implemented starting from 2018. The "one Standard and two Measures" clearly set out the requirements for training institutions in terms of teaching content, such as "not violating the education principles and the students' physical and mental development," focusing on reducing students' excessive extracurricular burdens. It attempted to establish a sound long-term management mechanism to protect the healthy development of young people and safeguard the legitimate rights and interests of students and parents.

2   Retrospective Review of the Policy of "Burden Reduction" of Basic Education in Shanghai

Through observation and research, it was found that after implementing the high intensity "burden reduction" policy, the in-class academic burden of Shanghai public primary and secondary schools has been relatively low, but the phenomenon of parents voluntarily "increasing the burden" has not been reduced. The academic pressure on primary and secondary school students after school remains high for a considerable proportion of students. For this reason, it is necessary to summarize the historical experience and understand the underlying causes of the problem of students' high workload.

Since 1993, due to the increasing burden of students' schoolwork, Shanghai has been pushing forward the reform of primary and secondary school curriculum and teaching materials as well as the admission examination system in order to reduce students' academic burden. As shown in Table 8.1, since 2003, Shanghai has spared no effort to regulate and adjust examination-oriented education and promote the policy of "burden reduction" of basic education. From 2003 to 2010, the policy's focus was on curriculum reform, school hours, school timetable arrangements, and after-school homework, all of which were directly related to students' academic burden. Since 2011, the focus of the "burden reduction" policy has gradually shifted from the direct academic burden to addressing the issue of balanced development compulsory education, promoting the equality of compulsory education through school districts or groups, and continuously strengthening the implementation of "zero starting point" (零起点) and "letter grade" (等第制) policy. From 2017 onwards, the policy began to pay attention to the impact of the enrollment of private schools and the disorderly operation of education and training market on the academic burden of students, and launched measures to address these issues, moving from single or multiple measures to comprehensive measures.

Looking back on the history of "burden reduction" over the past fifteen years, it is not difficult to see the policy history of decreasing the learning burden of public-school students and promoting "happy activities." However, along with years of effort came a boom in private primary and middle schools that parents "rushed to" and the rise of a prosperous and utilitarian education and training market. As a result, the extracurricular burden on children is still increasing.

TABLE 8.1 Comparison of "burden reduction" policies of basic education in Shanghai since 2003

Year	Policy	Contents
2003	The Shanghai Education Work Conference included "Reducing the burden as an important topic on the agenda."	Implementation of the new curriculum and new teaching materials at the beginning of junior high school in Shanghai (second-phase curricular reform).
2004		Fully implementation of the new curriculum and new teaching materials from the beginning of primary school in Shanghai, and 20% of the city's model municipal kindergartens and Level 1 kindergartens have also implemented the new curriculum.

TABLE 8.1 Comparison of "burden reduction" policies of basic education in Shanghai since 2003 (*cont.*)

Year	Policy	Contents
2005	The Shanghai Municipal Government has issued "Opinions on Reducing the Burden"	It was stipulated that no written homework for the first and second grades of elementary school, that the homework of the other grades of elementary school and the preparatory grade of the junior high school shall not take more than one hour to complete, and that the homework for first and second years of the junior high school shall take no longer than 1.5 hours. Schools may not use students' rest time to conduct group make-up classes, and they may not change the curriculum, difficulty level, or class hours at will.
2006	Curriculum plan for the academic year of 2006 for Primary and secondary schools in Shanghai	All primary and secondary schools must arrange their curricula according to their students' learning and living patterns and must strictly monitor the total number of weekly activities and academic class hours. All elementary and junior high schools are prohibited from scheduling early morning self-study. Schools shall ensure that primary and secondary school students have one hour per day for sports activities.
2007	Implementing the guiding principle of "Health First"	Five graded exams, including English for primary and secondary school students, were cut. Increase sleeping time for elementary school students and adjust the school schedule of the city's primary and secondary school students. The city's primary school students take two to four weeks to prepare for the first year of primary school in order to facilitate the transition from kindergarten to primary school (*Morning Post*).
2008	Some schools have introduced new policies to "reduce the burden"	Teachers are not allowed to assign repetitive, mechanical copying assignments; each assignment is to be completed within 40 minutes (to be implemented across the board from pre-junior middle school to the third year in junior middle school).

TABLE 8.1 Comparison of "burden reduction" policies of basic education in Shanghai since 2003 (*cont.*)

Year	Policy	Contents
2009	Notice from the Shanghai Municipal Education Commission	Requires the establishment of a system of public reporting on the status of curriculum implementation in primary and secondary schools, so as to effectively alleviate the problem of overburden with primary and secondary school students.
2010	Exploring a green indicator system for the quality of compulsory education	Focusing on both students' learning growth and study burden, guiding teachers to improve teaching quality, and paying attention to teacher-student relations.
2011	Implementation of the "New Quality Schools" project	To "run a quality school at the doorstep of every family" as the goal, not to select students, not to concentrate resources, not to pursuit rank and scores, to explore the path to promote the growth and development of each student. Pilot "Happy Activity Days" in primary schools throughout the city.
2012	Three major measures to effectively reduce students' schoolwork burden	(a) Further emphasize the responsibilities of governments at all levels. The Municipal Education Commission focused on the overall training of school principals on burden reduction. Make good efforts to ensure the examination-free admission of primary schools and junior middle schools, and enrollment based on school districts, so as to put an end to "admission based on the examination." (b) Improve the system of evaluation and supervision of schools in all districts and counties. (c) Continue to improve the monitoring system. Support and guide some districts and counties in carrying out pilot projects to monitor the "burden reduction."
2013	Implementation of the Ministry of Education's *Ten Provisions on Reducing the Burden of Primary School Students*	Provisions include eliminating written assignments in primary schools, introducing "zero starting point" teaching for new first-grade students, and the random and balanced placement of students and teachers in classes. Implementation of 'letter grade' evaluation and 'zero starting point' teaching.

TABLE 8.1   Comparison of "burden reduction" policies of basic education in Shanghai since 2003 (*cont.*)

Year	Policy	Contents
2014	The pilot of "curriculum standards-based evaluation" in primary schools	"Curriculum standards-based evaluation," full implementation of "zero starting point" and "letter grade" in primary schools.
2015	Seventeen districts and counties are fully piloting school district or group-based school operations	More than half of the city's elementary and secondary schools will be organized into school districts or groups.
2016	Full implementation of 'letter grade' evaluation system in primary schools	A "letter grade system" will also be introduced for grades 3 to 5 of primary school, replacing the traditional percentage scoring system of evaluation.
2017	Introducing comprehensive measures to treat both the symptoms and the root causes	Deepen the reform of school enrolment system; Regulate the teaching and examination management of private schools; Implementing the "zero starting point" and "letter grade system" for all primary schools; Establish credibility files on school principals and teachers; and vigorously monitor and rectify training institutions.

3   Reflections on the Issue of Burden Reduction

Similar to Shanghai, in October 2017, Jiangsu Education Department issued the "strictest" burden reduction order, *Opinions on Further Regulating School Management to Effectively Reduce the Academic Burden of Primary and Secondary School Students*, to carry out a new round of "burden reduction" work. The Opinion clearly states that the teaching progress should not be accelerated on will, student's homework should not be turned into parents' homework, implement grading-free homework and weekly no-homework-day, so as to reduce the burden of both students and parents. Abolish all forms of general, joint, or monthly examinations for compulsory education schools and first-year senior high schools. Cities and counties are not allowed to conduct unified examinations at class, grade, or school level for survey purposes. It is strictly forbidden to have Olympiad questions in the examination papers or treat Olympiad questions as bonus questions. It is strictly prohibited for schools to involve in extra-curricular training. The government should not set targets for schools on the rate of graduates advancing to further education. The Opinion required a fundamental change of the phenomenon of "reducing the burden of schools but increasing the burden of families, and reducing the burden in classes but increasing the burden out of classes."

Thinking of similar burden reduction orders issued in Jiangsu Province years ago, we believe this order is neither the first nor the last. Therefore, the discussion on the "fundamental question" of "whether reducing the schoolwork load is a true or false proposition" cannot be avoided. It is difficult to give a simple answer to this question, which has long been the subject of many different opinions. According to the general reactions of parents and society, the burden on students is indeed heavy. Even at the kindergarten level, there are quite a few children who attend more than two different types of training classes per week. As the school year progresses, the amount of time students spends on schoolwork, both inside and outside of school, increases, and very few children are able to go to bed before 10:00 p.m. every day or simply relax and play on the weekends. From this perspective, there is an actual need to reduce the burden of schoolwork on students, and the problem of overburdening students with schoolwork should be addressed. Then why burden reduction is considered a false proposition? The reason is that under the surface of the current overburden of basic education on students is the parents' "voluntarily addition of burden," such as the purchase of a house in a good school district with the whole family's resources, paying high tuitions to attend extracurricular tutoring, etc. Parents said that they felt "helpless," but had "no regret" for doing so. The high financial burden borne by families is actually parents "paying for" the unbalanced allocation of quality education resources.

3.1 *Parental Behavior*

For a family, parents' investment in their children's education is an autonomous family planning, and in general, it is a rational parental choice that does not affect significantly because of the education administration's "burden reduction order." Children's education process is divided into four interlocking stages: the transition from kindergarten to primary school, transition from primary school to junior high school, transition from junior high school to senior high school, and college entrance exams. To attend the best key high schools in Shanghai, one needs to enter a good private junior high school. In order to improve the competitiveness of enrolling in good private junior high schools, private primary schools have been focusing on examination-oriented education. In comparison, the admission rate to quality junior high school of public primary schools has been significantly lower. There is even a situation where "many parents spend a lot of money to buy a house in the good school district, only to find that they are not guaranteed to enroll in quality junior high school even if their children study in corresponding public primary schools. They end up sending their children to quality private primary schools." In the face of an overwhelming number of students, private schools have enough room to select the best students, and have higher requirements on the competence and ability of students than public schools, which directly leads to parents putting more burden on students.

As far as the government is concerned, it is not within the scope of its administrative authority to regulate parents' voluntary behavior of putting more burden on students. It can be said that as long as admission opportunities to key universities and key high schools are scarce, and as long as there are significant differences in test scores and admission rates between high-quality private junior middle schools and ordinary public junior middle schools, parents will not stop increasing their children's burdens voluntarily. What needs to be made clear is that parents seem to be voluntarily increasing children's burden, but in fact, they have no choice. The fundamental reasons are: first, the scarcity of quality educational resources and the imbalance distribution of quality educational resources between public and private schools; second, the fact that private schools have more independent admission rights, which violate administrative orders.

3.2   *School Behavior*

Public schools and private schools need to be discussed separately. Do public schools need burden reduction? From the survey of public-school teachers, it is generally considered that the curriculum requirements of public schools are already minimal. If we only consider meeting the syllabus requirements, in fact, the burden and pressure on students' learning are gradually decreasing, i.e., the academic requirements of the "90s" students are already lower than those of the "80s", and those of the "00s" are much lower than the "90s". As a result, public-school teachers often say that there is "no room to reduce." Another fact is that the more public schools reduce their academic burden, the more room is left for private schools and the training market. The booming development of education and training institutions can be attributed to a large extent to the strict implementation of the "burden reduction order" by public schools over the past 15 years. Parents generally believe that their children will not be competitive in the future if they only learn the content of public schools, and that they should never gamble with their children's future.

Therefore, this is a kind of "tragic" game, in which all the families involved can hardly escape the "prisoner's dilemma."

From the perspective of private schools, high academic standards are the basis for their high admission rates to further education. It is also the foundation upon which private schools are built. The two main ways for private schools to maintain a high rate of advancing to further education are to recruit the highest quality students and to provide rigorous academic training to students. As a result, private schools themselves lack the motivation to reduce students' academic burden. As they enjoy more autonomy in running schools, private schools are subject to fewer constraints and restrictions, making it difficult for the government's "burden reduction orders" to have the same restrictive effect. Private schools tend to admit students with "parents with high incomes," students of "well-off families," "bright and intelligent children," and students with "parents who spend a lot of time with them." This has been widely known. If this situation continues, the admission of students to private schools will be based on explicit criteria such as family background, parental achievement, and children's ability in verbal expression, which will inevitably exacerbate educational inequality and widen the gap between the rich and the poor.

3.3 Education and Training Institutions

Shanghai targets training institutions because the public intuitively considers training institutions as the primary source of "extra burden" on students. Problems such as incomplete access mechanisms and inadequate supervision have led to all kinds of chaos in the education and training market. However, is it really effective to reduce student's burden through regulating the training institutions?

The existence of education and training institutions, as commercial organizations, depends on school education and the students' selection system in school admissions. Therefore, education and training institutions are often referred to as "shadow education." As long as there is a demand from parents to send their children to academic training institutions, there is room and basis for training institutions to survive. The fundamental reason why it is challenging to reduce students' workload is that the relationship between parental demands and training institutions is not fully understood. Regulating the education and training market is a typical way of focusing on the "demand side," yet the key to reducing students' burden is on the "supply side." If the supply side remains unchanged, the demand side changes can only treat the symptoms but not the root cause. It may even lead to the phenomenon that the education and training market is monopolized by a few "giants" with higher charges after the large-scale clean-up and consolidation movement of the education and training market.

4 How to Continue the Work on Burden Reduction

Education in Shanghai leads the nation in the quality and equality level of education, but many problems still exist in reducing students' burden for systemic reasons. Many parents surveyed believed that the authorities' "heavy-handed" approach this time was a bit hasty. From a practical point of view, if public schools do not regain their dominant role in basic education, the current round of intense burden reduction order is highly likely to fail again.

The reasons behind this are: parents' anxiety about their children "not losing at the starting line" is the subjective reason why parents increase the burden on their children voluntarily; the shortage of quality education resources, and the imbalance in the allocation of quality education resources between public and private schools are the fundamental reasons why parents increase the burden on their children; the single test selection approach is the key reason to increase the burden on children by parents. Only by gradually solving these fundamental and crucial problems can we grasp the critical solutions for reducing students' learning burden.

4.1 *Strengthening the Dominant Role of Public Schools in Basic Education*

Basic education, especially compulsory education, is for the public good and should not be for profit. Therefore, the key provider for basic education should undoubtedly be public schools. Public schools are duty-bound to ensure education equality and nurture talents. This is also the basic reality in most countries around the world. The current phenomenon in which public schools are disadvantaged or even marginalized in the competition with private schools is abnormal and needs to be changed.

Many efforts are needed to re-establish the public-good nature of basic education and effectively improve public schools' operation and their quality of education. One of the key measures is to increase investment in education, substantially improve the salaries of teachers, and change the previous logic of financial investment, which was based on material goods but not human resources, so that financial resources can really be invested in students and teachers, thus providing a guarantee for the revival of public schools. In addition, the reform of the public primary and secondary school operating systems and the stimulation of the schools' intrinsic vitality are also important ideas and international experiences.

4.2 Reforming the Examination and Evaluation System and Promoting the Reform of the University Admissions System

The most fundamental approach to reduce students' burden is to change the current evaluation method based only on test scores in the examination-oriented education environment. Although Shanghai and Zhejiang proposed a new proposal of "two bases and one reference" in the college entrance examination reform, the high school academic level examination, which is one of the bases, is still converted into scores and added to the total score. Although the examination result is with letter grades in order to reduce the importance of each point, the result is still converted into numbers and included as a part of the total score. Thus, the score-based student evaluation system hasn't really changed.

By expanding universities' admission autonomy, universities can independently select students with academic potential according to the requirements of different disciplines and specialties. This is a key initiative to break the score-based evaluation system, and is a common practice in university admissions worldwide. China has written into the policy documents the autonomous recruitment of students by universities in accordance with the law, macro-management of the government, and two-way choice between universities and students. But in reality, due to corruption in the autonomous recruitment of students by some universities, this reform has not made much progress. As a matter of fact, most of the independent recruitment examinations are trustworthy, and various systematical and technical measures can be used to ensure the fairness of the admission process. We should not give up on this reform for fear of possible issues, but should continue to push it forward with confidence.

4.3 Restoration of Extracurricular Tutoring in Offered by Public Schools

After-school special interest activities and early education, which used to be offered in public schools, were unanimously welcomed by parents. However, the "blanket" ban on after-school tutoring, for the purpose of stopping "unwarranted charges," has resulted in pushing parents to privately-run training institutions. In the commercialized operation of training institutions, this kind of interest-based education can easily be turned into examination-oriented training, and parents have to pay dozens or hundreds more for it. It is an ineffective public policy to abruptly abolish after-school tutoring in public schools and depend on the commercial training market to meet parental and students' needs. In foreign countries, after-school "remedial education" is a common practice in public schools to satisfy certain kinds of educational demand. Public schools should actively involve in providing after-school tutoring for students in need, to enlighten students and cultivate their interests and capabilities.

4.4 Regulating the Management and Enrolment of Private Schools

In the context of implementing the new *Law of the People's Republic of China on the Promotion of Privately-run Schools*, schools at compulsory education level are not-for-profit schools, which are also responsible for ensuring equity in compulsory education. The Ministry of Education has made it a requirement that privately-run schools are also not allowed to select students through examinations. Localities are also changing the way privately-run schools recruit students to interview and lucky-draw. The key is for the government to exercise adequate supervision and oversight, to prevent private schools and training institutions from conducting test-taking training and becoming "training camps" that reinforce "examination-oriented education," and to guide them to become bases for well-rounded education with individual features and specialties.

As a fundamental solution to the competition for admissions to "junior high school," the Ministry of Education explicitly requires the implementation of the policy of allocating no less than 50% of the enrollment quota of model high schools to ordinary junior middle schools. However, in major cities such as Beijing and Shanghai, the implementation of this policy is still very unsatisfactory. There is a need to break the constraints of interest groups and truly implement this measure.

4.5 Granting Families the Right to Freely Choose School to Attend within Certain Limits

Due to the objective differences that exist with schools' qualities at the compulsory education stage, compulsory admission to nearby schools without examination deprives students and parents of the opportunity to choose schools they like to a certain extent. As a result, only families that can afford housing in a good school district can enjoy better public education resources, which leads to competition for housing in good school districts for families. The fair competition among students for quality educational resources through their own efforts is disrupted, exacerbating public fears of class entrenchment.

CHAPTER 9

Problems and Ways Out for Rural Education – A Discussion Inspired by Dr. Rozelle's Talk

Yang Dongping[1]

Abstract

Professor Rozelle's talk on rural education in China has aroused strong social reactions and in-depth theoretical discussions. This paper examines the major issues discussed, such as rural student dropout, children's health, the lack of early childhood education, and the positioning of high school education. It also discusses the underlying problems faced by rural education and the values and goals of educational reform. We argue that the "world of life" should be the foundation of the meaning of education, emphasizing the cultivation of non-cognitive skills and the development of individuality. Through learning by doing, independent learning, and individualized learning, education should cultivate a complete human being who could live independently in society and prepare for the future.

Keywords

rural education – school dropout – human capital theory – reflective education – life education

In mid-September, the video of a talk by Dr. Rozelle, a professor in School of Economics and Management at Stanford University, at "YiXi," titled *The Reality Is That 63% of Rural Children Have Not Been to High School for A Day, What to Do*, became a hit. Dr. Rozelle knows China very well. He and his team, REAP (Rural Education Action Program), have been conducting empirical research on economics, education, and health in rural China for 20 years. His talk revealed the weakness of rural education in China and made some startling discoveries. While it "exploded" into the news, it also provoked enlightening

---

[1] Yang Dongping 杨东平, Director of 21st Century Education Research Institute, and member of the National Advisory Committee on Education.

thoughts from the education community about the current state of rural education, its problems, and the way out.

1 Truthfulness of the Statistic: "63%"

The first controversy was over the validity of the number: "63%." Dr. Rozelle's talk was based on published results from a survey conducted by the REAP team he heads. The research team collected information on 24,931 students from 262 rural junior high schools, 46 general high schools, and 107 junior vocational schools in Shanxi, Shaanxi, Hebei, and Zhejiang provinces between June 2007 and November 2013. Survey results show that: the cumulative average dropout rate in junior high schools was 17.6%–31%; the dropout rate in high schools was 4.2%–7.4%; and the dropout rate in vocational schools was 29%–32%, resulting in a cumulative dropout rate of 63% at the secondary education level (i.e., including junior high school, senior high school, and secondary vocational school). That is, of the 100 students enrolled in the first year of junior high school, 31 dropped out by the end of the third year. Among the graduates from junior high school, 23 did not continue to senior high school, 25 went to regular senior high school, and 21 to vocational senior high school. By the end of the third year of senior high school, a total of 9 students dropped out, of which 2 were generally high school students, 7 were vocational senior high school students, and 37 finally graduated from senior high school.[2] An accurate description should be that the cumulative dropout rate at the secondary education level in rural poverty areas was 63%. For some reason, it was expressed in the talk as "63% of rural children do not go to high school for a single day," which was not the truth.

At a press conference held by the Ministry of Education on Sept. 28, Lv Yugang, director of the Department of Basic Education, argued that Rozelle's data came from a sample and were not up-to-date, thus not reflecting the reality and the complete picture. Statistics of Education Bureau show that in 2010, which was the year mentioned by Rozelle, the gross high school enrollment rate was 82.5% (an increase of 3.3% from the previous year); by 2016, the national high school enrollment rate reached 87.5%, with only nine provinces and regions in the country having a high school enrollment rate below 90%. In September 2017, the General Office of the State Council issued *Notice on Further Strengthening the Monitor of Dropouts and Raising the Student-retain-rate at Compulsory Education Stage*. According to the notice, the student-retain-rate

---

2 "Zhongguo nongcun zhongxue chuoxue diaocha, 中国农村中学辍学调查 [A Survey of Dropouts in Rural Secondary Schools in China]," *China Reform*, Issue 2, 2016.

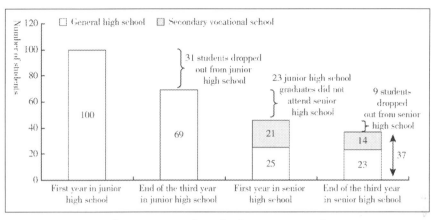

FIGURE 9.1 Survey on dropouts in secondary schools in poverty areas by REAP
SOURCE: REAP LECTURES

(巩固率) (i.e., the proportion of graduates to the number of students enrolled) for the national nine-year compulsory education was 93% in 2015, and reached 93.4% in 2016. We need to ensure to reach the target rate of 95% by 2020. The Notice also put forward three situations to avoid, including avoiding rural students dropping out of school due to learning difficulties or aversion to schooling, avoiding rural students dropping out of school due to poverty, and avoiding rural students dropping out of school due to the difficulty of going to schools far away. The government and related parties have the sole responsibility of monitoring dropout and ensuring students continue studying in schools. The Notice highlighted that the main reason for rural students dropping out of school at present is learning difficulties or aversion to schooling, while economic reasons have become secondary. In the process of precision-targeted poverty alleviation through education, "monitoring dropouts and keeping students in school" has become an important task.[3]

It is important to point out that dropout statistics, cumulative dropout rates from surveys, and the proportion of the population with high school education from censuses are different data that cannot be compared directly. Official statistics on dropout rates are cascaded through the administrative system and are subject to distortion. In many places, evaluations on local government performance regarding compulsory education require that "the annual dropout rate for primary school students should be below 1%; for junior high school students, below 2%," which often becomes the basis for statistical reporting.

---

3 "Quebao 2020nian jiunianyiwujiaoyu gonggulv da 95%, 确保2020年九年义务教育巩固率达 95% [Ensuring 95% Student-Retain-Rate of Nine-Year Compulsory Education by 2020]," *China Education News*, September 6, 2017.

In 2014, according to Liu Limin, Vice Minister of Education, "the dropout rate should be kept below 0.6% in primary schools and below 1.8% in junior high schools."[4] Field sample surveys can compensate for the bias in education administration statistics. In poor rural areas, ethnic minorities are more likely to drop out of school. The REAP team conducted a survey in ethnic minority rural areas in the west on 14,761 students in grades 4–5 from 181 schools in nine counties in the 2010–2011 and 2013–2014 school years, and found that "the dropout rate of all students in the sample was 2.5%, which was more than ten times the official dropout rate for primary school students (0.2%)."[5] In fact, it is not uncommon for rural schools in poor western areas to have three classes at the beginning of the first year of junior middle school but only two or one class left by the third year.

Another marginalized group with high dropout rates is the growing number of migrant children and left-behind children. According to the 2015 1% National Population Sample Survey results, in 2015, the number of migrant children was 34.26 million, and 68.77 million were left-behind children, bringing the total number of children affected by population mobility to 103 million, or 38% of children in China. The number of left-behind children living in rural areas reached 40.51 million, accounting for 59.9% of the total number of left-behind children and 29.4% of all rural children. In other words, three out of every ten rural children were left-behind children. At the same time, 28.26 million left-behind children were living in towns, accounting for 41.1% of all children left behind.[6]

2   Education Pathway for High School/Secondary Vocational Education

One of Rozelle's main arguments was that the low proportion of China's labor force structure with upper secondary education is an important obstacle to overcoming the "middle-income trap." This is shown in Figure 9.2.

---

4   "Xiaoxue chuoxuelv yao kongzhizai 0.6% yixia, 小学辍学率要控制在0.6%以下 [Primary School Dropout Rate to Be Kept Below 0.6 Percent]," http://politics.people.com.cn/n/2014/0214/c1001-24354865.html, February 16, 2014.
5   Cui Manlin, Lu Meichen, Chang Fang, Wang Huan, and Shi Yaojiang 崔曼琳、鲁美辰、常芳、王欢、史耀疆 "Shei zai chuoxue – laizi Zhongguo xibu shaoshuminzu nongcundiqu de zhengju, 谁在辍学——来自中国西部少数民族农村地区的证据 [Who's Dropping Out of School – Evidence from Ethnic Minority Rural Areas in Western China]," *Labor and Economic Research*, Issue 2, 2017.
6   United Nations Children's Fund "2015nian Zhongguo ertong renkou zhuangkuang baogao, 2015年中国儿童人口状况报告 [Population Status of Children in China in 2015]," http://www.chinadevelopmentbrief.org.cn/news-20233.html, October 11, 2017.

Country	Percentage in 2010 (%)
Turkey	31
Brazil	41
Argentina	42
Mexico	36
South Africa	28
China	24
Middle–income countries	32
High–income countries	74
From middle–income to high–income countries	72

FIGURE 9.2 Percentage of population with high school education in middle-income countries
* Countries and regions that transitioned from middle-income to high-income over the period of 50 years
SOURCE: ROZELLE'S TALK AT "YIXI"

In education statistics, upper secondary education includes general high schools and secondary vocational education. China's policy requires that the students' ratio in general high schools to students in secondary vocational schools be maintained at 1:1. In 2016, the number of students enrolled in secondary vocational education was 15,990,100, accounting for 40.28% of the total number of students enrolled in upper secondary education. The enrollment rate in China's general high schools was about 52%, and the rural general high school enrollment rate was about 35%. This was basically consistent with Rozelle's statement that "63% of rural children have never been to high school for a day." Therefore, the "high school" he was referring to were mainly general high schools.

With regard to the proportion of the population at the upper secondary level, national statistics show that between 2010 and 2014, the proportion of the population with the junior college education or higher increased from 8.75% to 11.01%, and the proportion of the population with upper secondary education (including technical secondary school) increased from 13.72% to 16.35%, an increase of 2.63%, showing that the dividends of education and human resources offset the impact of the decreasing demographic dividend.[7]

Upper secondary education, especially the aim and development of secondary vocational education, is a difficult issue and key for rural education. Secondary vocational education has formed a huge scale and complete system, with an enrollment of 5,933,400 students in 2016, accounting for 42.49% of the total enrollment at the upper secondary school level. Among the different types of secondary vocational education, students enrolled in general technical secondary schools accounted for 43.0%; vocational high schools accounted for 25.5%; technician schools accounted for 21.4%; and adult technical secondary schools accounted for 10.0%.[8] Among these, general technical secondary schools and technician schools in economically prosperous areas with industrial backgrounds or relying on enterprises are better developed, and their graduates are more suited to market needs. What is more problematic is the vocational high schools in rural counties in the central and western regions, which have been shrinking in recent years. In many places, vocational education centers, which cost a massive amount of money to establish, either exist

---

7 Zhang Xiaoge 张晓鸽, "Woguo yijing jinru rencai hongliqi: gaozhong ji yishang xueli renkou bizhongda, 我国已进入人才红利期：高中及以上学历人口比重大 [China Has Entered the Talent Bonanza: The Proportion of the Population with High School Education and Above Is High]," *Beijing Times*, December 11, 2015.
8 Ministry of Education "2016nian quanguo jiaoyushiye fazhan tongjigongbao, 2016年全国教育事业发展统计公报 [National Education Development Statistics Bulletin 2016]," http://www.moe.edu.cn/jyb_sjzl/sjzl_fztjgb/201707/t20170710_309042.html, July 10, 2017.

in name only, or are "sold in name only," enrolling students who plan to take the college-entrance exam. With the decrease in age-appropriate prospective students, some localities have reduced the enrollment of secondary vocational education and increased the enrollment of general high schools to respond to the public's needs. The reason is that the cost of running a secondary vocational school is several times that of a general high school. In addition, the secondary vocational schools in the rural areas in the central and western regions are far away from the market and cannot meet the demand of enterprises. With a lack of financial support, the quality of school education is low. Many students are also reluctant to study in secondary vocational education because they feel that the return rate is low. Although the State has adopted the policy of free secondary vocational education, it is still unattractive.

The repositioning of upper secondary education in the new historical phase of universal nine-year compulsory education and soon to be universal upper secondary education is an important issue. The research found that the personal income return rate with secondary vocational education is low relative to that with general high school education. Therefore, the World Bank recommends that countries shift more public investment in upper secondary education from secondary vocational education to general high school education.

The preference of Rozelle and his team on how to optimize the ratio and structure of public investment in general high school education and secondary vocational education is to prioritize the development of general high school education. This is not only because students do not welcome secondary vocational education, but also because general high school graduates have higher quality and better vocational adaptability than secondary vocational school graduates. In fact, due to the forced maintenance of the 1:1 ratio of general high school to secondary vocational education at the upper secondary education level, the development of general high schools is hindered because they cannot meet the public demand. In many rural areas, as only about one-third of junior high school graduates have the opportunity to go on to general high schools, the competition for the high-school-entrance examinations is even more fierce than that for the college-entrance examinations. There are even students repeating the third year of junior middle school to retake the examinations. As a result, some students who have no hope of further education have dropped out of school.

The opinion of the government authorities remains that the development of secondary vocational education should be continued by improving its quality and attractiveness. The *Thirteenth Five-Year Plan for the Development of the National Education Sector* proposes to "promote a vocational education model that integrates industry and education, adhere to the direction of running schools that are market-oriented, serve the development and promote employment. Vocational education should scientifically determine the training goals of vocational education at all levels and of all types, and innovate models for training technical and skilled personnel. We should promote integrated school-enterprise education, promote 'order-based' training and school-enterprise alternating training, and actively promote the modern apprenticeship system of joint school-enterprise recruitment and joint training."[9] One move to improve the attractiveness of secondary vocational education in recent years has been to increase secondary vocational students' opportunity to enter higher vocational schools. Along this line, vocational education will also establish a parallel system as a general academic system, with equivalent qualifications and titles to general education. Some have questioned this approach as a departure from the job-oriented purpose of vocational education, fearing it will turn vocational education into a new form of education for further studies.

A very constructive proposal to make vocational education more attractive has been put forward: regional integration and the relocation of vocational schools to large cities. An important reason why students are reluctant to go to secondary vocational education is the low rate of return on education. The return rate on education is related to where the schools are located. According to the analysis of several research teams in China, the return rate is higher in cities than in rural areas, with the highest rate of return on education in municipalities directly under the central government, followed by provincial capitals and then prefecture-level cities.[10] Due to the scale effects of big cities in the economic sense, more future job opportunities in China will be in big cities, which will play a much more important role in attracting and accommodating rural population than any small and medium cities. Setting up vocational education in large cities is conducive to improving the quality of vocational education in terms of its marketability and ability to meet demand.

---

9   State Council "Guowuyuan guanyu yinfa guojia jiaoyushiye fazhan 'shisanwu'guihua de tongzhi, 国务院关于印发国家教育事业发展 "十三五" 规划的通知 [Circular of the State Council on the Issuance of the Thirteenth Five-Year Plan for the Development of the National Education Sector]," http://www.gov.cn/zhengce/content/2017-01/19/content_5161341.htm, January 10, 2017.

10 Yu Jiantuo 俞建拖 "Pinkun nongcun ertong fazhan de zhenzheng tiaozhan: jian yu Luo Sigao jiaoshou shangque, 贫困农村儿童发展的真正挑战: 兼与罗思高教授商榷 [The Real Challenges of Child Development in Poor Rural Areas: A Discussion with Prof. Rozelle]," http://opinion.caixin.com/2017-09-20/101147740.html, September 21, 2017

It is also conducive to enabling migrant workers and their children to move to big cities through education and become new citizens.[11]

At present, China's upper secondary education, which separates general and vocational education, neglects the function of preparing high school students for successful careers and citizenship. Instead, general high schools have become "college preparatory schools," while vocational high schools "one-sidedly emphasize vocational skills and neglect basic literacy education." It is reasonable to take the route of comprehensive upper secondary education and establish comprehensive high schools that integrate general and vocational education. In this way, all high schools offer a variety of courses, including academic and vocational skills, and students can choose different types of courses on their own to determine their future career direction. However, this is a problem of "easier said than done," as all parts of China have been carrying out pilot reforms to establish comprehensive high schools, but in the intense environment of examination-oriented education, this reform has been difficult to make progress.

3   Child Health and Early Parenting

In Rozelle's talk, he argued that the reason why rural students are falling behind in school and why they are dropping out are pertinent to the issues of child health, child nutrition, and early parenting. This was very enlightening.

According to a large sample study on the health conditions of thousands of rural children in 19 provinces conducted by the REAP team, researchers found that anemia, parasites, and myopia seriously affect rural children's academic success. The total percentage of students with anemia, parasitic infections, or vision problems was 70%. Among them, 27% were anemic, 33% had parasite infections, and 20% were nearsighted. In addition, they spent two years (2013~2015) surveying cognitive delay in rural young children in western China. The study participants were 1808 children aged 6–30 months in Shaanxi Province, involving 351 villages and 174 townships. The Bayley Scales of Infant and Toddler Development (BSID) showed that 41% of Shaanxi's 18- to 24-month-olds surveyed were cognitively delayed, and 55% of the 25- to 30-month-olds were cognitively delayed. In 2015, a second BSID test was conducted in rural

---

11   Liang Jianzhang and Li Hongbin 梁建章、李宏彬 "Ruhe pojie nongcunjiaoyu de Luo Sigao nanti, 如何破解农村教育的罗斯高难题 [How to Solve the Difficult Problem Raised by Rozelle in Rural Education]," http://finance.sina.com.cn/review/sbzt/2017-10-01/doc-ifymmiwm3017146.shtml, October 1st, 2017.

Hebei province, just two hours' drive from Beijing, where 55% of children were also lagging behind in cognitive development. The results in Yunnan's remote areas were even more surprising, with more than 60% of the children failing the BSID test. Based on these results, Rozelle believes that rural students' low completion rate in high schools is related to the cognitive delays that exist in primary school and even younger when they were 0–3 years old. He warned that "more than 30% of China's future workforce may have permanent cognitive deficits," and that will become a burden to society.[12]

The association between children's nutritional and health status and academic achievement has previously been almost a blind spot in rural education research. Rozelle's research directly links the "first 1,000 days of life" and parenting between the ages of 0 and 3, to the academic achievement of rural students. He not only did research on this topic, but also took action to implement low-cost interventions such as offering nutrient tablets for anemia, deworming for parasites, lenses for myopia, and starting pilot projects to build early childhood education centers in rural areas.

One different opinion on this result is related to the intelligence testing of children. According to experts from the China Development Research Foundation, who have conducted similar studies, neuroscience research shows that 80–90% of children's brain development is complete between the ages of 0 and 3 years. However, there is no definitive consensus on the extent of such permanent deficits, and it is generally believed that interventions between the ages of 3 and 6 years, and even after school age, are effective. Considering that the fieldwork was conducted in a non-clinical setting, the term "permanent cognitive impairment" should be used cautiously. It is unfair to label 400 million rural people as cognitive impaired on the basis of a localized survey. And it is not academically rigorous to generalize the problem to hundreds of millions of people on the basis of a limited and localized sample.[13]

The problem of early child-rearing in rural areas is exacerbated by the intergenerational caregiving of the children left behind. Rozelle's solution, "let mothers stay in the rural areas," is seen as an unrealistic "fantasy." Whether

---

12 "Xianshi shi you 63% de nongcun haizi yitian gaozhong dou mei shangguo, zenmeban? 现实是有63%的农村孩子一天高中都没上过，怎么办？ [The Reality is 63% of Rural Children Don't Go to High School for a Day, What to Do?]," http://gongyi.ifeng.com/a/20170916/44686350_0.shtml, September 15, 2017.

13 Yu Jiantuo 俞建拖 "Pinkun nongcun ertong fazhan de zhenzheng tiaozhan: jian yu Luo Sigao jiaoshou shangque, 贫困农村儿童发展的真正挑战：兼与罗思高教授商榷 [The Real Challenges of Child Development in Poor Rural Areas: A Discussion with Prof. Rozelle]," http://opinion.caixin.com/2017-09-20/101147740.html, September 21, 2017

"mothers go back to the village" or "children go to the city" is as clear-cut as where secondary vocational education should be located. We need to invest more in rural education, including early childhood education, and at the same time, we need to rethink and change the policies of big cities that control the migrant population by limiting education opportunities. In fact, bringing rural youth from poor areas to the cities through education is the easiest and most effective way to alleviate poverty.

4 Underlying Causes of School Dropout among Rural Students

Rozelle's talk revealed the high dropout rate and low academic achievement of rural students, which addressed the public's concerns about the decline of rural civilization and rural education, and echoed popular perceptions about the new "belief of education is useless" and class entrenchment. The resulting discussion is not a professional clarification of facts and data, but rather questioning and reflection on the overall rural education crisis, which is perhaps more valuable.

The loss of rural students from basic education is, of course, related to the profound impact of early education, and problems of child nutrition and health, parenting, and intellectual development. But more directly, it is the damage caused by the deprivation of the opportunities to modernize and urbanize of the rural areas under a developmentist framework. Unlike the efforts to literalize the rural population in the first half of the twentieth century, the flow of educational resources has been cascading upwards now, despite the fact that education is now more widely available. The merging of rural schools, which began in 2001 with the mass consolidation of compulsory education and lasted a decade, is still ongoing, although the policy was halted in 2012. The "schools moving to the city" caused by the "school consolidation" has led to the concentration of rural primary and secondary schools in cities, counties, and towns at a much faster rate than the urbanization of the rural population. According to 2014 data, the population's urbanization rate was 55%, while the urbanization rate of primary school students was 68%, and the urbanization rate of junior high school students was 83%.[14] This has resulted in a pattern of "city schools crowded, town schools empty, village schools weak," with large class sizes in city schools and boarding schools in towns, whereas weak and small-scale schools in villages, leading to further widening of the urban-rural education gap.

---

14   Data from conference materials of the "4th China Rural Education Forum," October 2016.

As a result of the excessive consolidation of primary schools in rural areas, in the rural and mountainous areas of the central and western regions, the problem of rural students' long distances from schools, difficulties in attending school, and the high cost of schooling remain prominent. Because rural schools are too weak and of low quality, some rural parents are forced to choose to send their children to city schools. Parents are often required to accompany their children if they choose to attend schools in rural towns or counties, and the additional annual educational expenditure amounts to tens of thousands yuan, greatly increasing the education cost for rural students. Rural primary schools and teaching sites, small-scale schools in rural areas, had the last 20% of the most disadvantaged students in rural areas, further polarizing educational opportunities and quality. "Super Secondary Schools" have become a new landscape of upward migration of rural educational resources to the cities. Super Secondary Schools, mainly in prefecture-level cities and provincial capitals, are massive in scale. They recruit good-performing students and excellent teachers through illegal means. While creating the myth of extraordinarily high college-entrance ratio, those schools also lead to the decline of the majority of the high schools in the region, resulting in the so-called "downfall of the county schools" phenomenon, which substantially undermines the educational opportunities of rural students.

Thus, while we see that many rural high school students have been able to move up through the college-entrance examinations, it is crucial to recognize that many more students have left school prematurely in the process. This diversion is mainly happening in the transition from primary school to junior high school and from junior high school to senior high school. Based on the analysis of data from the 2008 National Comprehensive Social Survey (CGSS) of the Renmin University of China, 93.1% of students entering primary school but not junior high school were rural students, of whom 57.4% were from families whose economic situation was below the local average. 78.6% of students entering junior high school but not senior high school were rural students. Of these, 46.8% were from families whose economic status was below the local average. Of those who entered upper secondary school but did not enter university, 57.4% were from rural areas, of which 40.3% were from families whose economic situation was below the local average. The survey showed that the lower the age and educational stage, the more pronounced are the characteristics of the students' family economic and schooling backgrounds, and that compulsory education has a more substantial influence on students than upper secondary education.[15]

---

15 Ma Yuhang and Yang Dongping 马宇航、杨东平, "Chengxiang xuesheng gaodengjiaoyu jihui bupingdeng de yanbian guiji yu lujing fenxi, 城乡学生高等教育机会不平等的

Another apparent reason for the dropout of rural students is the damage caused by rigid examination-based education. The high intensity of test-taking training and difficult academic competition make many students fail in their studies and leave school early. The heavy burden of schoolwork and test pressure have caused a strong sense of learning burnout and exhaustion in a significant proportion of students. According to 2013 data, as many as 54.9% of eighth-grade students said that they were "easily irritated by studying," and 57.9% of eighth-grade students reported that "I often feel exhausted after studying for one day." The 2015 data shows that 11.4% of eighth-graders were reluctant to go to school and were at high risk of dropping out of junior high school.[16] They are not so much influenced by the "belief of education is useless" as they are "pushed" out of school by examination-oriented education.

The modernization model of urban centers, the upward shift of resources, and the widening gap between urban and rural areas make the competition between rural students and urban students on the single track of examination-oriented education, which is a "race of the tortoise and the hare" that is difficult to win.[17] In reality, going to school is the path for rural students to leave the rural area and change their social status. The inability of many rural students to achieve social status change through schooling is one of the reasons for the prevalence of the "belief of education is useless." For students who have difficulty furthering their education, such education is even more "useless," as it does not offer help for young people entering the labor market in terms of working skills or career development. This rootless and utilitarian education produces students who, even if they do leave the rural area, often cannot go far because they lack a positive mindset, the correct values, and the literacy to adapt to social change. Many of them cannot move to the city or return to the rural area, becoming "marginalized" and "suspended" in a state of uncertainty. Therefore, we need to rethink the goal of rural education. It should not only provide cheap labor for industrialization, but should return to the original intent of education. That is, to cultivate qualified citizens with sound personality, comprehensive competence, and self-development ability. Otherwise, how

---

演变轨迹与路径分析 [The Evolutionary Trajectory and Path Analysis of Inequality of Higher Education Opportunities for Urban and Rural Students]," *Tsinghua University Education Research*, Issue 3, 2015.

16　Data from the Centre for Monitoring the Quality of Basic Education, Ministry of Education.

17　Qiu Jiansheng 邱建生 "'Wujiao' yu 'wujiao' – Luo Sigao jiaoshou 63% yiwen duhou, "无教" 与 "误教"——罗斯高教授 63% 一文读后 ["No Education" and "Mis-education": Professor Rothko's 63% Post-Reading]," WeChat official account "Civil Education," September 20, 2017.

can students cope with the difficulties of life and society if they are not educated to be individuals with well-rounded personalities in schools?

This phenomenon does not start today, but is only now becoming more severe. As early as the 1930s, during the rural reconstruction movement, Yan Yangchu, who is known as the "Father of Mass Education," raised the question of "miseducation" and "no education." On the one hand, 80% of the population is uneducated. At the same time, school education is "foreignized" and "antiquated," and much of the education content is impractical. "So, there are sayings that 'education is misleading' and 'education is killing.'" "Many university graduates are unemployed, but the country is suffering from a shortage of talent."[18] Tao Xingzhi also warned that "China's rural education is going the wrong way! It tells people to leave the rural area and run to the city; it tells them to eat but not growing rice, to put on the dress but not growing cotton, to build houses but not planting trees; it teaches them to envy luxury but to despise farming; it teaches them to partake of profit instead of producing altruism; it teaches peasant children to become nerds; it teaches the rich to become poor and the poor to become even poorer; it teaches the strong to become weak and the weak to become even weaker."[19] What they sought was to build a living education suited to the practical life in the rural area! In the logic of modernization and urbanization, this criticism may seem backward and outdated, belonging to agricultural times; but in the postmodern vision of ecological civilization, its value and vitality will continue to be evident.

5 Rethinking the Values and Goals of Rural Education

Rozelle's analysis of rural education was from the perspective of promoting economic development and overcoming the "middle-income trap." His framework was based mainly on the theory of human capital. However, as Zhou Yisu, faculty of Education School of the University of Macau, argued, "the development of human capital is not necessarily the only path for education development. On the contrary, early childhood education and the nurturing of parent-child relationships are not only for tomorrow's workforce. It is not necessarily effective to arouse the empathy of ordinary readers for educational

---

18   Song Enrong 宋恩荣 "Yan Yangchu wenji, 晏阳初文集" [Yan Yangchu's Collected Writings]," Educational Science Press, 1989. Originally published in *Folk*, vol. 3, Issue 13, November 1936.
19   Tao Hsing-chi 陶行知 "Zhongguo xiangcunjiaoyu zhi genben gaizao, 中国乡村教育之根本改造 [The Fundamental Reform of Chinese Rural Education]," December 12, 1926.

issues."[20] This involves a different perception of the value, function, and goals of education.

In the process of nationalizing education, the school education formed in the era of industrialization was characterized by large-scale collective teaching and the hierarchical system. It pursued the utility of "improving social efficiency." Its pedagogical value took "scientific rationality" as the entirety of education. Because of its detachment from the world of the child and the world of life, this kind of education often leads to disregard and ignorance of humanity at the expense of the intrinsic goal of education, which is to nurture the whole person and develop individuality.

The reflection of education functions and goals is a holistic cultural phenomenon that has benefited from the latest scientific research results. A recent development in human capital theory is the recognition of the economic value of non-cognitive abilities, thus breaking with the traditional conception of IQ and test scores as the core content of human capital. Research has found that cognitive abilities, as represented by test scores, have a small absolute impact on earnings, with "test scores explaining only 18% of the impact of schooling on earnings." Non-cognitive abilities such as persistence, time management, communication, and cooperation have a much more important and lasting impact on children's future work and life than intellectual factors. Thus, "defaulting competence to cognitive ability and focusing only on the assessment of academic achievement may mislead the strategy and direction of educational investment."[21] Harvard Professor Gardner's theory of multiple intelligences is also an explorative revelation of the structure of human intelligence.

At the end of 2015, a recent UNESCO report, *Rethinking Education: Towards a Global Common Good?* proposes a rethink of the purpose of education. "The economic functions of education are undoubtedly important, but we must go beyond the strictly utilitarian vision and the human capital approach that characterizes much of international development discourse. Education is not only about the acquisition of skills, it is also about values of respect for life and human dignity required for social harmony in a diverse world." "Sustaining and enhancing the dignity, capacity, and welfare of the human person

---

20 "Rang 63% de nongcunhaizi shanggaozhong' bingfei Zhongguo jiaoyufazhan de da'an, 让63%的农村孩子上高中" 并非中国教育发展的答案 [Sending 63% of Rural Children to High School Is Not the Answer to China's Educational Development]." http://www.thepaper.cn/newsDetail_forward_1801631, September 21, 2017.

21 Zhou Jinyan 周金燕 "Renliziben neihan de kuozhan: feirenzhinengli de jingjijiazhi he touzi, 人力资本内涵的扩展： 非认知能力的经济价值和投资 [Expansion of the Concept of Human Capital: the Economic Value and Investment of Non-Cognitive Abilities]," *Peking University Education Review*, Issue 1, 2015.

in relation to others, and to nature, should be the fundamental purpose of education in the twenty-first century."[22] In the era of the Internet and artificial intelligence, this crisis and challenges have become even more severe. Raising a new generation with social adaptability and self-development so that human intelligence would overcome artificial intelligence, requires a focus on cultivating values, emotions, creativity, cooperation, etc. Thus, education needs to expand its narrow definition that only focuses on intellectual development and examinations and emphasizes the cultivation of core competence, comprehensive ability, and 21st-century skills.

This shift is happening in educational practice. The authors of *Redefining Education in the Developing World* argue that one of the key reasons for high dropout rates in developing countries is that there is a serious disconnect between what is taught and students' life, and that schooling is useless for improving lives and employment. For too long, education investors and researchers act based on the never-doubted assumption that "as long as test scores improve, the investment is worth it." Educational programs typically adopt traditional Western models of education, with an emphasis on math, science, language, and social studies, which may provide intellectual stimulation, but have little relevance in the lives of impoverished children. However, the development of healthy habits, such as hand-washing, and simple preventive measures, can significantly reduce disease and increase life expectancy. Thus, the authors believe that "what students in impoverished regions need are not more academic skills, but rather life skills that enable them to improve their financial prospects and well-being. These include financial literacy and entrepreneurial skills; health maintenance and management skills; and administrative capabilities, such as teamwork, problem-solving, and project management."

This new model of education, known as "school for life" (为生活而教), "shifts the goal of schooling away from the achievement of standardized learning outcomes toward making a positive impact on the economic and social well-being of students and their communities." The Entrepreneurship and health modules are mandatory curriculum components for primary school students, and teaching is based on a student-centered group learning approach. The combination of learning content that is relevant to learners' lives, application in practice, and student-centered teaching and learning processes will help students acquire a set of knowledge, skills, and attitudes, put into practice the

---

22   UNESCO, ed. "Fansijiaoyu: xiang 'quanqiu gongtongliyi' de linian zhuanbian? 反思教育：向"全球共同利益"的理念转变？[Rethinking Education: Towards A Global Common Good?]," Education Sciences Press, 2017.

abstract knowledge they learn through concrete activities, and increase their[23] confidence and sense of achievement in the process. After they graduate from school, they are more likely to be successful, whether they go to university or stay in a rural area.

Escuela Nueva (New School Plan) in Colombia was a pioneer in implementing this reform. It is based on a combination of theoretical and practical learning, individual and collective activities, learning and work, learning and play, teacher guidance, and student self-learning, so that students learn by doing. Through the *Study Guide*, which guides students' self-study, students are largely able to learn, practice, do activities on their own, and collaborate and help each other. At the same time, educators make full use of various educational resources, including the immersion of the natural environment and the assistance of the community and family. The model has been recognized by the World Bank as one of the most outstanding reforms in the world's developing countries, resulting in high-quality rural education not only in Colombia, but also influences education in many countries in South America and elsewhere. Its director, Vicky Colbert, won the 2015 World Innovation Summit for Education Award and was awarded the inaugural "Yidan Education Prize" in September 2017.

The philosophy of "school for life" is in line with Dewey's "education to prepare for life" and Tao Xingzhi's "education for life," which is not only beneficial to rural education, but also to the overall renewal and reform of education in China today. It inspires us to take the "world of life" as the foundation of education, emphasize the cultivation of non-cognitive skills and personality development. Through learning by doing, independent learning, and individualized learning, education should cultivate a complete human being who could live independently in society and prepare for the future.

---

23   Mark J. Epstein, Kristi Yuthas: Redefining Education in the Developing World, http://t.cn/RpDSWpD.

CHAPTER 10

The Establishment of "Double First-Class" (双一流) Universities in China and Issues to Prevent

Xi Youmin[1] and Zhang Xiaojun[2]

Abstract

The "Double First-Class" initiative officially started in 2016. With the announcement of the first round of "Double First-Class" universities list, all universities in the country joined the pursuit of being in the first-class. The paper reviewed the basic features of the first phase of the "Double First-Class" universities construction plan and the list announced, as well as the comments of the society on this major initiative. Based on the review, this paper puts forward several major issues that need to be cautious about in the current "Double First-Class" universities construction. First, to prevent the emphasis on scientific research but neglect undergraduate teaching; second, to prevent the rush to pursue targets at the expense of essential construction; third, to prevent the destruction of the overall educational ecology for the sake of local goals; fourth, to prevent the overemphasis on quantifiable indicators and departure from the systematic innovation of the education system; and fifth, to prevent the loss of school features in the pursuit of unified achievement indicators.

Keywords

Double First-Class – undergraduate education – educational reform – educational ecology

The construction of "Double First-Class" universities in China has not only made the leaders of many universities "sleepless at night" and a large number

---

[1] Xi Youmin 席酉民, Professor, Ph.D. Advisor, Executive President of the Xi'an Jiaotong-Liverpool University, and Vice President of the University of Liverpool, UK.
[2] Zhang Xiaojun 张晓军, Leader of Jiaotong-Liverpool University, Dean of Institute of Leadership and Educational Advanced Development.

of academicians and professors "lose sleep and forget to eat from anxiety," but also stirred up the whole society and aroused public discussions. How to make the "Double First-Class" initiative, which shoulders the historical mission of leading education and influencing future development, lives up to its mission and prevents potential problems in the process has become a topic of deep concern.

1 The Initiation of the "Double First-Class" Universities Construction in China

In recent decades, the development of higher education in China has primarily relied on project-driven initiatives, such as the famous "211 Project", "985 Project", and "2011 Project". In June 2016, the implementation of many years of "211 Project" and "985 projects" officially became history, and "2011 Project" seemed to be temporarily dormant. The successor is the current heated construction of "Double First-Class" universities.

On November 5, 2015, the State Council promulgated the *Overall Plan for Promoting the Construction of World-Class Universities and World-Class Disciplines* (hereinafter referred to as "Double First-Class"), with the goal that by 2020, several Chinese universities will be among the world's top universities and a number of disciplines in Chinese universities will be among the world's top disciplines. By 2030, more universities and disciplines will be among the world's best, with several universities will be among the top universities in the world, a number of disciplines will be among the top disciplines in the world, and the overall strength of higher education will be significantly enhanced. By the middle of the twenty-first century, the number and strength of first-class universities and disciplines will be leading the world, and China will become a strong country in terms of higher education. The specific strategy will be to encourage and support the differentiated development of different types of high-level universities and disciplines, with five-year cycles. In 2016, a new round of construction started, and five construction and five reform tasks were identified, including building a first-class faculty, cultivating top-notch innovation talents, advancing scientific research, passing on and innovating the outstanding culture, promoting the translation of research findings, and strengthening and improving the Party's leadership of universities, improving the internal governance structure, realizing breakthroughs in key points, building a social participation mechanism, and promoting international exchange and collaboration. "Double First-Class" has become a guiding policy for school development and discipline construction nationwide in provinces, cities, local, and all kinds of universities. All of a sudden, all kinds of planning and activities to strive for "Double First-Class" hot wave rolling.

The fundamental purpose of "Double First-Class" construction is to build a strong nation through higher education. The initiative was based on national strategic needs, with the important aspect of constructing world-class disciplines. Undoubtedly, since the implementation of the "211", "985" projects, Chinese colleges and universities have made significant progress in constructing first-class universities and first-class disciplines. However, "there is a growing discontent in society about the "solidification of status" in colleges and universities. The emphasis on highlighting the construction of first-class disciplines in the promotion of 'Double First-Class' is to avoid repeating the policy aberration of the past."[3] Thus, the "Double First-Class" construction strategically attempts to construct a logically more equitable development opportunity for Chinese universities, and is greatly welcomed by the universities that have yet to enter the national priority construction projects. As Mr. Liu Guangming wrote in his blog on blog.sciencenet.cn, the "Double First-Class" policy is quietly changing the development ecology of China's higher education, and will "promote the formation of a virtuous ecology for the coordinated development of higher education." After the announcement of the "Double First-Class" construction plan, it has attracted great attention from the whole society. As someone who really cares about education, while actively using a new policy to promote education development, we must think cautiously and beware of its possible adverse effects. For example, the international competition in higher education has put different pressure on developing key universities and ordinary universities. Such difference is difficult to eliminate in the short term. In addition, the difference in access to resources and equity in getting resources between different types of universities is even greater. The "Double First-Class" initiative may bring the "Matthew effect" to China's higher education, which may lead to more unbalanced development of regional higher education and different types of universities, and different competitive trends in the development of academic disciplines. Therefore, Mr. Liu argues that the development of "Double First-Class" will create an unfavorable ecological system that will hinder the coordinated development of higher education in China.

---

3   Chu Zhaosheng 储召生 "Renqing 'shuangyiliu' de miao he gen, 认清 "双一流" 建设的杪和根 [Recognize the Details and Root of "Double First-Class" Construction]," *China Education Daily*, May 9, 2016.

2 The Discussions Triggered by the "Double First-Class" Universities Construction List

On September 21, 2017, the Ministry of Education, the Ministry of Finance, and the National Development and Reform Commission issued the *Notice on the Announcement of the List of Universities and Disciplines for Building World-Class Universities and First-Class Disciplines*.

The "Double First-Class" list includes 42 universities, including 36 in Class A, 6 in Class B, and 95 in first-class discipline development. The relevant government official explained that the "Double First-Class" initiative is different from the previous "985 project" and "211 project"; it is a brand-new initiative. The uniqueness of the "Double First-Class" initiative is that the universities have greater autonomy. For example, Professor Huang Daren, former president of Sun Yat-sen University, believes that universities now have the organizational right to build first-class disciplines. Secondly, the universities on the "Double First-Class" list do not stay on the list and receive financial subsidies from the government forever, but are dynamically adjusted in a five-year cycle. In addition, the list is for universities to build "Double First-Class" rather than "Double First-Class" universities, which places more emphasis on construction rather than identity and label. Although there are many differences compared with the previous initiatives, the list immediately became a hot topic of higher education and even the society upon release. In addition to simple cheering for universities included in the list and showing regret for those not included, the discussion of the first phase of the "Double First-Class" construction contains the following views.

First, probably the most discussed issue is the state's rationale to organize such a university building campaign through administrative means. In recent years, an important topic of reform in the field of higher education has been de-administration, repositioning the relationship between the government and the university, separating management, operation, and evaluation, and returning the autonomy of operation to the university. However, this project of using administrative forces to guide universities' running, which plays a decisive role in the allocation of university resources, has to some extent deviated from the general direction of the reform. Many in the education sector have questioned whether such an administrative push can actually promote universities to the top tier. In particular, the usual practice of quantitative evaluation of achievements by administrative means may not be able to deeply touch the essence of building first-class universities, thus making it challenging to guide universities on a sustainable path of healthy development. Although it is desirable from the nation's perspective to support a number of universities and disciplines to reach world-class as soon as possible, building world-class universities and disciplines quickly through the simple cycle of investment and evaluation may deviate even further away from the goal, especially in terms of cultivating people.

Second, since the "Double First-Class" construction is fundamentally related to the allocation of national school operation resources, the issue of fair and balanced allocation of educational resources has also attracted a great deal of attention. In addition to the applause for the inclusion of Zhengzhou University, Xinjiang University, and Yunnan University in the list of "Double First-Class" construction, a large number of questions have also been raised about the highly inequitable distribution of resources. Over the past few decades, the resources for higher education, despite having undergone several major adjustments to the distribution model, have been allocated to a very small number of universities based on the concept of great care for a few universities. This allocation approach has made it difficult for a large number of universities that do not stand out in performance statistics to receive a share of the resources, thus preventing them from getting basic support for the development and delaying development opportunities due to a lack of resources. This raises the question of whether it is worth advocating the development of a very small number of universities to the first-class, at the expense of the development of a large number of universities in general.

Third, society is very concerned about the goals pursued by the current "Double First-Class" initiative. Although the national strategy of recent years clearly indicates that the current stage of higher education reform should promote the development of connotation and put the improvement of teaching quality as the core of reform, the current Double First-Class construction allocates resources more on the basis of university's scientific research achievement. This leads students to continue to follow the path of the "985 project" in the past and continue to focus on publishing papers desperately, deviating from the mission of times for the universities to set their basic goal as "establishing morality and cultivating people."

In addition, there has been much discussion about the procedures for "Double First-Class" development, the implementation plan, etc. These discussions are important for a deeper understanding and assessment of the role of the "Double First-Class" initiative. In any case, however, a new round of "Double First-Class" development is already on the way. Regardless of its effect on China's higher education reform, we need to think about making the most of this project to promote higher education and university development, especially to avoid possible problems. Therefore, the next part of this paper will focus on preventing the adverse effects of this project as much as possible in the process of "Double First-Class" construction.

3   The Five Issues That "Double First-Class" Construction Needs to Prevent

In our view, there are five potentially relatively large negative impacts.

The first is that undergraduate education will be underestimated, intentionally or unintentionally, in the pursuit of the explicit performance indicators of the "Double First-Class." Undergraduate education is the basis of university education, which is difficult to measure and compare through quantitative indicators. The performance indicators of "Double First-Class" are often directly linked with the achievements of scientific research. The basic indicators for the ranking of world-class academic programs by disciplines and the selection of "Double First-Class" are basically measured by the scientific research level of a school and discipline, especially the number and impact factor of papers published, but these indicators rarely involve undergraduate education. Many countries in Europe and America, which are world leaders in undergraduate education, have realized the seriousness of this problem, and "rebuilding undergraduate education" has gradually become the direction of their higher education reforms. The university's development strategy attaches more importance to the education of undergraduate students and the quality of undergraduate education. Many insightful scholars in China are also calling for and emphasizing the importance of undergraduate education in constructing "Double First-Class." Mr. Zhong Binglin pointed out that first-class undergraduate education is an important foundation for building a world-class university. "A world-class university must possess advanced educational concepts and an independent university spirit. It should be able to cultivate leading and innovative talents for all walks of life, conduct original scientific research, and have an important impact on the socio-economic and cultural development of the country and even the world."[4] In practice, however, this potential impact should not be underestimated. The development of "Double First-Class" universities has yet to enhance the evaluation of undergraduate education development.

The second negative effect is that it will further exacerbate the academic impetuousness of higher education, making it difficult for researchers to focus on research and innovation and increasingly depriving the tranquil atmosphere of the university campus. The lessons from the previous higher education development projects are already abundant in this regard. Over the

---

4   Zhong Binglin and Fang Fang 钟秉林、方芳 "Yiliu benkejiaoyu shi 'shuangyiliu' jianshe de zhongyao neihan, 一流本科教育是"双一流"建设的重要内涵 [First-Class Undergraduate Education Is An Important Component of The Construction of 'Double First-Class' Universities]," *China University Teaching*, Issue 4, 2016.

past two decades, China's higher education, driven by various projects, has witnessed a dramatic growth in many quantitative indicators, but has meanwhile gradually lost the ability to think and practice the essence of education. Nowadays, colleagues in higher education pay more attention to various indicators and the number of talents such as "Thousand Talents" and "Yangtze River Project Talents," and seldom think about issues such as, what kind of students are prepared for the future, what kind of good teachers are really needed by universities in this era, how students learn, and how universities can better support students' learning. The state has devoted its efforts and resources to higher education, but in reality, it is not uncommon to hear criticisms about the loss of direction in higher education reform, and complaints about the dismantling and re-packaging of academic disciplines in universities motivated by the "Double First-Class" initiative. Many scholars and educators are already very anxious about this phenomenon, slowly killing the university spirit. Mr. Ren Yuzhong of Peking University called out that "universities should protect the fundamentals." At present, under the interferences of all kinds of world university rankings, education, including the government's resource allocation and university development strategies, is often misled by those rankings, and only a few universities can hold their ground. The world-renown first-class university, Kyoto University in Japan, which has produced nine Nobel Prize winners and is famous for the "Kyoto School," is a representative of universities with unique characters. With "freedom" academic style and "harmony" school philosophy, experiences of Kyoto University are worthwhile for us to think about and learn from.

The third negative effect is that it may violate the laws of education and science and disrupt the sustainable development of universities and disciplines. The construction of "Double First-Class" will help outstanding scholars to find a sense of belonging. However, nowadays, many universities are eager to meet the standard of "Double First-Class" in a short period of time by assembling and re-packaging. As a result, they spare no expense to recruit famous professors and talents, or even purchase a discipline. Even though they have met the "first-class" standards in terms of indicators, the systemic ecology of education has been destroyed as an educational institution. In an ecological environment where one is free to follow his or her research interests and can study peacefully for a long time, all junior scholars have the potential to become great scientists, and the persistent pursuit of interests may give birth to important scientific discoveries and technological innovations. However, with the mechanism of allocating resources based on various "university building projects and initiatives," the evaluation system that emphasizes scientific research over education, and the various types of talent projects that emphasize selection over cultivation, we will lose the opportunity to develop many impactful universities. This is highly detrimental to the long-term sustainable development of universities and disciplines! In the ecosystem of "Big Education," symbiosis is the core mechanism, where mutual benefit and win-win situation is the only way to create value for talent development. Stakeholders may lack the foundation and motivation to work together systematically for the sake of students' learning and growth, which leads to the failure of self-organization of the ecosystem and makes the long-term sustainable development of universities impossible.

The fourth negative effect is that it will deprive Chinese education of the opportunity to stand on the same starting line with the world's top universities to explore the future of education, to catch up with the world's advanced educational concepts, and possibly lead the future of education. In other words, it may seem to be the quickest way, but in fact, is the slowest way or even "the opposite way." "The "Double First-Class" initiative is being embraced with enthusiasm by everyone from departmental universities to local undergraduate institutions. It seems that the university will be abandoned by the times if it does not participate in "Double First-Class," and the president of the university will be considered to be lack ambition and responsibility. Thus, many schools or leaders lose rational thinking and go with the flow. From the preparation stage of the "Double First-Class" initiative, many university leaders and professors have devoted resources to all kinds of "first-class" planning. Of course, the positive value of doing so is no doubt, but it is also an indisputable fact that in this process, universities invest lots of energy and time into things that deviate from the main business. The "knowledge- and content-oriented" and "examination-oriented" education and passive learning, which was already outdated in terms of educational philosophy and practice, is getting even worse. In the face of globalization and the era of the Internet and the Internet of Things, knowledge storage, dissemination, sharing, and robotics, and artificial intelligence penetrate into all areas of learning, living and working, etc. This has changed people's lifestyle and learning behavior, challenging the traditional way of learning and education. At this critical moment, if the "Double First-Class" initiative is not properly implemented; if objectively (non-subjective consciousness) and in practice underemphasize education; if the energy and vision of educational leaders, academicians, professors, and teachers focus only on the "data and ranking" for the sake of the first-class, neglecting or deviating from the fundamentals of the university, pulling away from the focus on educational reform and grasping educational trends and reshaping teaching and learning models, we may actually drift away from building truly first-class universities.

The fifth negative effect is that it may mislead some general universities regarding their operational objectives and feature development. In the announced "Double First-Class" list, the names of some colleges and universities that were not prominent in the past "985" and "211" projects' lists appear. It has brought tremendous development opportunities to many universities. Currently, the assessment of "Double First-Class" with the research quality as the primary perspective does not focus on a university's contribution to students' learning and growth. Therefore, it can be predicted that this education initiative, which is more inclusive and opens opportunities to all universities, will bring more universities into a unified track of discipline and academic development. As a result, those local colleges and universities that could not meet the requirements for "985" and "211" projects in the past will focus their attention on several ESI indicators that have the potential to become the "world-class academic disciplines", but neglect their own educational features and the main task of educating students. One of the reform goals for the next ten years proposed in the *National Plan for Medium- and Long-term Education Reform and Development (2010–2020)* is to "focus on the reform of systems and mechanisms, encourage localities and schools to boldly explore and experiment, and accelerate the pace of reform in important fields and key areas. We will innovate the talent training system, school operating system and education management system, reform the evaluation and entrance-examination system, reform the teaching content, methods and means, and build a modern school system." Premier Li Keqiang recently proposed three "further steps" in his comments on education: further deepening comprehensive education reform, further narrowing the urban-rural, regional and inter-school gap in the allocation of educational resources, and further improving teaching and research quality. Universities should have a clear understanding of their targets and roles. Many universities should switch to practical application-oriented training and take the road of feature development. But the inappropriate pursuit of "Double First-Class" will not only deviate from the state-led reform direction, but also make many schools deviate from their own healthy development route!

People are the foundation of universities. Universities must be people-oriented, nurturing students, and must pay attention to spiritual and cultural cultivation. In his essay *A Scholar's Quest*, management guru March once wrote: "A university is only incidentally a market. It is more essentially a temple – a temple dedicated to knowledge and a human spirit of inquiry. It is a place where learning and scholarship are revered, not primarily for what they contribute to personal or social wellbeing but for the vision of humanity that they symbolize, sustain, and pass on." He argues that "higher education is a vision, not a calculation. It is a commitment, not a choice. Students are not customers; they are acolytes. Teaching is not a job; it is a sacrament. Research is not an investment; it is a testament."[5] These insights on universities and higher education are a slap in the face to an increasingly fickle and secular higher education!

4   Expecting More Soberly Thought-Out Activists

Problems described in the previous section may seem like platitudes, but shouldn't find the solution to these old "stubborn" problems be a new concern of the national education strategy, taking advantage of the "Double First-Class" initiative being vigorously carried out by the whole nation? Reflecting on the current grievances and daily work of our university leaders, professors, and teachers, looking at their energy and time allocation, and then a little research on those veritable top universities in Europe and the United States, briefly comparing what their leaders, professors, and teachers do and their time and energy allocation, we can easily see that many of our efforts may have deviated from the university's fundamentals. We should not wait for the completion of the "Double First-Class" initiative and then face these old problems again with the next "great project."

Education, the greatest and most complex of all human endeavors, needs calm, independent thinkers, and also those who dare to go against the grain and those who can break free from the tide, and especially those who can follow the trends, follow the rules and dare to be maverick in the rounds of different movements! Xi'an Jiaotong-Liverpool University (XJTLU) was established in this particular era, and has the unique opportunity to rethink education, reshape teaching and learning, and redefine the university on the same starting line as the world's top universities. It has the advantage of an international platform and global integration of resources. It is willing to explore the future of education "alone," to build a new type of university organization based on appropriate web-based technologies, and to create a mechanism and form of operation symbiotic with the development of society. In particular, in the face of educational reshaping, XJTLU has been implementing the educational philosophy of "aiming at students' healthy growth, being interest-oriented and learning-centered" and advocating "research-oriented" education. In addition to the existing professional elite education model, it has opened a new training model of high-end applied elite education that integrates schools, business

---

5   By James March, translated by Ding Dan 丁丹, March on Management, Oriental Press, 2010.

corporations, and industry. It has built a three-level symbiotic academic ecosystem of nature, knowledge, and society, in order to achieve the great mission of XJTLU on education, research, social services, cultural leadership, internationalization, and influence educational reform! In fact, as long as we explore and do well what universities should be doing according to future trends, we are already on the way to building a first-class university.

CHAPTER 11

A Review of the Changes in Education Funding over the Last Two Decades in China

Hu Ruiwen[1] *and Cui Haili*[2]

Abstract

In the two decades from 1995 to 2015, China's total education expenditure increased 20 times, and its proportion of GDP increased from 3.1% to 5.2%, effectively guaranteeing the development of China's education. However, while government investment in education continued to maintain a high growth rate, the growth rate of multi-channel education investment declined significantly. Given the limited room for growth in China's governmental financial investment in education, it is necessary to deepen the reform of the education financing system, mobilize the enthusiasm of the government, enterprises, and individuals, and broaden the sources of funding for education, so as to provide an adequate financial basis for the modernization of education.

Keywords

investment in education – the governmental investment increases as the private investment recedes (国进民退) – diversified supply

Education investment is a fundamental and strategic investment that supports the country's long-term development and is the financial foundation of education development. The growth of China's financial investment in education and investment in education through multiple channels between 1995 and 2015 has greatly ensured the rapid development of education in China, promoting the expansion of education at all levels and in all categories and the improvement of the quality of education. In particular, the sustained and

---

1 Hu Ruiwen 胡瑞文 is a member of the National Advisory Committee on Education, former President of the Shanghai Academy of Education Sciences, and a researcher.
2 Cui Haili 崔海丽 is a doctoral candidate in education policy at East China Normal University.

TABLE 11.1 Average annual increase rate in China's fiscal and non-fiscal education expenditure, 1995–2015 (at constant prices)

unit: %

Years	GDP	Total education expenditure	Fiscal education expenditure	Non-fiscal education expenditure
1995–2005	9.2	13.5	11.3	18.7
2005–2015	9.6	11.2	14.3	3.6

SOURCE: *CHINA STATISTICAL YEARBOOK*, AND *CHINA STATISTICAL YEARBOOK OF EDUCATION EXPENDITURE*, RELEVANT YEARS (SAME BELOW)

rapid growth of fiscal education funds (the average annual growth rate for both decades remained above 10%) has played a baseline guarantee role for the increase in the popularity of education at all levels, the improvement in the school-running conditions for basic education, and the financial support for needy students in China. Unfortunately, however, contrary to the trend of rapid growth in fiscal education funds, the growth rate of non-fiscal education investment was slow and declined sharply during the decade between 2005 and 2015, limiting to a large extent the growth rate and scope of total education funding (See Table 11.1).

1 Analysis of the History of Investment in Education in China

Human resources are a vital factor in promoting economic and social development. In the early 1990s, the level of coverage of compulsory education in China was very low, and the gross enrolment ratio at the senior high school and higher education levels were far below the average of developing countries. According to the 1990 census, the average number of years of education for the working-age population was only 6.8 years, and the proportion of the population with a senior high school education or higher was only 14% (of which less than 3% had post-secondary education). At that time, the overall low level of education and the low quality of the workforce was a serious constraint on China's economic growth. In order to achieve leapfrogging economic development, it is fundamentally dependent on the extraordinary development of education and human resources. The Communist Party and the State Government have made education development and human resources development their top priority, establishing a strategy for prioritizing education development, and a strategy for revitalizing the country through science and education and strengthening the country with talents, making education a priority area for economic and social development, giving priority in planning, investment, and development. The government has also mobilized resources from both the Government and society to work together to develop education through such strategies as diversified school operation and reform of the financing system. Those strategies increased the impact of education investment on providing a fundamental guarantee for the development of the education sector.

During the period 1995–2015, total investment in education nationwide increased from 187.8 billion yuan to 3,612.9 billion yuan, with an average annual growth rate of 14.5%; per capita investment in education increased from 155 yuan to 2,641 yuan, with an average annual growth rate of 15.2%. In absolute terms, the proportion of education investment in national GDP increased from 3.1% to 5.2%, an increase of 2.1% (See Table 11.2). The sustained and rapid growth in education expenditure over the past two decades has effectively guaranteed the development of education at all levels and of all kinds in China. Between 1995 and 2015, China's nine-year compulsory education student-retain-rate rose from 55% to 93%, the gross high school enrolment rate increased from 22.3% to 87%, and the gross enrolment rate for higher education increased from 6.7% to 40%. According to the midterm evaluation of the fifth anniversary of the implementation of the *National Education Plan*, the overall development level of China's education has now entered the middle to upper ranks compared to other counties around the world, providing strong human resource support for the country's economic and social development.

TABLE 11.2 Progress in investment in education in China, 1995–2015 (at relevant year prices)

Year	Total investment in education (billion yuan)	Per capita education expenditure (Yuan)	Total input as a percentage of GDP for the year (%)
1995	187.8	155	3.1
2000	384.9	304	3.9
2005	841.9	644	4.6
2010	1,956.2	1,459	4.9
2015	3,612.9	2,641	5.2

In the first decade from 1995 to 2005, both government investment and private investment in education increased. In the early 1990s, in order to fill the gap between the development of education and the inadequate supply of education resources, and to promote the steady growth of education spending, the Party Central Committee and the State Council issued the Outline of China's Education Reform and Development Plan in 1993. The Plan aimed to systematically promote reform of the school operating system, the investment system, and the management system for education in China.

During this period, China's investment in education established a new system based on government appropriations, cost-sharing of tuition and miscellaneous fees for non-compulsory education, and social inputs such as donations and fundraising. Specifically, urban and rural education fees were surcharged with different proportions, making them the second-largest source of financial funding for education, in addition to fiscal appropriations. In addition, the government implements a policy of cost-sharing and tuition for university and high school education. Diversified non-governmental education programs were vigorously developed, promoting and encouraging enterprises, economic entities, conglomerates, and groups with various forms of ownership to invest in education and to establish non-government-run private schools of all levels and types. The government also mobilized the initiative of society and individuals to develop school-run industries and paid services, increased social donations and fund-raising, and other types of investment in education, so that both public and non-fiscal education funding have achieved extraordinary growth. Over those ten years, the state's financial investment in education has increased by 2.65 times, while non-fiscal investment in education has increased by 5.98 times. The rapid growth of the two kinds of investment has jointly promoted the basic realization of the goal of "universal ninth-year compulsory education" and the rapid expansion of the number of students in ordinary high schools and colleges.[3] Regarding the structure of education investment, the proportion of non-fiscal social and private investment in education rose from 24.8% to 38.7% of total investment in education, the highest level in history. Correspondingly, the proportion of governmental fiscal investment in education to the total investment in education has decreased, demonstrating the good results of the reform of China's education system.

---

3   Between 1995 and 2005, the number of students enrolled in ordinary high schools in China increased by 2.4 times from 7,138,000 to 24,091,000; the number of students enrolled in ordinary colleges and universities increased by 4.4 times from 2,906,000 to 15,618,000.

TABLE 11.3 Trends in the structure of education investment in China, 1995–2005 (at relevant year prices)

Year	Total expenditure on education (billion yuan)	The proportion of fiscal expenditure on education (%)	The proportion of non-fiscal education expenditure (%)				
			Total	Tuition and fees	Social donations	Organizer investment in private schools	School self-financing income
1995	187.8	75.2	24.8	10.7	8.7	–	–
2000	384.91	66.6	33.4	15.5	3.0	0.4	14.5
2005	841.88	61.3	38.7	18.4	1.1	0.7	18.5

Note: Some data are missing for 1995.

2   Trends in Investment in Education, 2005–2015

During the decade from 2005 to 2015, China's fiscal investment in education has maintained a high growth rate, and its proportion in total education expenditure has increased considerably. Although the absolute amount of investment by society, enterprises, and individuals has increased year by year, its proportion in total investment in education has fallen sharply, showing a trend of "increases of the governmental investment but recedes of the private investment." This failed to achieve a dual-track development driven by both the government and the private sector. The main manifestations are as follows.

2.1   The Average Annual Growth Rate of Multi-Channel Funding for Education Is Much Lower than in the Previous Decade

Between 2005 to 2015, China's fiscal education expenditure showed rapid growth of its own: the average annual growth rate of public fiscal education expenditure continued to remain at a high level of more than 10% (higher than the growth rate of GDP in the same period), but the growth rate of social and private education investment only reached an average of 3.6% (See Table 11.4).

In terms of the growth in the amount of education expenditure, between 2005 and 2015, fiscal education investment increased from 516.11 billion yuan to 2,922.15 billion yuan, a 4.7-fold increase (in current-year prices). However, non-fiscal education investment increased only from 325.77 billion yuan to 690.77 billion yuan, a 1.1-fold increase. The increase in non-fiscal education investment over the decade was only about a quarter of the increase in fiscal education investment (See Table 11.5).

TABLE 11.4 Average annual growth rate in fiscal and non-fiscal education expenditure in China, 2005–2015 (at constant prices)

unit: %

Years	GDP	Total education expenditure	Fiscal education expenditure	Non-fiscal education expenditure
2005–2015	9.6	11.2	14.3	3.6
Of which: 2005–2010	11.2	12.7	17.4	3.3
2010–2015	7.9	9.6	11.2	3.9

Note: The 2005–2015 growth rate is the average of the growth rates for the periods 2005–2010 and 2010–2016.

TABLE 11.5 Growth in the amount of education investment in China, 2005–2015 (at relevant year prices, in billions of yuan)

	Total education expenditure	Fiscal education investment	Non-fiscal education investment
2005	841.88	516.11	325.77
2015	3,612.92	2,922.15	690.77
2015/2005	4.3 (times)	5.7 (times)	2.1 (times)

2.2   *Significant Decline in the Share of Social and Personal Investment in Total Education Expenditure*

From the point of view of the structure of education investment, the proportion of education investment from non-government sources in China's total education funding in 2015 was 19.1%, equivalent to only half of the level a decade earlier (in 2005, the proportion was 38.7%), showing a significant decline. Among the three sources of non-government funding, the proportion of tuition and fees in total education investment fell from 18.4% in 2005 to 12.3% in 2013; the proportion of education funding raised by schools through social services and other means also fell from 18.5% in 2005 to 9% in 2013; the proportion of social donations and fund-raising in total education investment fell from 1.1% in 2005 to 0.3% in 2013; the proportion of investment by private school operators in total education decreased from 0.7% in 2005 to 0.5% in 2013.

A REVIEW OF THE CHANGES IN EDUCATION FUNDING 183

TABLE 11.6   Trends in the structure of education investment in China, 2005–2015 (at relevant year prices)

Year	Total education expenditure (billion yuan)	The proportion of fiscal education expenditure (%)	Total	Tuition and fees	Social donations	Organizer investment in private schools	School social service and self-financing
			\multicolumn{5}{c}{The proportion of non-fiscal education expenditure (%)}
2005	841.88	61.3	38.7	18.4	1.1	0.7	18.5
2010	1,956.19	75.0	25.0	15.4	0.6	0.5	8.5
2013	2,386.93	77.9	22.1	12.3	0.3	0.5	9.0
2015	3,612.92	80.9	19.1	–	–	–	–

Note: Part of the 2015 data is missing.

2.3 Decline in the Proportion of Household Expenditure on Education for Urban and Rural Residents

Between 2005 and 2015, the proportion of education expenditure in the total annual consumption expenditure of China's urban and rural residents both showed a downward trend, which was mainly reflected in the following: on the one hand, the per capita income of China's urban and rural residents increased by 2.0 times and 2.5 times respectively during the decade; however, the per capita education expenditure of urban and rural resident families only increased by 0.9 times and 1.2 times, both of which were lower than the growth rate of annual per capita income (See Table 11.7).

TABLE 11.7   Trends in per capita income and expenditure of urban and rural residents in China, 2005–2015 (at relevant year prices, in yuan)

Urban residents	Annual per capita income	Per capita education expenditure
2005	10,493	571
2015	31,195	1,069
2015/2005	3.0 (times)	1.9 (times)

Rural residents	Annual per capita income	Per capita education expenditure
2005	3,255	254
2015	11,422	553
2015/2005	3.5 (times)	2.2 (times)

On the other hand, the proportion of education expenditure to total annual household consumption expenditure for both urban and rural residents have shown a declining trend. According to international research, with economic development and rising income levels, the relative proportion of material consumption in total consumption of residents should decline, while the proportion of non-material education, culture, and health consumption should increase. In 2015, the Engel coefficient (the proportion of total food expenditure in total personal consumption expenditure) of China's urban residents fell by 7% points, while that of rural residents fell by 12.4% points, which should provide more room for growth in education and health spending by residents. However, statistics show that the proportion of total consumption expenditure on housing, transportation and communication, household equipment, and health care for both urban and rural residents in China between 2005 and 2015 showed a rising trend to varying degrees, but the proportion of consumption expenditure on education showed a downward trend. As shown in Tables 11.8 and 11.9, the proportion of urban residents' education consumption fell from 7.2% in 2005 to 5.0% in 2015, while the proportion of rural residents' education consumption fell from 9.5% to 6.0%.

TABLE 11.8　Analysis of the structure of per capita consumption expenditure of urban residents

unit: %

Types of per capita consumption expenditure	2005	2010	2015
food	36.7	35.7	29.7
clothing	10.1	10.7	8.0
Housing	10.2	9.9	22.1
Household equipment, supplies, and services	5.6	6.7	6.1
Health care	7.6	6.5	6.7
Transport and communications	12.5	14.7	13.5
Cultural and recreational services	6.6	7.2	6.1
education	7.2	4.9	5.0

TABLE 11.9   Analysis of the structure of per capita consumption expenditure of rural residents

unit: %

Types of per capita consumption expenditure	2005	2010	2015
food	45.5	41.1	33.1
clothing	5.8	6	6.0
housing	14.5	19.1	20.9
Household equipment, supplies, and services	4.4	5.3	5.9
Health care	6.6	7.4	9.2
Transport and communications	9.6	10.5	12.6
Cultural and recreational services	2.1	3.1	4.5
education	9.5	5.3	6.0

3   Analysis of the Reasons for the Decline in Non-Fiscal Investment in Education

The situation of investment in education is influenced by a nation's economic and financial system, education management system, historical background, education philosophy, social awareness, and many other factors. This development in China's education investment structure over the past decade is closely related to the lack of uniformity in the understanding of China's educational research community and governmental authorities of the general environment for education development, the gap between supply and demand, the attributes of different types of educational products, and the lack of vigorous policy reform.

3.1   *Insufficient Awareness of the Dual Nature of Educational Service*

With regard to the definition of the attributes of education, over the past 30 years since the reform and opening-up, the academic and educators in China have had heated debates from different perspectives on the nature of education as a public endeavor or a business. As an important part of the national economy, education has the characteristics of public endeavor and for public benefit, and should follow the special laws of education; at the same time, part of education has the characteristics of business and commodity, and market mechanisms can be introduced appropriately.

The public welfare nature of education services reflects the importance that the Government and the people attach to the social benefits of education, focusing on the public nature, standardization, and equity of education products or services in order to maintain harmony and equality in social development. The business and commercial nature of education services reflect the fact that some education service activities may obtain returns higher than the costs, that regulation by market-oriented means can produce greater social and economic benefits, and that emphasis is placed on the individuality, characteristics, and quality of products or services in order to meet the needs of different education consumer groups.

The public and business nature of education is reflected in three types of service products: public service products (mainly compulsory public education provided by the government), semi-public service products (mainly non-compulsory academic education in which the government and individuals share the cost), and private products (mainly high-end, high-cost, high-quality, selective schooling and education and training designed to enhance competitiveness). Thus, except for compulsory and military education, market mechanisms can be introduced at all levels of education, allowing for varying degrees of "commercial presence," thus enabling more of the limited public financial resources for education to be spent on compulsory education and on supporting disadvantaged groups and promoting educational equity.

Since the mid-1980s, China has referred to the provision of various services for production and consumption as the tertiary sector, with education as one of its areas. In 1992, the *Decision on Accelerating the Development of the Tertiary Sector* by the State Council of the Central Committee of the Communist Party of China emphasized that education belonged to the tertiary sector and was a basic industry with an overall and pioneering impact on the development of the national economy. The 1999 Third National Education Conference clearly stated that "education should be placed in a strategic position of priority development as a pioneering, overall and fundamental knowledge industry and key infrastructure." In addition, the *Provisions of the CPC Central Committee and the State Council on Deepening Education Reform and Comprehensively Promoting Quality Education* also stated that "social forces are encouraged to provide services for schools and develop education industry." All these policy documents show China's deepening understanding of the education industry and provide a policy basis and guarantee for the joint development of public and private education.

However, at the beginning of the 21st century, the theoretical community has become increasingly opposed to the idea that non-compulsory education has certain business attributes, believing that the functions and responsibilities for developing education and guaranteeing education equality should be borne entirely by the government, denying the important auxiliary role that the market should play in the allocation of educational resources. This, to a certain extent, influences public opinion and the decision-making of government departments in charge, hindering the process of diversification of the school operation and school financing. The 2010 *Outline of the National Medium- and Long-term Education Reform and Development Plan (2010–2020)* clearly stated that "social investment is an important component of investment in education. We should fully mobilize the whole society to actively engage in developing education, expanding the access of social resources to education, and increasing investment in education through multiple channels". However, all parties face the same problem in China: inconsistency in understanding the history of education system reform and not enough open-mindedness have been essential factors influencing the in-depth reform of China's education financing system and preventing private capital from entering the education market.

3.2 Inaccurate Estimation of the Educational Development Environment at the Primary Stage of Socialism

In the late 1980s and early 1990s, China's government, society, and the general public all agreed that education in China was "one big, two poor and three heavy," and a consensus was formed that "education for the people should be provided by the Government and the people together," which mobilized the Government and society to jointly provide education for the people. This alleviated the shortage of state funding for education, expanded the scale of schools at all levels, and improved the conditions in which schools operate.

At the turn of the century, especially after China acceded to the World Trade Organization (WTO), the rapid development of China's economy and the implementation of the tax-sharing system strengthened the financial co-ordination capacity of governments at all levels, which promoted the rapid growth of local fiscal expenditure at all levels and closed the gap between supply and demand in education to a certain extent. However, the regional, urban-rural and inter-school disparities that have emerged in the overall development of education, especially at the compulsory education stage, continue to highlight the structural gap between supply and demand in education funding. It has become one of the Government's essential responsibilities in the new era to ensure educational equity and "run quality education that satisfies the public."

Although government fiscal expenditure has played the major role in investment in education, and have performed the function of investment management in educational institutions at all levels, China is still, and will remain for a long time, in the primary stage of socialism, which is the basic status of education in China. Given the immense but not strong enough economy, there is a need for enormous governmental financial support for the development of social undertakings and the improvement of people's livelihoods, and the gap between supply and demand in State finances for education will be long-standing. At the same time, as education at all levels becomes more universal and equitable, the main issue in the development of education in China has changed from "being able to go to school" to "being able to go to a good school." The major concern is that the imbalance-developed and inadequate-supplied education cannot meet the public's demand for quality education. The fostering and operation of high-quality, featured education require more resource input and higher operating costs. However, the government's public financial capacity is limited. It can only undertake basic education public services and cannot provide education at all levels and types, especially high-quality, featured education that costs far more than the average, making it difficult to rely solely on government financial resources to truly meet the people's increasingly diversified demands for quality education. The overemphasis on the Government's financial responsibility for education development and its function as a guarantor has led to an underestimation of the desire and potential of enterprises, society, and families in educational consumption, restricting the operation of education through market mechanisms and the contribution of increased input from multiple sources to the growth of education spending.

3.3 Inappropriate Administrative Interventions Affecting Society's Motivation to Expand Investment in Education

During the period 2005–2015, within the public education finance system framework, the central government emphasized that more public finance should be allocated to areas that relate to people's livelihoods. As part of the national reform of the education system, the central government set the goal that fiscal expenditure on education should achieve 4% of GDP, making the promotion of the reform of the education public finance system one of the important contents of the Twelfth Five-Year Plan. Through the efforts of many parties (especially through the use of some administrative means), the goal of increasing investment in education was finally achieved, with fiscal investment in education accounting for 4.2% of GDP in 2015. This provided a solid material basis for realizing free compulsory education, improving rural schooling conditions, and promoting educational equity.

However, at a time when the government was trying to increase its investment in education, the opposing ideas towards some content in the *Private Education Promotion Law*, which allows for appropriate returns from operating education institutions, has discouraged the positive momentum of private education development. The tuition rates for high schools and universities have remained unchanged for a decade, which has reduced the proportion of cost-sharing for families at the non-compulsory education level. Denying the reform of the diversified system of public education advocated in the 1993 Outline of National Education Reform and Development (e.g., a few public schools should explore the reform of the self-financing system, key schools should establish branch schools and privately-run schools), stopping the policy for a limited number of lower-enrollment-test-score students to enroll in better high schools through paying higher tuition or extra charges, and the reduction of policy incentives for education donations and fund-raising have led to a significant decline in the enthusiasm of China's society, enterprises and private individuals to invest in education, resulting in a drop of 0.8% in the proportion of multi-source education investment in GDP compared to 2005. The proportion of non-fiscal education investment in total education investment dropped from 39% to 19%, showing a sharp contrast between the relatively rapid growth of fiscal education expenditure and the accelerated decline of non-fiscal education investment.

4 The Overall Financial Needs and Situation for Promoting Education Modernization

At present and in the longer term, relatively insufficient educational resources will not be able to meet the public's enormous demand for quality education. In order to resolve this issue between supply and demand and to achieve the overall goal of educational development, it is necessary to raise large amounts of educational funding through multiple channels. In the years to come, given the limited room for growth in fiscal investment in education, greater emphasis should be placed on mobilizing enterprises' enthusiasm, society, and individuals to invest in education by deepening the reform of the education system and mechanism.

4.1 *Investment in Education in China is Lower than that of Middle- and High-Income Countries*

Despite China's outstanding achievements in education spending growth, there is still a large gap compared to countries with higher levels of education development, and it is not yet sufficient to meet China's demand for funding to promote education equity and improve education quality. Statistics show that China's per capita education expenditure in 2014 was US$650 (converted to US dollars according to average purchasing power), less than one-third of the average level of OECD in 2011. In terms of relative value, government public expenditure is the main indicator of a country's government investment "effort" in education. With this indicator, China was 1% lower than the OECD average level, lower than the United States, South Korea, and other high-income countries, as well as lower than Brazil, Mexico, and other upper-middle-income countries. At the same time, the ratio of social and private inputs to GDP was much lower than that of the United States and South Korea.

In terms of the amount of per-student education expenditure, there is also a large gap between China's education at all stages and that of OECD. Taking higher education as an example, the average per-student expenditure on higher education in OECD countries in 2011 was US$13,958, more than twice as much as China's per-student expenditure on higher education in 2014. The high level of per-student expenditure on higher education provides a solid guarantee for the development of popularized and even universalized higher education in these countries and the improvement of education quality (See Table 11.11).

TABLE 11.10   International comparison of education investment

	Per capita education expenditure (PPP dollars)	The proportion of total education investment to GDP (%)	Of which: (%) Government investment	Of which: (%) Social and private investment
OECD countries	2,213	6.1	5.2	0.9
High-income country				
USA	3,416	6.9	4.7	2.2
Korea	2,186	7.6	4.8	2.8
Chile	1,359	6.9	4.3	2.6
Upper-middle-income country				
Brazil	1,253*	*	5.9	*
Mexico	1,072	6.2	5.1	1.1
China	650	5.24	4.24	1.0

Note: 2015 data for China, 2011 data for all other countries, data for Brazil refers only to public expenditure on education per capita (* indicates data unavailability).
DATA FROM *EDUCATION AT A GLANCE 2014: OECD INDICATORS*

TABLE 11.11   Comparison of per-student expenditure at all stages of education in China in 2014 and that of OECD in 2011 (PPP dollars)

	Primary schools	Junior high school	High school	Universities and colleges
OECD countries	8,296	9,377	9,506	13,958
United States	10,958	12,338	13,143	26,021
South Korea	6,976	6,674	9,696	9,927
China	2,263	3,074	3,158	6,266

SOURCE: *CHINA EDUCATION EXPENDITURE STATISTICS YEARBOOK 2015; EDUCATION AT A GLANCE 2014: OECD INDICATORS*

The Nineteenth National Congress report put forward China's strategic goal of "accelerating the modernization of education and building a country with strong education." To achieve the development tasks of expanding the scale of education, narrowing the education gap, and improving the quality of education, we should raise the per capita education expenditure and per-student education expenditure at all levels to at least half of the 2011 OECD average level. According to simple calculations, by 2030, the total demand for education investment nationwide will need to reach at least 6.0% of GDP, which means that China is still facing a huge funding gap in achieving the strategic goal of modernizing education.

4.2   *Growth in GDP and Fiscal Revenue Slows Down, Making it Difficult to Maintain the Rapid Growth in Fiscal Education Spending Seen in the Previous Period*

During the period 1995–2015, the state's fiscal investment in education achieved an average growth rate of nearly 13%. However, since 2012, the country's economy has moved from a high growth phase to a medium to the high growth phase, with the GDP growth rate remaining at an average of 7.3% and the fiscal revenue growth rate stabilizing, which will have an impact on the growth of China's public education expenditure. In 2012–2015, the average growth rates of fiscal revenue and fiscal education expenditure were 8.2% and 8.6%, respectively. China's economy will be keeping moderate to high growth rate, which will affect fiscal revenues to some extent, as well as the growth rate of public funding for education (See Table 11.12).

TABLE 11.12   Analysis of the relation between the annual growth rate of GDP and total fiscal education expenditure, 1995–2015 (all at constant prices)

unit: %

Years	GDP	Fiscal revenue	Fiscal expenditure on education
1995–2005	9.2	15.0	11.3
2005–2012	10.4	14.9	18.3
2012–2015	7.3	8.2	8.6

At the same time, in terms of the State's fiscal expenditure structure, between 2007 and 2015, the proportions of fiscal expenditure in the three major categories of government expenditure on public services, social and people's livelihoods, and economic had stabilized in general[4] (See Table 11.13). Although in the future, the State may reduce the proportion of government expenditure on public services and expenditure on economic, and expand the proportion of expenditure on social and people's livelihood, the room for increasing the proportion of expenditure on social and people's livelihood will not be very large.

TABLE 11.13   Analysis of the three major expenditure categories of state fiscal expenditure, 2007–2015

Year	Public fiscal expenditure (billion yuan)	Public service	Social and people's livelihoods	Economic and others
2007	4,978.14	31.7	50.0	18.3
2009	7,629.99	25.0	53.3	19.7
2011	10,924.78	21.6	58.4	17.8
2013	14,021.21	20.9	60.5	16.4
2015	17,587.78	20.5	62.6	16.9

The proportion of expenditure by three major categories (%)

---

4 National public fiscal expenditures can be divided into three sectors: the first sector is government public service expenditures, including government administration, foreign affairs, national defense, public security and debt expenditures; the second sector is social and people's livelihood expenditures, including education, science and technology, culture, health, employment and social security, environmental protection, urban and rural affairs, affordable housing and disaster relief; the third sector is expenditures on economic, infrastructure and others.

Among the public fiscal expenditure on social and livelihood services, there is an urgent need to increase the share of public expenditure on health and social security and employment, given they have long been relatively low in fiscal expenditure (1/2.2 and 1/1.4 of public expenditure on education in 2015, respectively) (See Table 11.14). Therefore, even if the country increases the share of fiscal expenditure on all social and livelihoods services, the proportion cut to education will likely be modest.

In the period ahead, although China's fiscal investment in education will continue to grow, it may have a slowing growth rate and limited room for increment. Given the limited room for growth in fiscal education spending, there is an urgent need to deepen the reform of the education investment system and the school-operation system, actively tap the potential of educational consumption in society and the market, promote "the increment of investment from both the government and private," and raise the level of assurance that education investment provides for education development.

5 Deepen the Reform of the Education System and Promote Diversified Resource Supply

In the face of this reality, we should promote in-depth reform of the education system, strengthen policy guidance, in order to allow the market to take charge, mobilize the multifaceted enthusiasm of the Government, enterprises, and the general public. In addition to the steadily increasing government's fiscal investment in education, we should do everything possible to increase investment in education throughout society, gradually adjusting the ratio of fiscal investment to multi-channel education funding to 7:3. In that way, if the proportion of total investment in education in society to GDP will increase by around 0.3% every five years, we will have enough material foundation to realize the goal of modernizing education.

5.1 *Dynamically Adjusting Non-Compulsory Education Tuition and Fees, and Increasing the Proportion of Private Contributions for Regular Senior High Schools and Higher Education*

A strict distinction should be made between compulsory and non-compulsory education in terms of funding resources. Specifically, the government should strengthen the guarantee of balanced basic public education services (e.g., free compulsory education, universal pre-school education subsidies, free secondary vocational education, etc.). At the same time, a reasonable cost-sharing mechanism for non-compulsory education should be improved, and the tuition fees for regular high schools and higher education should be dynamically adjusted.

TABLE 11.14   Structure of State fiscal expenditure in the category of social and livelihood expenditure 2007–2015

Year	The proportion of social and people's livelihood expenditure to public fiscal expenditure (%)				
	Total	Education	Science and technology	Culture, sports, and media	Social security and employment
2007	50.0	14.3	3.6	1.8	10.9
2009	53.3	13.7	3.6	1.8	10.0
2011	58.4	15.1	3.5	1.7	10.2
2013	60.5	15.7	3.6	1.8	10.3
2015	62.6	14.9	3.3	1.7	10.8

The tuition standards for regular high schools and higher education institutions in various regions need to be scientifically calculated and appropriately adjusted based on multiple factors, such as the rate of increase in the per-student cost of education, the state of economic and social development, the trend of price changes, and the expected level of growth in per capita disposable income of the population. And a dynamic tuition adjustment mechanism should be established. At the same time, for students from economically disadvantaged families, a series of student-support policies should be set up and perfected, such as risk compensation for State student loans, work-study grants, interest-free loans on campus, tuition fee reductions and special hardship subsidies, etc. Local government should set up different proportions of student-support coverage, such as 15% and 20%, according to the strength of its own economic and social development, the number of poverty students, and the proportion of State support, ensuring access to non-compulsory level education for students with financial difficulties.

5.2   Using the Privately-Run Schools Promotion Law as an Opportunity to Mobilize Enterprises and Individuals to Run Education

Taking the revision of the *Law on the Promotion of Privately-run Schools* as an opportunity, the Government should actively revise and improve policies and related laws on the entry of social and private capital into the field of education services, optimizing the ecological environment for the development of privately-run education, encouraging innovative institutional mechanisms

th care	Environmental protection	Urban, rural, agricultural, forestry, and water affairs	Subsidized housing expenditure
	2.0	13.4	–
	2.5	15.5	1.0
	2.4	16.1	3.5
	2.6	17.5	3.2
	2.7	18.9	3.3

for the operation of schools by social forces, and ensuring that institutional transitions are smooth. This will push forward reform of private education in a standardized and orderly manner and stimulate the vitality of private school operation. On the basis of continuously improving the quality of public education, diversification of education service delivery mechanisms is being realized, so as to fully satisfy the individualized and differentiated educational needs of the public, effectively promoting the development of public education services and improving the quality of education services.

Several measures could be adopted to promote the diversification of education service supply. For instance, we should explore the joint operation of schools by public schools, enterprises, and various social organizations to attract social capital. Key public schools can set up private schools and branch schools to attract social capital to involve in the group-school-operation led by high-quality public schools. We should encourage retired senior principals and teachers to use their educational experience and personal brands to run schools, which will improve school-operating efficiency, and increase private investment in education. We should also encourage private, foreign, and other social capital to invest in education in ways permitted by laws and regulations, such as money, land-use rights, and securities, and to set up mixed-ownership schools. The government should promote the development of high-quality social education institutions and expand the coverage of high-quality education resources to meet the public's educational needs through the government's purchase of education services (e.g., by purchasing student quota or providing subsidies).

5.3 *Improving the Education Donation System Suited to China's Conditions and Attracting the Participation of Private Capital*

We should actively liaise with overseas alumni and successful industrialists to expand overseas donations. Meanwhile, we should improve the incentive mechanism for educational donations, simplify the approval process, implement the provision of the pretax deduction for individual educational donations, allow donors to receive reasonable returns to enhance the sense of accomplishment and enthusiasm for donating to education. In addition, we should establish and improve the management and use of donations and supervision mechanisms to ensure transparency, openness, and efficiency in the use of donated funds (or goods).

In short, relevant policies should be formulated to actively mobilize capital from all sectors of society, including private and individual capital, to enter the field of education. We should make use of market mechanisms to expand investment in education and education consumption, which will help to reduce the Government's public financial burden. Consequently, the financial resources released can be allocated to the development of compulsory education in rural areas, poor areas, etc., or invested in free secondary vocational education, student subsidy programs, and financial assistance for poverty students. This will improve the efficiency of the government's provision of public education services.

CHAPTER 12

Report on "Innovative Small and Micro Schools" (创新小微) in China

Yang Jin[1]

Abstract

This study aims to present the current situation of China's "innovative small and micro schools," explore the motivations for the emergence of this educational phenomenon, analyze the educational demands of this group, investigate their educational manifestations and operation processes, sort out the difficulties encountered in the development process and the support needed, and understand their educational achievements. On this basis, I put forward targeted policy and legal recommendations to promote the healthy development of this innovative educational phenomenon and to promote educational reform in China.

Keywords

educational innovation – educational practices – "innovative small and micro schools"

Over the past three decades, education worldwide has moved in the direction of innovation and diversity, with the emergence of "charter schools" in the United States in the 1990s; the first batch of "free schools" being established across the United Kingdom in 2011; and the adoption of the three Acts on Experimental Education in Taiwan in 2014, etc. In China's mainland, more and more parents and educators are beginning to rethink and act upon the existing education system, and several "innovative small and micro schools" have emerged. These schools have opened the public's eyes to more possibilities for educational development, and they have become a new force for educational reform.

---

[1] Yang Jin 杨晋 is the Project Manager of the Center for Educational Innovation at the 21st Century Education Research Institute.

It should be noted that this study is more focused on full-time schools (students at 7–18 years of age) with the following features: not taking "tests-taking" as the primary purpose of education; respecting the differences of each child and encouraging their individual development; aiming to develop children's personality, mental and physical health, future-oriented and lifelong learning ability; and exploring the diverse and innovate educational practices in conjunction with the school's educational philosophy and educational objectives. Given the small size of these schools currently (most of them have less than 200 students), we tentatively call them "innovative small and micro schools."

With the help of the China Homeschooling Alliance website,[2] the China Innovative Education Exchange, and the 21st Century Education Research Institute, the study collected data and information from 142 schools. After screening, a group of "Chinese classics recitation schools," Waldorf schools,[3] educational camps that do not have full-day programs, and preschool only institutions were excluded from the study. Finally, 27 schools were identified as study objects, 4 of which could not be reached. Therefore, the final survey was conducted in 23 schools. The research was conducted in 23 schools. One hundred twenty-three questionnaires were distributed to the founders/heads of the schools and the parents of the students in the schools, and face-to-face or telephone interviews were conducted with the founders/heads of the schools. At the same time, field visits to some representative cases were conducted to obtain more information.

1 Overview of "Innovative Small and Micro Schools"

1.1 *School Size: Most Schools Have Fewer than 50 Students, with an Average Teacher-Student Ratio of 1:2*

In terms of the number of students, only one of the 23 schools has more than 200 students, with a total of 380 students, while most of the rest have 11–50 students. Four schools have ten students or fewer. All these schools have small class sizes and very high teacher-student ratios, which are well above public school standards (see Table 12.1). Most of these schools are facing a shortage of students and unfilled classes to a certain extent. In interviews with school founders/directors, most of them expressed that they hope to maintain a teacher-student ratio of 1:4 to 1:5 in the future.

---

2 China Homeschooling Alliance website: http://chinahomeschooling.com/forum.php.
3 Waldorf schools Directory: http://box.hiwaldorf.com/guide/term/mainland.

TABLE 12.1   Teacher-student ratio in "innovative small and micro schools"

Teacher-student ratio	Number of schools
More than 1:2 (inclusive)	9
1:2-1:3 (inclusive)	6
1:3-1:4 (inclusive)	4
1:4-1:5 (inclusive)	2
Less than 1:5	2

1.2   *Time of Establishment and Regional Distribution: Most Are New Schools; Beijing, Sichuan (Chengdu), and Guangdong Are Active Regions*

Of the 23 schools that participated in the study, the oldest school has been established for 12 years, and the newest one just opened in October of 2017. Figure 12.1 shows that many "innovative small and micro schools" have been opened since 2010.

Beijing, Sichuan (Chengdu), and Guangdong are the regions where the development of "innovative small and micro schools" is active, as shown in Table 12.2, with nearly half of the schools located in suburban areas, seven in urban centers and five in rural areas. There is one "mobile" school that does not yet have a physical campus, where the choice of learning location is determined by the requirements of teachers, teaching content, and teaching format. Interviews revealed that the school has plans to establish a headquarters based in Shenzhen and is in the process of creating a space for growing children to learn more deeply and practice projects of interest to them.

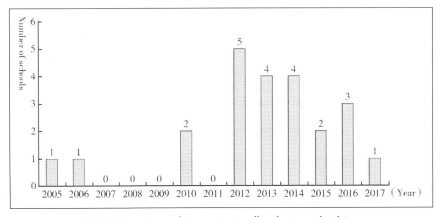

FIGURE 12.1   Establishment year of "innovative small and micro schools"

TABLE 12.2 Geographical locations of "innovative small and micro schools"

School location	Beijing	Chengdu	Shenzhen	Guangzhou	Foshan	Dongguan	Hef
Number of schools	6	3	2	1	1	1	1

Note: One of the schools has two campuses in Qingdao and Xiamen.

1.3 Funders and Motivations: Three-Quarters of the Schools Have Been Established to Address Schooling Issue of Their Own Children

Nearly three-quarters of the schools studied were founded in order to provide schooling for founders' own children, all of whom attend or have attended their own schools. Among the schools, seven were founded and run jointly by the parents. As a result, for ten schools, the highest grade currently offered is the grade attended by the founder's children. As the children grow older, the number of grades in the school increases.

1.4 School Age Distribution: Most Schools Are for Children in the 5–12 Age Group

Most students in those schools are currently in the 5–12 age group, with only ten schools have a secondary school section. The schools mainly offering elementary education have expressed a general desire to continue offering secondary education in order to establish a relatively complete teaching system and to address parents' anxiety about the difficulty for their students to continue education in the public school system.

1.5 Main Recruitment Method: "Word of Mouth"

Most of the "innovative small and micro schools" rely on friends' recommendations and word-of-mouth referrals from parents. With the development of new media, WeChat groups on parenting, childcare, and education related topics and friends' circles are becoming the main ways for parents to know about these schools. Each school has its own WeChat public account, which regularly shares the school's educational philosophy and daily learning activities. Five schools have posts dedicated to branding and new media operations.

These schools also hold regular "open days" for the purpose of recruitment, where interested parents are invited to visit the school to experience the atmosphere and environment and are introduced to the school's educational philosophy and teaching practices. The school founders/directors generally

Xiamen	Qingdao	Ji'nan	Guiyang	Xinxiang	Wenzhou	Xi'an	Zhangjiajie
1	1	1	1	1	1	1	1

believe that the parents and the school are in a mutual selection process and hope to attract families who truly understand the school's educational philosophy. Schools may consider not admit children, whose parents' educational philosophy is opposite to or seriously inconsistent with that of the schools.

2 Educational Philosophy and Teaching Practice of "Innovative Small and Micro Schools"

After analyzing the philosophy, mission, and vision of these schools, it was found that the following points were mentioned very frequently: 1. education should be about people; 2. education is about life and needs to return to life and establish a connection with life; 3. protect children's innate curiosity and guide them to become active learners and lifelong learners; 4. with Chinese culture and philosophy as the core, and connect with the pluralistic reality of the world; 5. education requires the collaborative participation of the family, the community and society.

In the interviews with school founders, the shared education objectives for the innovative small and micro schools are "to develop a sound personality; to learn effective communication and teamwork; to have a healthy body and good habits; to have the ability to face the unknown future."

The realization of educational philosophy and goals depend on everyday teaching, curriculum activities, and learning assessments. Without a suitable vehicle, the best ideas cannot be realized.

2.1 The Daily Curriculum of "Innovative Small and Micro Schools"

Considering the distinct characteristics of children of different school age groups, I divide these schools' daily teaching and learning activities into two categories: "12 years and under" and "12 years and above".

2.1.1   Elementary School (12 Years and Under)

2.1.1.1   *Basic Literacy Courses*

Basic literacy courses generally consist of Chinese language, English, Mathematics and Social Studies, and Science, with some schools incorporating basic literacy courses into 'Thematic Learning,' covering multiple subjects.

Most of the school founders/directors claimed that their schools usually refer to the curriculum standards set by the Ministry of Education for each subject, and many schools use the Chinese language and mathematics textbooks published by the People's Education Press or other versions, with teaching materials selected from the textbooks and expanded in teaching practice. Some schools choose their own learning materials, especially for Chinese language courses. "School H studies the *Thousand-Character Classic*, the *Three-Character Classic*, and the *Sound and Rhyme Enlightenment* in the first grade; the second grade selects snippets from the textbooks used back in the Republic of China and classic articles from past dynasties, as well as excerpts of poetry from the *Book of Poetry*; the third-grade studies the *Analects of Confucius* and a hundred poems selected from the Han, Wei, and Six Dynasties; and the fourth grade begins to read chapters from the *Great Learning*, the *Doctrine of the Mean*, and *Mencius* intensively." These schools emphasize the development of reading habits and provide a variety of extended reading materials and reading lists, taking into account the teaching schedule and children's interests.

The math program values the formation of a child's thinking models and learning in real-life scenarios. "School A has a student-run restaurant where the children themselves do all the bookkeeping. The teacher does not provide a sophisticated bookkeeping template, but allows the child to build their own logical bookkeeping system through practice, where many skills, including the ability to calculate, are naturally exercised." Other schools have opted for Khan Academy's math program, which uses a database to learn each child's learning status and understanding in order to provide targeted guidance and practice.

English teaching can be divided into two categories: one is to create a bilingual environment for children from an early age, where each class has a foreign teacher to encourage children to listen and speak more; the other is that "students exposed to English too early will easily confuse the Pinyin and English alphabet. Therefore, during the child's language-sensitive period, more attention should be paid to the development of the child's language foundation (oral muscles, accurate pronunciation, etc.). English learning is added to the curriculum after children's language thinking is basically formed."

2.1.1.2   *Theme-Based/Project-Based Learning*

"Theme-based/project-based" learning is a common teaching method in these schools, emphasizing "active learning by the students." Projects should not be designed based on the teacher's preference or ability, but rather on the student's interests, ability level, and growth needs. Teachers work together with students to explore and select possible learning topics/projects. In the process, children are encouraged to be "problem-aware" and ask questions and find ways to solve problems independently, with teachers playing more of a coaching role to guide learning skills. For example, M School carries out "theme-based learning" with different themes for different grade levels. Specifically, in Year 1, the major themes are weather changes and plant growth. In Year 2, the major themes are animals and ecology, etc. Each theme is broken down into sub-themes. At the start of each learning period on a specific theme, teachers would spend two to three weeks with students asking questions about the theme and categorizing the questions. For the following weeks, teachers would lead students to explore the theme and find solutions through various approaches.

2.1.1.3   *Sports and Outdoor Activities*
Physical education (PE) and outdoor exercise are high priorities at these schools, with over 80% of schools offering daily PE classes. In addition to regular sports like running, jumping, and ball games, many schools also offer courses that emphasize skills such as rock climbing, field cycling, and sailing. These kinds of training not only pay attention to children's physical development and improving their flexibility and agility, but also focus on the development of character, perseverance, and teamwork.

2.1.1.4   *Arts Courses*
In addition, art classes such as music, art, and drama are also essential. These schools provide students with the opportunity to be exposed to different cultures and arts, to help discover their potential and interests, and to develop the ability to perceive and create art. To their credit, these schools are especially protective of children's imagination and creative talents and do not impose standardized restrictions.

2.1.2   *Secondary School (12 Years and Above)*
Ten of the schools in the study provide classes to students aged 12 and above. At this stage, children are developing their own goals, so schools focus more on providing a supportive environment that encourages them to explore and learn for themselves.

More than half of the schools have personalized learning plans for each student. They often adopt a "mentorship system" in which the student chooses his or her own mentor. The mentor is more of a coach, a supporter, not providing knowledge directly to the student as much as possible, but helping them to discover what they are really interested in, encouraging them to hypothesize, explore, experiment, find the truth, and providing necessary but not excessive support.

For example, after a student comes up with a goal, his or her mentor may spend several days or even a week going over and clarifying the goal with the student: "Why do you have this goal," "How are you going to implement this goal," "What kind of support do you need as you work towards this goal," "What learning resources can you find to help you reach this goal," "What other support and resources do you need," etc. Once these are sorted out, the mentor would communicate regularly with the student about their progress, provide the support the student needs, etc. Of course, if it's something that both the mentor and the student are interested in, they will learn together.

Schools that do not fully implement personalized learning still have some mandatory classes, such as Chinese, English, math, social sciences and humanities, science, and technology, but they are not standardized or paced the same for all students. Instead, teachers will set different learning objectives for each student, taking into account their interests and areas of expertise as well as their different plans for the future. In these ten schools, PE class is mandatory for every student, with PE class and outdoor activities every day to ensure that students get enough exercise.

In addition, several schools pay special attention to vocational education, hoping that students can have a broad understanding of various types of occupations. Considering their own preferences and expertise, students can have more in-depth thinking of their future development. Only in this way, students will have clear enough goals and self-awareness, and enough internal drive to encourage them to continue learning and improving themselves, regardless of whether they choose to proceed to higher education, employment or entrepreneurship after graduation.

2.2   *Featured Curriculum of "Innovative Small and Micro Schools"*
2.2.1   Life Skills and Sustainable Lifestyles

At M School, cooking, sewing, plumbing, and electrical work are all taught by specialized instructors, and students get hands-on practices. The founders of the school hope every child to have the ability to live entirely independently when they graduate from elementary school. This also includes maintaining sustainable lifestyles such as waste separation, organic composting, rainwater collecting, etc., all of which are included in the curriculum.

2.2.2   Learning of Traditional Culture as Represented by Solar Terms

In schools that value traditional Chinese culture, living according to solar terms is a crucial part of the curriculum. At P school, teachers encourage children to acquire original knowledge from nature, integrate the concepts of solar terms into students' lives and learning, guide students to lead a rhythmic and regular life, and experience the essence of Chinese culture in the day-to-day solar-term-based life. At M school, in addition to the 24 solar terms, students are also taught the 72 pentads. Students are asked to analyze which pentads are related to plants and animals, and which are non-living phenomena. More importantly, teachers lead students to observe and think about how people came to these conclusions thousands of years ago, and how to obtain accurate and valid data. This will give students a deeper understanding of Chinese culture and allow them to apply this way of thinking to their lives in the future.

2.2.3   "Non-traditional" Learning

Unlike many schools that view online games as a scourge, X school offers courses in "game art" and "games and history," and even a *"Arena of Valor"* project-based course in which teachers and students participate together. "In this project, teachers and students work together as game teams to learn and discuss ways to improve tactics. The homework might be writing a paper to analyze one of their avatars' combat level, the problems that arise and how to improve, etc. Students really run it like an eSports club, getting sponsorships and participating in tournaments. In the process, students develop skills such as expression, communication, teamwork, etc., while giving them a deeper understanding of 'eSports' as a profession."

2.2.4   "Mixed-Age" Learning

Since the number of students in these "innovative small and micro schools" is generally small, students of different ages have more opportunities to interact and learn from each other.

"On 'Food Day,' students divide work and collaborate according to their ages and interests." "On 'School Fest,' senior students perform school cultural stage plays for the junior students." "During wild camping trips, the older kids volunteer to help the younger kids set up tents and cook," and so on so forth.

Compared to public schools, where students primarily study with peers of similar ages, children in these schools have more opportunities to interact with children of other age groups. This helps better develop their social skills and empathy, and enable them to learn to help and care for others in practice.

2.2.5   Read Ten Thousand Books, Travel Ten Thousand Miles

School trips and off-campus activities are important ways for students in these schools to gain real practical experience in society and nature and to establish a link between learning and life. These schools have outings weekly or bi-weekly and organize national and international study tours every year. Unlike many walkabout excursions, these outings and school trips are more carefully designed by teachers with specific learning purposes, guiding the child to observe nature, architecture, people, and society.

2.3 Evaluation of the Teaching Effectiveness of "Innovative Small and Micro Schools"

These "innovative small and micro schools" generally see the need to evaluate the effectiveness of teaching and learning in order to understand the progress and status of diverse students, to improve teaching methods, and to provide more individualized support for different students.

2.3.1 Multiple Evaluators: Teachers, Students, and Parents All Involved, Combining Evaluation and Self-Evaluation

Most schools invite multiple evaluators to assess students' overall development. Teachers need to record all aspects of children's development and status in their daily learning life and provide regular feedback to parents. At the same time, children are encouraged to learn to evaluate themselves and each other to develop self-awareness.

2.3.2 A Variety of Evaluation Methods and Tools: Paper-Based Examinations, "Breakout" Examinations, and Project Presentations

Most schools still use 'paper-based tests' as a form of assessment, but the purpose of the test is not to score, rank, or compare children, but rather to assess how well each child has mastered the knowledge, how well the teaching objectives have been met, and what next steps are needed to support and tutor different children.

There are a few schools that take "breakout-form exams based on constructing realistic scenarios." Breakout exams at G school include knowledge points, knowledge structure, psychology, willpower, logic, intuition, and physical fitness. The purpose is not only to test, but also to make the test the most efficient course, where children feel the power of their previous learning, emotions, and willpower, so that they are more motivated to grow. Each child is accompanied by an observer during the test-taking process to track and record the child's performance at all test levels. This also provides parents a platform to fully observe their child's development.

For project-based learning, most schools adopt a "project presentation" approach for evaluation. At the end of the project, children are provided with an open forum to present their work, reflect on the project, any problems encountered, and the solutions. Each student is required to conduct self-assessment, mentor assessment, and group assessment, and is encouraged to improve and build on based on the assessment results.

2.4   Graduate Prospectus

Since these "innovative small and micro schools" are generally established for a short period of time, they only have a few graduates. Most of the students in these schools are under 12 years of age, and many schools have no graduates yet. However, most of the parents of students in these schools have expressed their hope that the schools continue to operate secondary education sections and that they would be willing to keep their children in these schools.

According to feedback from schools with students over the ages of 12, most graduates chose to apply for further study abroad, and many of the graduated students were admitted to top foreign universities. There have also been one or two students who have taken the domestic college-entrance exams. Some have chosen to start their own businesses or find direct employment after graduation. These students have generally found their own interests and specialties in secondary school and are able to choose a major according to their interests and their future development plan.

It is well worth keeping an eye on the developments of graduates from these schools in the long run.

2.5   Formation and Support of Teaching Staff

The recruitment and development of teachers are at the heart of "innovative small and micro schools."

2.5.1   Key Indicators for Teacher Recruitment: "Love of Children" and "Love of Learning"

When we talked to the founders/principals of these schools about what skills and characteristics are most important when hiring teachers, the most frequently cited skills were "love of children" and "love of learning."

"'Love of children' comes first. Teaching methods and techniques can be trained and learned, but without love and respect for children, all techniques would become indifferent and cold." These schools do not require every teacher to have a professional background related to education when recruiting teachers, and not even emphasize the teacher's professional and academic qualifications that much, but hope that the candidates are willing to be a teacher and like this career. With internal drive, teachers are more willing to learn, improve and perfect themselves, and can grow and gain in the process of teaching and working with children.

2.5.2 Emphasis on Internal Teacher Training and Exchange Mechanisms, Experienced Teachers Taking a Mentoring Role

It is essential for schools to provide professional training and support for teachers. Firstly, each school has internal training and experience-exchange mechanisms that encourage learning, sharing, and reflecting on each other's experiences within the team. Secondly, they also provide information and opportunities for teachers to undertake external training, which they can choose according to their needs. Some schools also implement a "mentorship system" among their teachers, in which experienced teachers act as mentors for junior teachers after they join the school. Under this system, mentors not only share their teaching experience, but also provide support for the difficulties faced by junior teachers in the process of self-development, helping them grow in all aspects.

2.5.3 Teachers Are Given Full Trust and Freedom, Independent Explorations Are Supported

In addition to training in professional skills, these schools generally give teachers a great deal of trust and freedom. They are encouraged to develop new courses and projects, to experiment with different teaching methods, to choose their own teaching materials, to control the pace of teaching, and to enrich the content and form of the classroom.

3 Overview and Feedback from Families Who Chose "Innovative Small and Micro Schools"

3.1 *Types of Students and Families Selecting "Innovative Small and Micro Schools"*

Questionnaires were sent to parents of students attending these schools to understand parents' main motivations to choose "innovative small and micro schools."

3.1.1 Parents Disagree with the Educational Philosophy of In-System Traditional Schools

Survey results show that most of the parents of these children were born after 1975, have bachelor's degrees or above, and many of them have studied abroad. Most of them were once "successful" under the examination-oriented education system, but they do not want their children to regard the college-entrance examination as their only goal, and put a lot of energy into repeated examination skill training for preparation for the college-entrance examination. They

REPORT ON "INNOVATIVE SMALL AND MICRO SCHOOLS"

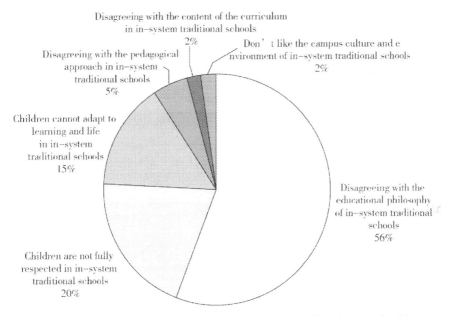

FIGURE 12.2   Main reasons for parents to choose "innovative small and micro schools"

want their children to be well-rounded and mentally and physically healthy, rather than becoming a "testing machine."

3.1.2   Children Are Not Fully Respected in In-System Traditional Schools

Some children had experienced verbal and even physical punishment from teachers in in-system traditional schools, and had been physically and mentally hurt. During interviews with parents, some parents said that the teachers at their children's previous schools did not take their children's feelings into account. For example, sharing their children's test scores and rankings publicly in parents' WeChat groups. This is not good for the healthy development of children. They would prefer to choose a school that respects their children and is more student-centered.

3.1.3   Children Are Unable to Adapt to Study and Life in In-System Traditional Schools

There are also children who may have mental or intellectual delays or disabilities, or who have physical disabilities, or who are considered by the general public to be "problem children," such as aversion to school, inability to follow classroom rules, and disruption of other students' studies. Parents have no

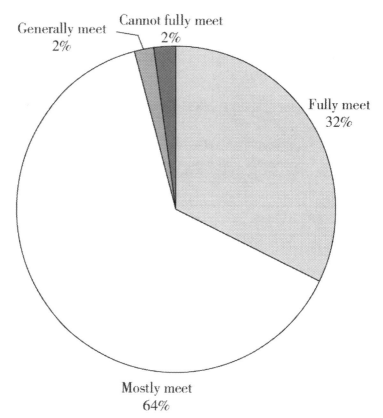

Does the study and living arrangement at school meet your expectations?

FIGURE 12.3 Parents' satisfaction rate with their children's school

choice but to send their children to these innovative schools outside the system when they have "nowhere else to go" and "no school to go to."

3.2 Parents' Feedback on Their Children's School Learning and Life

Figure 12.3 shows that 95% of parents believe that the school their child currently attends meets their expectations.

Only 2.44% of the parents were not satisfied with their child's academic outcome, and the reason for their dissatisfaction was that their child's knowledge was not comprehensive or systematic enough (see Figure 12.4). Regarding their child's school life (see Figure 12.5), 12.2% of parents were "not very satisfied" or "not satisfied." The majority of parents were not satisfied with the "inadequate facilities and the school environment."

REPORT ON "INNOVATIVE SMALL AND MICRO SCHOOLS" 211

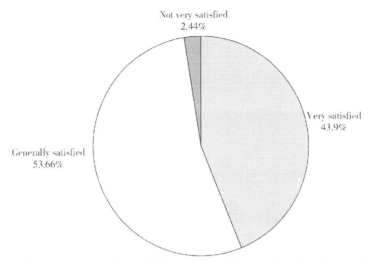

In general, are you satisfied with your child's academic achievements since he or she entered this school?

FIGURE 12.4 Parents' satisfaction rate with their children's academic outcomes

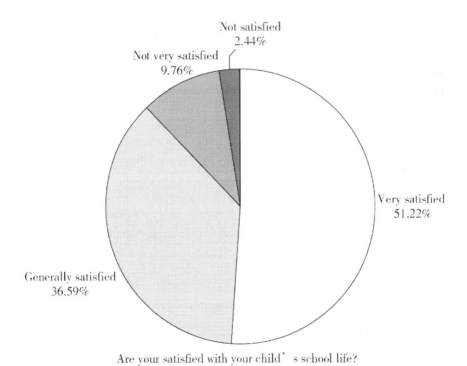

Are your satisfied with your child's school life?

FIGURE 12.5 Parents' satisfaction rate with their children's school life

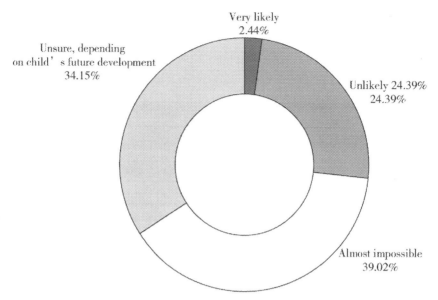

How likely will you send your child back to in–system traditional schools in future?

FIGURE 12.6   Likelihood of parents sending their children back to the institutional system

When asked whether there was a possibility of sending their children back to an in-system traditional school in the future, 24.39% of parents answered it was unlikely, 39.02% said it was almost impossible, and 34.15% were unsure, depending on the future development of their children (see Figure 12.6). This shows that most parents were satisfied with this type of school, with more than half of them not considering sending their children back to the in-system traditional schools.

3.3   *Students' Feedback on Their School Learning and Life*

Children's satisfaction with their learning and life is an essential indicator for evaluating the "innovative small and micro schools." Due to the young age of students in most of these schools, we did not conduct the survey directly with the students, but instead designed two questions in the parent questionnaire to reflect the children's satisfaction level with their school learning and life through the parents' observation and daily communication with their children.

According to the survey results (see Figures 12.7 and 12.8), in general, the children's satisfaction rate with their studies and life was similar to or even

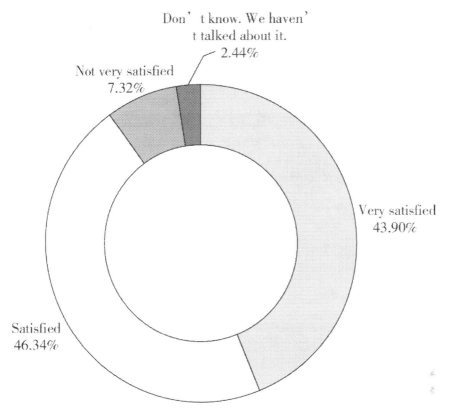

Is your child satisfied with his or her academic achievement?

FIGURE 12.7   Students' satisfaction rate with their learning outcomes

slightly higher than that of their parents. In interviews with some parents, parents reported that their children "love going to school. The child even once insisted on going to school when he was sick". "My child often asks me during the holidays why the school hasn't started yet." "In terms of learning, my child has become more proactive and loves to read." "My child likes and admires Mr. ZH very much. He thinks he is very knowledgeable and interesting in class, which greatly inspired his interest in humanities and history, and he is willing to actively explore and learn" ... These feedbacks showed children's attitude towards school learning and life from multiple dimensions.

In addition, a few parents chose "don't know, haven't communicated" in the questionnaire. These parents should pay more attention to their children's development and communicate more with their children.

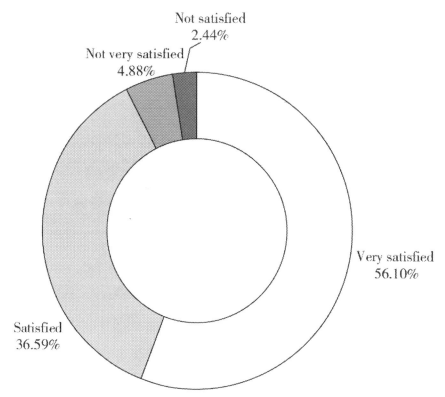

FIGURE 12.8   Students' satisfaction rate with their school life

4   Issues and Challenges for "Innovative Small and Micro Schools"

4.1   *Hard to Obtain a School Operation Qualification* (办学资质)

On January 18, 2017, the State Council issued *Several Opinions on Encouraging Social Forces to Establish Education and Promote the Healthy Development of Private Education*, which clearly stated that "relaxing the requirements for operating schools – the government shall not restrict social forces in running education, as long as laws and regulations are not broached, the interests of third parties, public, and national security were not violated. However, it is not easy for these "innovative small and micro schools" to obtain school operation qualifications. As of the writing of this report, none of the "innovative small and micro schools" surveyed have obtained the school operation qualification, due to their failure in meeting requirements for the number of students in their classes, school space, etc. But most of the school founders/directors are working hard to obtain the qualifications.

4.2   Establishing a Stable Team of Teachers

These "innovative small and micro schools" have high requirements for teachers' abilities in curriculum design, classroom management, diverse teaching methods, understanding children's development, and providing psychological support. During the recruitment process, it was found that most of the teachers who had worked in the in-system traditional schools were already used to the previous teaching mode, and sometimes could not adapt to the innovative teaching methods. However, teachers without education-related professional backgrounds were enthusiastic and willing to learn, but they lacked teaching experience and needed a long time to learn.

Therefore, it is also a huge challenge for these schools to recruit the right teachers and build a stable team of teachers.

4.3   Striking a Balance between the Education Philosophy and the Diversified Needs of Parents

Most parents who sent their children to innovative small and micro schools agree with the schools' education philosophy. However, there were still various concerns and requests that arose during the actual teaching process. For instance, although parents were aware that the school was not able to provide student school registration records for their children, they still came in every now and then to inquire about student registration records. Some parents can't help but compare their child to other children studying in in-system schools at the same age, worrying that they don't know enough words or memorize the multiplication table.

The founders/principals of these schools generally expressed that they understood parents' concerns and anxieties and spent a lot of time communicating with them. However, finding a balance between parents' diverse educational needs and the school's educational philosophy in a short period of time is a challenge for these schools.

4.4   Student Recruitment

Currently, most of the enrollment of "innovative small and micro schools" remains at the stage of word-of-mouth among parents, and many schools do not have full classes. Relying on the development of new media, social media is becoming a platform for these schools to self-publicize and exhibit, which is one of the important channels for recruiting students. But the fact is that the dissemination effect is still very limited, and it is difficult to reach a wider group of parents. In addition, most of these schools have difficulty providing a "student school registration record" for their students, making it difficult for many parents to decide to enroll in these schools. Moreover, the high tuition compared to public schools, especially at the compulsory level, also make some parents hesitant to send their children to these schools.

4.5 Other Issues

The development of the Internet has provided these schools with a wealth of teaching resources, but many school founders/principals said that it is not easy to find an excellent curriculum or one that can match the students' needs. It takes a lot of time for teachers to select, experiment, and improve it. More energy and time are needed to build a perfect curriculum system for their own schools.

Many founders/principals of "innovative small and micro schools" have the dual-role of school runner and teacher. They need to take care of student admissions, teacher recruitment, finances, daily operations, etc. Also, they need to devote their energy to daily teaching, curriculum development, and interaction with students. How to find a balance between these two roles is a challenge for many founders/directors.

5 Recommendations

5.1 *Promoting Reform of the Primary and Secondary School-Operation System, Opening Up Opportunities for Private Schools and Encouraging the Diversified Development of the Educational Ecosystem*

The Third Plenary Session of the eighteenth Central Committee pointed out a clear direction for education reform and development: "Further promote the separation of management, operation, and evaluation (管办评分离), expand the autonomy of schools in school operations, improve the internal governance structure of schools, and encourage social forces to run education." It also provides an important basis for promoting reform of the school-operation system, the purpose of which is to stimulate the vitality of public schools, open-up education to society, and enable social forces outside the system to grow. These innovative schools have explored a variety of new forms of school operation from the perspective of solving their own or society's practical problems. They contain tremendous reform momentum and educational wisdom. The government should adapt to this change, value and protect the enthusiasm of diverse subjects, encourage all kinds of local, private, pluralistic, and open educational reform exploration, further open-up education, expand social participation, expand the concept of innovation and entrepreneurship from the business sector to the education sector, encourage innovation and entrepreneurship in education just as it supports small and micro enterprises, lower the threshold for the establishment of schools, encourage idealistic and aspiring principals and teachers to establish small and micro schools and kindergartens to meet diverse educational needs.

5.2 *"Innovative Small and Micro Schools" Should Strengthen Their Teaching Team*

Innovative schools should have their own positioning, develop a system to recruit featured teachers, train, evaluate, and develop them. They should give full play to the advantages of all kinds of teachers and form "self-organized" teaching and research study groups that integrate the junior teachers' enthusiasm and diverse backgrounds with the teaching experience of the senior teachers to stimulate more innovative classrooms and teaching practices. At the same time, there should be a conscious effort to organize, accumulate and share these experiences to promote sustainable teacher development.

5.3 *More Emphasis Should Be Placed on Home-School Cooperation in "Innovative Small and Micro Schools"*

Parents are essential resources of the school. Innovative small and micro schools can learn from the experience of public schools to form a systematic and institutionalized "parents' committee" to ensure parents' right to participate in school work and make full use of parents' resources, so that parents can be fully integrated into the school work and gradually understand the school's education philosophy. Schools should promote more timely communication between school management and parents to gradually improve parents' educational literacy and ease their anxiety. Parents' committees can also monitor and evaluate the school's performance and form a feedback mechanism with the school in order to promote the positive development of the school.

5.4 *Strengthen the Communication and Cooperation among the "Innovative Small and Micro Schools," Expand Their Impact, and Promote Bottom-Up Educational Change*

As an emerging education phenomenon, the scales of "innovative small and micro schools" are still very small. Thus these schools should communicate more, share experiences, and provide support to each other. In July 2017, the Innovation Education Exchange (IEE) was founded by seven organizations to provide a communication platform for these "innovative small and micro schools." The IEE promotes the sharing of experience in curriculum system, teacher training, and other aspects and hope to jointly develop a teaching evaluation system, and to establish an internal "student school register" certification system within the "innovative small and micro schools." The certification system will help build a complete education system from kindergarten to high school. Ultimately, this will form a synergy that will drive a bottom-up change in China's education.

CHAPTER 13

The Current Status and Issues of the Compulsory Education: Insights from the National Report on Monitoring the Quality of the Compulsory Education in China

Wei Xiaoman,[1] Li Mian[2] and Huang Fuping[3]

Abstract

The *National Report on Monitoring the Quality of Compulsory Education in China* objectively presents the status of students' development in all aspects of moral, intellectual, physical, and aesthetic development at the compulsory education stage. In general, students have positive values in life and good standards of behavior. They have good academic performance in language, mathematics, and science, and mostly enjoy the curriculum. In addition, most teachers are liked by their students. The report pointed out several issues with compulsory education, such as the prioritization of academic performance over physical and aesthetic education, the inadequacy of students' comprehensive ability, the heavy burden of schoolwork on students, the need to improve teachers' educational background, and the low utilization rate of educational resources in schools, and etc. The report also proposed several areas for improvement, including: accelerate the implementation of the concept of comprehensive education, further promote the reform of the education evaluation system, standardize the management of compulsory education schools, and improve teachers' quality.

Keywords

compulsory education – quality monitoring – school workload – educational evaluation – teachers' quality

---

1 Wei Xiaoman 韦小满 is a professor at the Center for Collaborative Innovation in Monitoring the Quality of China's Basic Education, Beijing Normal University.
2 Li Mian 李勉 is a lecturer at the Center for Collaborative Innovation in Monitoring the Quality of China's Basic Education, Beijing Normal University.
3 Huang Fuping 黄福平 is a research assistant at the Center for Collaborative Innovation in Monitoring the Quality of China's Basic Education, Beijing Normal University.

In July 2018, China's first national compulsory education quality monitoring report was officially released to the public. The *National Report on Monitoring the Quality of Compulsory Education* (hereafter referred to as the *National Monitoring Report*) presents an objective picture of the development of students in all aspects of moral, intellectual, physical, and aesthetic development at the compulsory education stage, meanwhile focusing on the issues and deficiencies of the compulsory education. It also puts forward suggestions to improve the quality of compulsory education based on the current status. The report's release helps guide the public in establishing a correct view of education quality, provides essential data for the Government's refined management and scientific decision-making, and offers accurate guidance for improving educational practice and enhancing education quality.

1 Main Achievements in the Compulsory Education in China

The National Monitoring Report presents an objective picture of the achievements of compulsory education in terms of students, curriculum, teachers, schools, etc., in the following five major areas –

1.1 Students Have Positive Life Values and Exhibit Good Behavioral Standards

According to national monitoring data, both fourth- and eighth-grade students believe that the most critical factor for achieving success is personal efforts, with 47.9% and 62.7% respectively choosing it. These percentages were much higher than other options such as family background, help from others, luck or opportunity, and others. This shows that primary and middle school students are more convinced of the importance of personal efforts to succeed and want to achieve success through their own efforts rather than relying on external factors. This finding reflects the fact that some social beliefs that family background and power are the most important factors for success have not had a significant impact on students and that schools, teachers, and families have played an influential role in values education.

According to national monitoring data, 93.6% of fourth- and 97.3% of eighth-grade students have performed well in complying with social morality. This fully demonstrates that abiding by public morality has become a conscious daily behavior of the vast majority of students. In this regard, the good performance of students shows that moral education at schools has played a positive role, with remarkable achievements.

1.2 Students Perform Well Academically in Language Arts, Mathematics, Science, and etc.

Language, mathematics, and science are essential academic subjects for primary and middle school students. These subjects' national curriculum standards set out the basic requirements for students' knowledge and skills, processes and methods, affective attitudes, and values. Following the national curriculum standards, the National Monitoring Report measured students' academic performance in language, mathematics, and science. Adopting internationally accepted procedures and technical methods, The National Monitoring Report classified students' academic performance into four different levels, including "to be improved, medium, good and excellent". The National Monitoring Report shows that 81.8%, 84.6%, and 76.8% of fourth-grade students reached the medium or higher levels in language, mathematics, and science, respectively. For eighth-graders, 79.6%, 78.9%, and 83.6% achieved the medium or higher levels in language, mathematics, and science, respectively. This result shows that most students in China have a good grasp of the relevant curriculum knowledge and skills, and have met the corresponding requirements of the national curriculum standards. This reflects several advantages in the basic education curriculum and teaching in China. First, the curriculum content is systematically developed. In addition, teachers teach knowledge in a purposeful and planned manner, with a classroom teaching centered approach. Finally, teachers can effectively and efficiently help students master the relevant curriculum knowledge. At the same time, students in China have invested a great deal of time in their studies. They have a solid grasp of foundational knowledge and basic skills, thus achieving better results overall.

1.3 Students Mostly Enjoy the Curriculum

According to the National Monitoring Report results, the proportions of fourth-grade students who liked moral education, language, physical education, music, and art were 89.8%, 93.8%, 92.9%, 89.6%, and 88.6%, respectively. The corresponding proportions for eighth-grade students were 83.5%, 89.1%, 87.3%, 87.9%, and 81.8% respectively. Two main reasons contributed to the fact that more than 80% of the students enjoyed the courses they studied. First, the curriculum contents are attractive to students. The curriculum design was in line with students' cognitive development and learning habits, and the content of the courses was intriguing to students. Second, the teaching format of the courses was favored by the students. Teachers taught courses in varied, lively, and authentic format. Interest is the best teacher. Students' interest in the curriculum will help to mobilize their enthusiasm, initiative, and creativity in learning, and focus their attention on the course content and knowledge learning, resulting in constant improvement in learning efficiency and quality.

1.4 Most Teachers are Liked by Students

According to the national monitoring data, the proportions of fourth-grade students who liked their class teachers, moral education teachers, language teachers, and physical education teachers were 91.6%, 90.8%, 94.7%, and 90.5%, respectively; the corresponding proportions for eighth-graders were 79.6%, 82.1%, 87.4%, and 84.7%, respectively. The majority of the students liked the class teachers and teachers of the subjects they studied, which means that they recognized most of the class teachers and subject teachers. Such recognition is comprised of two aspects. First, the recognition of the teacher's ability and teaching approach. Students welcome teachers for their good professional knowledge and ability to facilitate students' learning effectively. The second is the emotional identification with the teacher. Teachers create a respectful, equal, and harmonious teacher-student relationship, which the students recognize. Therefore, for teachers, good teaching skills and harmonious teacher-student relationships can significantly enhance teachers' personal charisma and increase their popularity among students. The favorable relationship among class teachers and subject teachers stimulates students' interest in the subjects concerned and improves their performance both academically and in other areas.

1.5 Strong School Culture and Nurturing Environment

Building a healthy environment is an essential part of moral education. A good moral education environment subtly influences students with positive education and proper guidance, which helps guide the development of students' ideological and moral consciousness and character and cultivate students' good behaviors and habits.

In terms of creating a moral education environment, the National Monitoring Report shows that more than 90% of primary schools and 90% of junior high schools adopt "socialist core values" as school mottoes and school philosophy. 82.3% of primary schools and 90.1% of junior high schools have statues, pictures, or mottoes of great men. 76.1% of primary schools and 85.2% of junior high schools have portraits and stories of figures related to traditional Chinese virtues. These results indicate that primary and middle schools share the concept of building a nurturing environment, attach importance to the construction of a moral education environment, and take concrete actions to implement relevant national and local policies and regulations.

Cultural and sports activities are important elements of campus culture and an essential venue for moral education in schools. By giving full play to the educational function of cultural and sports activities, teachers and schools can greatly guide and promote the cultivation of students' moral consciousness and moral behaviors and habits. National monitoring results show that primary and secondary schools have all carried out a wide variety of cultural and sports activities on campus. Among these, sports games and individual sports competitions were the most frequently held, with 68.1% of primary schools and 86% of junior high schools holding such competitions. The above monitoring results indicate that most schools attach importance to campus cultural and sports activities. They promote the development of campus culture through the design and implementation of diverse activities. This enables schools to better implement and embody the philosophy of nurturing students with culture and further enhance their moral education effectiveness.

2 Major Issues in Compulsory Education in China

Identifying problems and deficiencies can clarify the directions for quality enhancement and improvement. In addition to objectively presenting the achievements made in the current process of improving the quality of compulsory education, the National Monitoring Report also focuses on the deficiencies that still exist in compulsory education. It provides an important reference for the next stage of education quality improvement. Specifically, there are the following five main issues.

2.1 The Phenomenon of Emphasizing Academic Performance While Neglecting Physical and Aesthetic Education Still Exists

According to the *Experimental Program for Curriculum Setting in the Compulsory Education* (2001) by the Ministry of Education, the number of per week classes for language, mathematics, physical education, and art in the fourth grade should be 6, 4–5, 3, and 3 respectively. However, according to national monitoring data, 72.0% of schools had more than six classes for language, 67.2% had more than five classes for mathematics per week for fourth-graders. The percentage of schools with less than three fourth-grade-classes per week was 44.3% for physical classes and 12.9% for art classes. The above monitoring results imply that the number of hours of language and mathematics classes in schools exceeds the national standard seriously, while the number of hours of physical education and art classes is obviously insufficient. Given the total class hours, more hours in language and mathematics education will inevitably lead to reduced physics and art education hours. To a certain extent, this also reflects the fact that the idea of emphasizing academic education at the expense of physical education and aesthetic education is still deeply rooted in the field of education.

The goal of implementing all-around education and promoting students' all-round development has been proposed for many years, and various policies and measures have been actively introduced at the national and local levels to promote all-around education. Despite all these efforts, we have to recognize that all-around education is still quite far from being fully implemented. The "baton" of the middle school and college entrance examinations formed over the years has had a tremendous guiding effect on primary and middle schools' educational practice. Specifically, the exam results and higher education entrance rate have been critical criteria for evaluating schools and teachers, thus making schools and teachers have to take the exam subjects as the most important thing in teaching, resulting in more class hours being allocated to examination subjects. Such one-sided notions and practices run counter to the goals and intentions of all-around education and are detrimental to students' all-round development. We need to correct and address this issue from a variety of perspectives.

2.2   *Insufficient Comprehensive Ability Hinder Student Development*

The national monitoring results show that students have a good grasp of foundational knowledge and skills, but are relatively week in their comprehensive ability. For example, science classes aim at developing students' scientific understanding, scientific inquiry, and scientific thinking skills. Among those aims, students are relatively strong in scientific understanding, whereas they need to improve in scientific inquiry and scientific thinking skills for both fourth- and eighth- grade students.

Specifically, 75.7% and 74.9% of fourth-graders achieved a medium or higher level of scientific inquiry and scientific thinking skills, respectively. These percentages were about 5% lower than that for scientific understanding. For eighth-graders, 83.0% and 76.3% achieved medium or higher levels of scientific inquiry and scientific thinking skills, respectively, which were 4.1 and 10.8 percentage points lower than that of scientific understanding, respectively.

Among the above three abilities, students' relative strength in scientific understanding indicates that students can understand and master the foundational science knowledge and are capable of learning science. However, lower ratings in scientific inquiry and scientific thinking ability reflect the fact that students need to improve their higher-level, more comprehensive, and more creative abilities, which are necessary for effectively carrying out scientific research and applying scientific methods to propose and solve problems. On the one hand, this is restricted by the current curriculum setting and implementation, which prioritizes the systematic teaching of knowledge, leaving insufficient room for the development of students' comprehensive and applied ability. On the other hand, teachers put less emphasis and effort into comprehensive ability development, and their professional abilities need to be improved. At present, China's teacher education system does not provide sufficient support for the cultivation of students' comprehensive abilities.

With the continuous development of China's economy, there is a higher demand for people's comprehensive ability. Therefore, as the "base" of the education system, basic education must emphasize and put more effort into cultivating students' comprehensive ability to effectively change the current status, where students showed weakness in comprehensive and applied ability. Only in this way will education achieve the goal of cultivating talents to build an innovative country.

2.3 Excessive Burden of Schoolwork on Students

The burden of schoolwork is measured based on several important indicators, including time spent on homework, participation in out-of-school academic classes, and academic stress.

The National Monitoring Report investigates the performance of mathematics (2015) and language (2016) on each of these three indicators. Because the data were collected in different years, scores for language and mathematics cannot be aggregated. According to the national monitoring results, students spend a relatively long time on homework. For example, the proportions of fourth-graders who spent on average more than half, one, and two hours each day on mathematics homework alone were 33.6%, 14.7%, and 4.4%, respectively. On average, for language, 40.4%, 21.5%, and 8.7% of fourth-graders spent more than 0.5, one, and two hours per day, respectively. In addition to completing homework assignments, some students were attending extracurricular tutoring classes. Specifically, 43.8% of fourth-grade students attended mathematics tutoring classes, and 37.4% attended language tutoring classes. Those tutoring classes bring an extra burden to students.

Studies have shown that the amount of time students spend studying, and their academic performance are not positively correlated. In other words, students who spend longer time studying do not necessarily have better academic performance. On the contrary, overly long study hours may have negative impacts on students, such as students tend to suffer from stress and sleep deprivation.

The national monitoring results show that 30.7% of fourth-grade students report feeling stressed in mathematics studies, and 69.3% of them sleep less than the national standard of 10 hours. This is detrimental to the physical and mental health of students. In addition, spending too much time studying results in insufficient time for students to develop their other abilities and interests, which will hinder their well-rounded development. This situation is caused by the current education quality evaluation system that unilaterally emphasizes academic achievement. In particular, several factors contribute to this issue. First, schools, teachers, and parents all overly emphasize students' academic learning and put forward strict and excessive-high requirements for students' academic learning. Second, students are lack of adequate learning strategies and not getting enough guidance from their teachers. Finally, extracurricular education and training institutions are not well-regulated and carry out illegal activities. Therefore, a comprehensive approach at multiple levels is needed to address students' excessive schoolwork burden effectively.

2.4   *The Teachers Teaching Quality Needs to Be Further Improved*

Problem-based teaching transforms the traditional "filled class" and "ducking" teaching. This approach advocates students to carry out independent learning, in-depth investigation, and group cooperation under the teacher's guidance. It facilitates the understanding and mastery of knowledge and skills, and promotes the development of innovative thinking and creative skills.

National monitoring data indicate that 63.0% of fourth-grade science teachers, 61.2% of eighth-grade physics teachers, 75.5% of eighth-grade biology teachers, and 80.7% of eighth-grade geography teachers are at low or relatively low levels in terms of their ability in problem-based teaching.

Science is a subject that emphasizes inquiry and discovery. Therefore, problem-based teaching is of paramount importance, and it poses a major challenge for science teachers. Due to the long-standing dominance of the "exam-oriented education," the primary purpose of classroom teaching has been systematically, efficiently, and effectively helping students master knowledge. An effective way to achieve this goal is the traditional teaching format, where teachers pass knowledge to students. Therefore, this traditional unidirectional teaching approach has become the main-stream in teaching practice. Such teaching philosophy significantly restricted teachers' teaching practice, and inhibit the enhancement of teachers' ability to carry out problem-based teaching activities.

In addition, the school curriculum, assessment system, and teacher training do not provide enough support for the implementation of problem-based teaching. As a result, teachers do not have enough space and resources to carry out problem-based teaching. To a large extent, all these prevent teachers from developing their abilities and carrying out problem-based teaching.

Teachers' professional knowledge is a prerequisite for effective teaching and learning. Only with a considerable amount and quality of professional expertise, can teachers present supplicated knowledge comprehensibly and organize classroom activities that are conducive to student learning.

Taking moral education as an example, national monitoring results show that 79.0% of fourth-grade teachers and 71.3% of eighth-grade teachers felt that they don't have sufficient professional knowledge to meet teaching needs, especially in the areas of legal knowledge, geography, and mental health. The moral education class is a comprehensive course involving all aspects of students' learning and life. Therefore, teaching this course requires knowledge of multiple majors or subjects. Moreover, in recent years, many new contents have been incorporated into the moral education class materials, including knowledge of the law and mental health. This has posed an even more serious challenge to most moral education teachers, especially part-time teachers. As a result, many teachers increasingly feel that their expertise does not meet the requirements to teach this course.

With the further advancement of curriculum reform, the curriculum in primary and middle schools will become more and more comprehensive. Consequently, the corresponding requirements for teachers' professional knowledge will become higher and more challenging. We have to seriously consider and address the important issue of providing enough support for teachers to update their existing knowledge system to meet the new requirements.

2.5 Low Utilization Rate of Educational Resources in Schools

The national monitoring data show that 37.2% of fourth-graders and 50.5% of eighth-graders had not yet visited their school library during the semester of this assessment among students in schools with libraries. Concerning science labs, 39.1% of fourth-grade science teachers, 39.7% of eighth-grade physics teachers, and 59.4% of eighth-grade biology teachers reported never or rarely using them in schools equipped with science labs. Besides, a significant proportion of students or teachers reported that they never or rarely used other special classrooms and teaching equipment resources.

As China continues to raise investment in education in recent years, we have seen significant improvements in educational facilities and equipment in primary and middle schools. However, the aforementioned national monitoring results indicate that the schools need to make better use of their educational resources.

The reasons for the low utilization of the resources are related to students, teachers as well as schools. For students, the heavy academic workload makes them spend the most time on schoolwork, leaving little time to make full use of resources such as libraries. As for teachers, they seldom use the relevant resources in their teaching because of two major reasons. First, teachers are required to complete excessively heavy teaching tasks within a specified period of time. However, they will have to spend more time teaching if they chose to use those educational resources, which prevents them from using those resources. Second, some teachers are incapable of managing and using the resources for effective teaching and learning. As far as schools are concerned, the management and human resources support for educational resources are not enough to guide, encourage and facilitate students' and teachers' use of relevant resources, thus also affecting the use of relevant resources. The low utilization rate of educational resources in schools is not only a waste of resources but also impedes the further development of educational activities. How to make good use of educational resources and promote the integration of resources and teaching practice are the focus of the next stage of education, teaching, and resource management work.

3   Reflections and Suggestions on the Reform and Development of the Compulsory Education

The National Monitoring Report has objectively reported the achievements, existing issues, and deficiencies in the work to improve the quality of compulsory education, providing a basis for further advancing compulsory education reform and development. Regarding the existing issues and weaknesses, we need to work comprehensively on the teaching philosophy, education system, management, and teaching practice to promote healthy development and quality improvement of compulsory education.

3.1   *Accelerating the Implementation of the Idea of Whole Person Education*

In terms of curriculum development and implementation, schools must strictly follow the National Curriculum Program requirements with regard to the ratio of class hours for each subject. In particular, schools must ensure that courses in physical education, aesthetic education, and comprehensive practical activities are offered in full length, and are not crowded out or reduced at will.

Teachers should adopt innovative teaching methods to reduce the burden and stress of students' learning. They should find ways to stimulate students' learning interest and involvement, and facilitate their overall development.

Concerning the integration of academic disciplines, it is necessary to strengthen the links between academic disciplines, integrate the educational content of related fields, and carry out interdisciplinary thematic educational activities. Schools should promote the integration and coordinated development of moral education, physical education, academic education, aesthetic education, and labor education, and bring into play the overall effect of comprehensive education.

In terms of school management, the concept of whole-person education should be carried through every detail of school management. Schools should actively create a favorable atmosphere and environment to provide strong support for students' all-round development.

In the area of family education, training, communication, and guidance for parents should be strengthened, so as to convey to them a comprehensive view of education quality and students' whole-person development. We need to facilitate parents to gradually construct a family education approach that is compatible with school education, thus leaving enough room for the all-round development of students.

3.2   *Further Promoting Reform of the Education Evaluation System*

In terms of the concept of evaluation, we need to change the current focus on test scores and enrollment rates. Instead, we need to establish a comprehensive educational evaluation concept and direct our education focus on cultivating students' comprehensive quality and personality development.

For the evaluation content, we should make efforts to build a comprehensive evaluation system that reflects students' overall development. The main contents of the education quality evaluation should cover students' moral development, academic development, physical and mental development, and artistic accomplishment.

Assessment methods should combine progressive and summative assessments, focusing more on the extent of student progress and school progress, thus changing the practice of emphasizing results alone but ignoring developmental changes in the process.

In terms of parties involved in the evaluation, schools, teachers, students, and parents shall all participate in the evaluation. Obtaining relevant information and data from multiple channels will improve the comprehensiveness and objectivity of evaluation.

3.3   *Standardize and Guide the Management of Compulsory Education Schools*

We should strengthen the supervision of the legality of school management systems and school-running practices. Guidance should be provided to schools in terms of formulating and perfecting management systems and regulations according to the law to ensure order in the management of school teaching. In addition, we need to push schools to strictly implement and comply with the Party's and the National education guidelines and policies and the relevant laws and regulations to ensure that school-running and management practices are carried out under the law.

We should guide schools to establish a mechanism for guaranteeing teaching quality. With this system, school leadership should fully understand the current situation regarding students' development, curriculum, teaching materials, and teaching practice. Based on the knowledge of the current status, schools should be able to identify and analyze existing issues and adopt targeted measures and approaches to improve education in a timely manner.

We should also promote the establishment of a sound management system for the maintenance and use of educational and teaching resources in schools, so that they are fully open to students and teachers. Schools should make it convenient for students and teachers to use educational resources. In this way, the usage rate of those facilities will also be raised.

3.4 *Improving Teachers' Quality*

We should organize and implement specific teachers' quality monitoring programs based on the requirements of primary and middle school teachers' professional standards. This will allow us to gain a comprehensive understanding of the current situation, existing issues, and deficiencies of the teachers. Such knowledge will provide the basis to help clarify the direction for teacher education, policy improvement, and the enhancement of the overall quality of the teaching force.

We should comprehensively upgrade teachers' quality. We should provide teachers training in a variety of areas such as curriculum standards, educational philosophy, professional knowledge, and teaching methods. In addition, we should organize experts from relevant universities and local teaching and research experts to provide follow-ups and guidance for teachers, so as to help them improve their teaching skills effectively. It would also be helpful to make full use of new technologies such as "Internet + education", which will allow us to create a new platform for education and teaching services. Such a digital platform will create a favorable environment for teachers to discuss and exchange ideas for effective teaching and improving students' learning outcomes.

With regard to the future improvement and development of national monitoring, it is necessary to further improve the monitoring system and build a monitoring model that integrates regular monitoring with targeted monitoring. In addition to the ongoing routine monitoring of the quality of education in the six disciplines, including moral education, language, mathematics, science, physical education, and art and their relevant influencing factors, targeted monitoring should also be carried out in the light of relevant hotspot issues and in accordance with the specific needs of national and local education reform and development. Those targeted monitoring will help the national and local authorities gain an in-depth understanding of the existing issues and their causes and provide reference and a basis for the formulation of precise strategies to solve the problems.

Simultaneously, a sound system for promoting the implementation of education policies and an education accountability system, both based on monitoring results, should be established. At the school level, we should further encourage the application of monitoring results in school management and educational practice. This involves helping schools and teachers effectively improve their work based on monitoring results to continuously improve schools' management and education quality.

CHAPTER 14

Special Education in China: From Ensuring Access to Improving Quality

Feng Yajing[1]

Abstract

In recent years, China's special education has made remarkable achievements in multiple areas, such as constructing more special education schools, raising the professional level of special education teachers, improving the standardization and effectiveness of teaching in special education schools, and increasing higher-education opportunities for persons with disabilities. The focus of developing special education has gradually shifted from ensuring educational opportunities for all children with disabilities to effectively improving the quality of education and providing every child with disabilities with developmentally appropriate education and rehabilitation services. On this basis, in the future, emphasis should be placed on the development of special education at the non-compulsory education stage, raising the level of support for children with disabilities who are learning in regular classrooms (LRC) (随班就读), and further ensuring the quality and benefits of special education teachers.

Keywords

special education – guarantee opportunity – improve quality

In recent years, the Communist Party of China (CPC) and the State Government have attached unprecedented importance to the development of special education. A series of major initiatives have been introduced to promote the development of special education, so that the focus of special education development in China has gradually shifted from ensuring educational opportunities for children with special needs and increasing school enrolment

---

[1] Feng Yajing 冯雅静, Ed.D., is an assistant researcher at China Academy of Education Sciences. Her main research interests are special education and inclusive education.

rates to improving the quality of education services, truly providing each child with special needs with education and rehabilitation services appropriate to his or her development. Both the quantity and quality of special education have been greatly improved. At the Fifth Plenary Session of the 18th Central Committee of the CPC, the Central Committee of the CPC clearly stated that "we should provide high-quality special education." Following the "care for special education" initiative at the 17th National Congress and the "support for special education" brought up at the 18th National Congress, higher expectations for special education have been made in China, which focuses on "high quality," implying that children with special needs should not only be able to "enter" and "stay" in special education schools, but also, more importantly, "learn well." In this sense, the development of special education in China has entered a new historical phase.

1 Important Initiatives for the Development of Special Education in China in Recent Years

In recent years, China's initiatives to promote the development of special education have mainly focused on several areas, including continuing to improve the special education system, determining the direction of development of inclusive education, introducing curriculum standards for three types of special education schools, and developing educational resources, reforming education and teaching methods to improve relevance and effectiveness, and strengthening the construction of special education teacher teams. The government has announced and implemented several special laws and regulations, such as the *Regulations on Education for People with Disabilities* (残疾人教育条例) (revised in 2017), The *Plan for Promoting Special Education: 2014–2016* (特殊教育提升计划), *Guidelines for Regular Schools on Special Education Resource and Classrooms Constructions* (普通学校特殊教育资源教室建设指南), *Administrative Provisions on the Participation of People with Disabilities in the National College-entrance Examination* (*Interim*) (残疾人参加普通高等学校招生全国统一考试管理规定（暂行）), and the *Second Phase of the Plan for Promoting Special Education* (2017–2020) (第二期特殊教育提升计划). In addition, initiatives to promote special education have also been reiterated in other education-related policy documents (e.g., the *13th Five-Year Plan for National Education Development* (国家教育事业发展"十三五"规划) and the *Guidelines on Accelerating the Development of Education in the Middle and Western Regions* (关于加快中西部教育发展的指导意见), etc.), which have made significant achievements.

1.1 *Improving the Special Education System*

In recent years, with the smooth implementation of the construction, renovation, and expansion of special education schools in China, the number of special education schools has increased significantly. Children with special needs are generally guaranteed with education opportunities at the compulsory education level. However, the development of special education at the non-compulsory education level is still relatively lagging behind. Therefore, the active development of special education at the non-compulsory level to gradually complete the special education system, and provide continuous and complete education services for people with disabilities have become the focus of the relevant policies in recent years. This will help fully meet the needs of preschool children with disabilities, as well as post-compulsory education to improve the quality of life and self-fulfillment of people with disabilities.

The *Plan for Promoting Special Education: 2014–2016*, issued in 2014, required that preschool education for children with special needs be incorporated into local preschool education development plans and included in major national preschool education projects. It encouraged special education schools to hold senior high sections (classes) for students with disabilities and vigorously develop senior high school education for persons with disabilities that focuses mainly on vocational education. In addition, it encouraged higher education institutions to set up special education colleges, and required regular college majors to actively enroll students with disabilities who meet the requirements. At the same time, in April 2015, the Ministry of Education and the China Disabled Persons Federation jointly published the *Administrative Provisions on the Participation of People with Disabilities in the National College-entrance Examination (Interim)*, which made it convenient for students with disabilities to participate in the college-entrance examination and was one of the important measures to improve the special education system. In July 2017, the Ministry of Education and seven other departments jointly issued the *Second Phase of the Plan for Promoting Special Education (2017–2020)*. It supported "regular kindergartens to accept children with disabilities," proposed that "regular senior high schools and secondary vocational schools should expand the scale of enrolment of students with disabilities by LRC or organizing special education classes," and required "regular higher education institutions to actively recruit candidates with disabilities who meet the admission criteria, making necessary renovations to create a barrier-free environment, and providing support and assistance to students with disabilities in their studies and lives." All these showed the State Government's concern for and attention to the development of special education at the non-compulsory education level.

1.2 Setting the Direction for the Development of Inclusive Education

The main direction and measures for the development of special education in China in recent years have been the vigorous development of inclusive education and the expansion of the scale of LRC in regular schools. In the context of the international trend of the development of inclusive education, China has gradually realized that, although the large-scale construction of special education schools can provide educational opportunities for a large number of children with special needs within a short period of time, it is not a long-term solution to the sustainable development of special education. Instead, truly high-quality special education should be organically integrated with general education. Therefore, the only way to achieve high-quality special education is to open the doors of regular schools to students with disabilities. The newly revised *Regulations on Education for People with Disabilities* in 2017 stated in the General Provisions that "we shall improve the quality of education for persons with disabilities, actively promote inclusive education, provide general education or special education to persons with disabilities according to their types of disabilities and their ability levels, giving priority to the general education approach." This further established the development direction of inclusive education in China in regulations. In addition, the *Plan for Promoting Special Education: 2014–2016* required the gradual establishment and improvement of a support system for LRC for children with special needs. In January 2016, the General Office of the Ministry of Education issued the *Guidelines for Regular Schools on Special Education Resource and Classrooms Constructions*, which provided national standards and scientific basis for the construction of resource classrooms. The *Second Phase of the Plan for Promoting Special Education (2017–2020)* further emphasized that "the majority of children with special needs should enjoy LRC in regular schools, with special education schools taking an important role and home visits and distance education playing a supplementary role. We should promote inclusive education comprehensively."

1.3 Putting More Efforts on the Development of Curriculum and Teaching Materials for Special Education Schools

The curriculum is the medium and means of special education implementation and is the core of quality improvement. In order to comprehensively improve the effectiveness and standardization of education in special education schools, the Ministry of Education issued the *Curriculum Standards for Compulsory Education in Schools for the Blind* (2016 Edition) (盲校义务教育课程标准), the *Curriculum Standards for Compulsory Education in Schools for the Deaf* (2016 Edition) (聋校义务教育课程标准), and the *Curriculum Standards for Compulsory Education in Schools for Students with Intellectual Disabilities (2016 Edition)* (培智学校义务教育课程标准) at the end of 2016. Those Standards have been implemented since the fall semester of 2017. Meanwhile, further research and development of corresponding teaching materials have been carried out. The reform of teaching and evaluation of special education has also been promoted comprehensively, and more efforts have been put into the development of relevant teaching resources. These are important initiatives and achievements of curriculum development in the field of special education in recent years, which has provided guidance and standards for the relatively unregulated teaching in special education. They have made teaching in special education schools more scientific, and provided essential references for the improvement of the teaching quality for children with special needs.

1.4 *Developing a Team of Special Education Teachers*

In recent years, the State has attached great importance to the critical role of building a team of special education teachers and enhancing the professionalism of special education teachers. It has been proposed that "by 2020, an adequate, well-structured, well-qualified and compassionate team of special education teachers will be formed". In order to achieve that goal, the following measures have been implemented. First, the Ministry of Education issued the *Professional Standards for Special Education Teachers (Trial)* (特殊教育教师专业标准 (试行)) on August 21, 2015. The document stipulated the professional quality of special education teachers in terms of professional philosophy and ethics, professional knowledge, and professional competence, which provided a basis for pre-service and in-service training for special education teachers, and laid the foundation for the introduction of a certification system for special education teachers in the future. Second, expanding the scale of training for special education teachers. Higher education institutes were encouraged to offer special education programs, and provide more professional training opportunities for in-service special education teachers nationwide through a combination of group training and distance training. Third, general education programs were required to offer special education-related courses, so that general education teachers are more equipped to teach children with special needs enrolled in LRCs. Fourth, ensuring subsidy assistance for special education, attract more future special education teachers, and pay attention to their mental health.

1.5 *Increase Funding for Special Education*

In recent years, China had increased government funding for special education. On the one hand, it has raised the standard of per-student public funding for students with disabilities. The *Plan for Promoting Special Education: 2014–2016* required for the first time that "the per-student public expenditure standard for special education schools at compulsory education level shall reach RMB 6,000 per year within three years". The *Second Phase of the Plan for Promoting Special Education (2017–2020)* further advocated that "applicable areas can increase annual budget based on the percentage of students with severe and multiple disabilities enrolled". On the other hand, the funding for students with disabilities at all school levels was increased. The *Second Phase of the Plan for Promoting Special Education (2017–2020)* proposed to "address the special needs of students with disabilities, coordinate resources to provide preferential support to students with disabilities, and raise the level of subsidies. Students with disabilities from economically disadvantaged families will receive free education at the senior high school level. Priority will be given to funding students with disabilities in pre-school and higher education, and the level of funding will be gradually increased. Establish and improve policies on subsidies for special study materials, education and training, and transportation fees for students with disabilities." The significant increase in the standard of per-student public expenditure and the improvement of funding policies have provided important guarantees for the improvement of the quality of education for children with special needs, ensuring that every child with disabilities does not drop out of school due to financial difficulties.

2 Major Accomplishments in Special Education Development in Recent Years

In recent years, with the Central Committee of the CPC and the State Council attaching great importance to and giving strong support to special education, China's special education has achieved leaping development. A series of important achievements have been made in the development of special education in China. Not only has the number of special education schools and the enrolment rate of children with special needs in compulsory education increased significantly, but the initial transition from guaranteed education opportunities and scale expansion to quality and connotative development has also been realized. China has now placed equal emphasis on ensuring access to education for children and adolescents with disabilities and on improving the quality of education. From improving the level of development of children and adolescents with disabilities in all domains, to raising the professional skills and optimizing the structure of special education teaching staff, to facilitating an inclusive education environment, the development of special education is no longer limited to providing special children with access to education, but has made the improvement of quality of education and level of development a more important goal.

2.1 Significant Increase in the Number of Special Education Schools

All parts of China are actively carrying out the construction, renovation, and expansion of special education schools, and actively implementing the requirement of "building a special education school in a county with more than 300,000 people". This has led to a significant increase in the number of special education schools in China since 2012, from 1,853 in 2012 to 2,107 in 2017, an increase of 254 (13.7%). Of these, 200 special education schools were built in 2012–2015 alone, with a relatively high increase rate, while the increase rate has slowed down in the past two years, implying that the task of building, renovating, and expanding special education schools has basically been completed (See Figure 14.1). The increase in the number of special education schools represented the increase in the total amount of special education resources in China, which has led to a significant increase in the compulsory education enrollment rate of children with special needs in China.

2.2 Significant Increase in the Number and Gradual Diversification of Students with Disabilities in Schools

Except for a small decline in 2013, the number of students with disabilities in schools nationwide showed a rapid increase during the period 2012–2017, from 378,800 in 2012 to 578,800 in 2017, an increase of 200,000, or 52.8%. This indicated that the right to compulsory education for children with disabilities in China has been effectively guaranteed in recent years, with a significant rise in school enrolment rates, and expanded scale of special education. In terms of disability types, the number and proportion of students with visual and hearing disabilities have shown a year-on-year decline, with the number of students with visual disabilities falling from 10.8% in 2012 to 6.5% (i.e., only

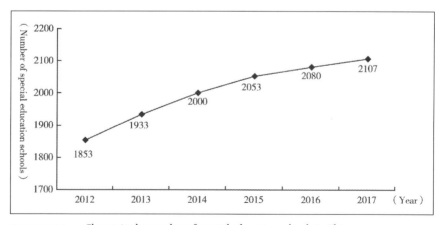

FIGURE 14.1   Change in the number of special education schools in China, 2012–2017

37,600) in 2017. Between 2012 and 2017, students with hearing disabilities fell from 101,100 to 89,800, a decrease of 11,300. The number of students with intellectual disabilities has increased year by year, but the proportion first increased and then decreased, accounting for about half of all students with disabilities in school. On the contrary, the number and proportion of students with "other disabilities," including physical disabilities, mental disabilities (including autism), speech disabilities, etc., showed a large increase, increasing by 10.7% from 2012 to 2017 (i.e., 138,300 in 2017), accounting for nearly a quarter of all school children with disabilities (See Figure 14.3). On the whole, the types of

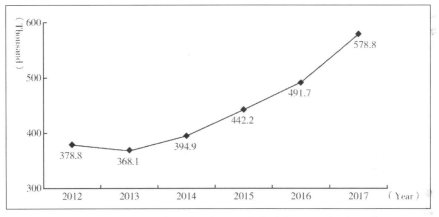

FIGURE 14.2   Change in the number of students with disabilities in schools in China, 2012–2017

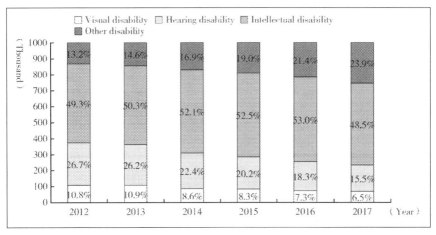

FIGURE 14.3   Changes in the types of students with disabilities in schools in China, 2012–2017

students with disabilities in China's schools have undergone obvious changes in recent years, with the proportion of students with visual and hearing disabilities gradually decreasing, while the number of children with other types of disabilities besides visual, hearing, and intellectual disabilities gradually increasing, which indicated a more diversified student body.

2.3 Expansion of the Scale and Optimization of the Structure of Special Education Teachers

Teachers are an important intellectual resource for the development of special education, and an increase in the number of teachers is a necessary condition for ensuring educational opportunities for children with disabilities. China's special education teaching staff is composed of full-time teachers, administrators, teaching assistants, and supporting staff. Figure 14.4 shows that since 2012, the total number of teaching staff in special education schools has increased year by year, from 53,615 in 2012 to 65,138 in 2017, an increase of 21.5%. At the same time, the number of full-time teachers has increased from 43,697 to 55,979, an increase of 28.1%, which exceeded the increase rate in the total number of teaching staff. In addition, the proportion of full-time teachers in the total number of special education teachers in China increased from 81.5% in 2012 to 85.9% in 2017, and the proportion of administrative, teaching assistants, and supporting staff decreased year by year, indicating that the professionalism of the entire teaching team gradually increased and the structure of the team was gradually optimized (Figures 14.5).

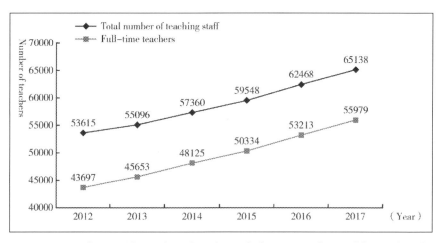

FIGURE 14.4 Change in the total number of special education teachers and the number of full-time teachers in China, 2012–2017

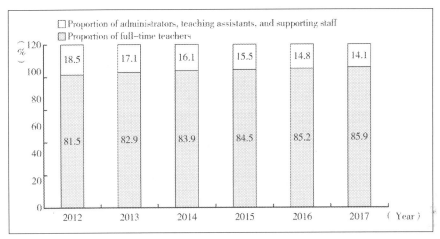

FIGURE 14.5   Change in the proportion of full-time special education teachers and administrative, teaching assistants, and supporting staff in China, 2012–2017

2.4 *Gradual Improvement in the Professional Skills of the Special Education Teachers*

2.4.1 Significant Increase in the Proportion of Full-Time Teachers Who Have Received Professional Training in Special Education

Many full-time special education teachers have been transferred from general education teaching positions. Therefore, professional training on special education needs to be offered to them in order to enhance their ability to teach children with disabilities. From 2012 to 2017, with the development of various types of training at all levels, such as national training and provincial training, the proportion of full-time special education teachers in China who have received professional training in special education increased from 58.4% to 73.3%. In other words, more than 70% of special education teachers have had relevant training experience, which signified a great improvement on the overall professional level (Figure 14.6).

2.4.2 Continuous Improvement in the Educational Level of Full-Time Special Education Teachers

From 2012–2017, the overall educational level of full-time special education teachers in China has improved significantly. The number of teachers with graduate degrees doubled, with a total of 1,246 in 2017, and the proportion also increased from 1.4% to 2.2%. The most significant increase was in the number of teachers with bachelor's degrees, which increased from 22,480 to 36,624, an increase of 62.9%, and the proportion also increased from just over half to 65.4%, making them the backbone of China's full-time special education

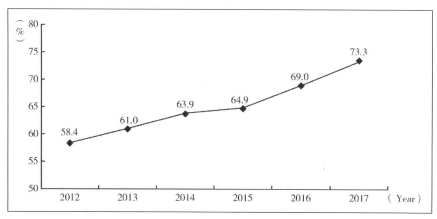

FIGURE 14.6　Change in the proportion of full-time special education teachers who have received special education professional training in China, 2012–2017

teaching force. On the contrary, the percentage of teachers with a junior college degree was only about 30% in 2017, and teachers with a high school degree or less accounted for a very small percentage. In general, the education level of full-time special education teachers in China has increased significantly in recent years, with most teachers holding a bachelor's degree, and more teachers with graduate degrees becoming full-time special education teacher, which ensured the overall professional level (See Figures 14.7 and 14.8).

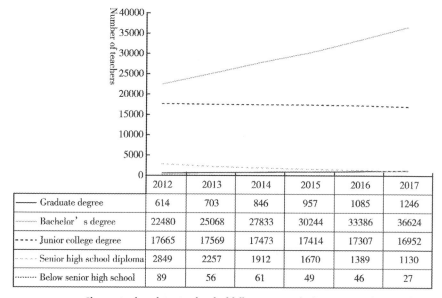

FIGURE 14.7　Change in the education level of full-time special education teachers in China, 2012–2017

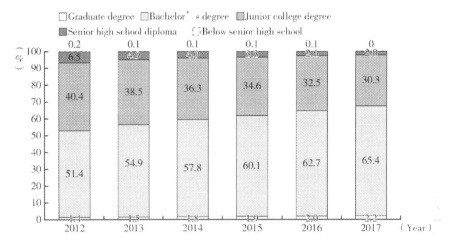

FIGURE 14.8   Change in the proportion of full-time special education teachers with different degrees in China, 2012–2017

2.5 Significant Improvement in the Relevance and Effectiveness of Special Education

The individual differences of children with special needs put forward higher requirements for a more individualized and targeted instruction. Truly effective teaching should be able to correctly respond to the individualized needs of children with special needs and provide them with teaching content that meets their requirements through teaching strategies that are suitable for their physical and mental development and learning characteristics. In recent years, many relevant policies included requirements such as deepening special education teaching reform and emphasizing heterogeneity and targetedness in special education, which are important measures and ways to improve the quality of special education. At present, individualized education has received unprecedented attention and emphasis in most special education schools in China. Each child with special needs will undergo a professional and systematic assessment when they enter the school. Parents, teachers, and relevant professionals work together to establish an "Individualized Education Plan" (IEP) for him or her based on the results of the assessments after joint discussions. The plan includes background information of the child (type and degree of impairment, parents' education levels, address of residence, etc.), the current level of development in each domain, the long-term and short-term goals on the basis of the assessment results, the special services needed, and the corresponding assessment methods, etc. In other words, it is a "customized" education plan for each child with special needs. The curriculum, rehabilitation services, and interventions for children with special needs after they enter school are all based on the IEP. The curriculum combines IEP with inspiring, engaging, and cooperative instruction methods to promote active thinking, independent learning, and collaborative learning among children with special needs. In addition, where teachers' workloads permit, special education schools try to increase the proportion of class hours for individual training sessions, so as to ensure that each child with special needs is able to receive appropriate education to the maximum extent possible and to give full play to his or her potential.

2.6 Increasing Opportunities for Students with Special Needs to Receive Higher Education

Access to higher education for students with disabilities can help them realize their potential, gain self-confidence, and ultimately improve their quality of life. The increase in opportunities for special students to receive higher education is also an important manifestation of the improvement in the quality of special education in China, which implies the improvement of the comprehensive competence of students with special needs and the continuous improvement of the support and guarantee system for special education. Since 2012, the opportunities for students with special needs to receive higher education in China have continued to increase, and the number of students with disabilities enrolled each year increased from 8,363 in 2012 to 12,663 in 2017, an increase of more than 50%. With the continuous improvement in the quality of teaching in special education senior high school classes and the effective implementation of relevant support policies, the number of students with disabilities taking the national college entrance examination and enrolling in higher education institutions with the help of various examination facilitation policies has increased drastically over the past few years. In 2017, a total increase of 3,589 students was seen compared to 2012, an increase of 49.6%, accounting for 83.5% of the total increase. This indicated that in recent years, most of the students with disabilities in higher education were enrolled in general colleges and universities, with the proportion of students with disabilities enrolled in general colleges and universities accounted for about 85% of the total student with disabilities receiving higher education. However, the number of students with disabilities enrolled in special education colleges did not increase much, but has maintained a relatively stable and slow rate of increase in recent years (See Figure 14.9).

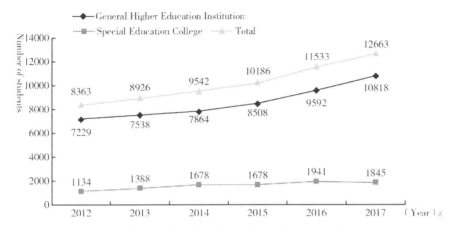

FIGURE 14.9 Trends in the number of students with disabilities enrolled in a university in China in recent years (2012–2017)
DATA SOURCE: *2012–2017 STATISTICAL COMMUNIQUE ON THE DEVELOPMENT OF THE WORK ON PERSONS WITH DISABILITIES*, HTTPS://WWW.CDPF.ORG.CN/SJZX/TJGB/

3   Experience in the Development of Special Education in Recent Years

As mentioned above, in recent years, thanks to China's constant attention and strong support, the total amount of special education resources in China has increased significantly, the professional level of the special education teaching staff has been greatly enhanced, and the quality of education received by children and adolescents with disabilities has been significantly improved. These accomplishments should not only be credited to the international trends of special education development, which provided effective reference and lessons for the development of special education in China, but also are the achievements from China's efforts in exploring strategies for sustainable special education development based on societal realities. The direction of development of special education, conditions, and guarantees, key factors, effective approaches, etc., are all worthy of in-depth summary and consideration.

3.1   *Adhering to Preferential Policies and Special Provision for Special Education*

The level of development of special education is an important indicator of a country's social civilization. However, amongst all levels of education in China, special education is still the sector where the most development is needed. In order to truly modernize education and meet the educational needs of all children, including children with special needs, special education should be given special attention and support. Therefore, when formulating and introducing policies, preferential policies have been adopted for special education. China has drafted and implemented a series of policies to tackle the challenges faced in special education, which enabled special education development rapidly in a relatively short period of time. For example, The *Plan for Promoting Special Education: 2014–2016* and the *Second Phase of the Plan for Promoting Special Education (2017–2020)* have been issued consecutively, providing specific and detailed provisions on the overall goals, key tasks, and major measures for the development of special education within a certain period of time in stages, thus enhancing the level of attention paid by education administrative departments and schools and effectively improving the level of policy implementation, ultimately promoting the improvement of the quality of special education. In addition, the promulgation of policies such as the *Guidelines for Regular Schools on Special Education Resource and Classrooms Constructions* and the *Administrative Provisions on the Participation of People with Disabilities in the National College-entrance Examination* have solved such pressing problems as the supportive measures for LRC and the participation of persons with disabilities in national college-entrance examinations, effectively guaranteeing the educational opportunities and quality for students with special needs.

3.2 *Promoting Development through Inclusion and Promoting General and Special Education Integration*

Although the number of special education schools has increased significantly in recent years with the implementation of the construction, renovation, and expansion of special education schools in China, the education provided by special education schools cannot truly meet the needs of special children in terms of school enrolment rates and their academic and social development. Therefore, to improve the quality of special education in China, regular schools need to open their doors to children with special needs and vigorously promote inclusive education. The responsibility of providing quality education to students with disabilities needs to be shared collaboratively by special education schools and regular schools, while regular schools are taking the lead. The practice and achievements of the development of inclusive education internationally also fully prove the correctness, necessity, and feasibility of general-special education integration. In recent years, the relevant policies issued in China have clearly reflected the strong support for the LRC, with regulations and requirements on the development of the teaching force, the provision of professional resources, the provision of facilities and equipment, and the guarantee of per-student public funds. As a result, LRC in China no longer remains at the stage of piecemeal attempts and experiments, but is promoted as a basic education policy and gradually becomes standardized. The quality of education received by LRC children with special needs has also been improved. Therefore, the right choice for improving the quality of education and the quality of life of children with special needs is to steadfastly pursue the path of integrated development, thereby bringing about an effective reform of the entire general education system, promoting the deep integration of general education and special education, and continuously improving the support system and guarantee mechanism for LRC.

3.3 Prioritize Teaching Resources, Vitalizing Special Education Internal Development Drive

Great importance must be attached to the key role of teacher quality for special education to achieve further development and improve its quality. In recent years, developing the special education teaching force has received great attention in relevant policies as a breakthrough and key factor in improving the quality of special education. Consequently, the scale of the special education teaching force has increased, the structure has been optimized, the academic qualifications and professional titles of full-time special education teachers have improved, and more and more teachers have received professional training in special education. A team of special education teachers with sufficient quantity, reasonable structure, and high competency has gradually formed, which further guarantees the professional level and standardization of education in special education schools. In the future, the strengthening of special education teacher force should be taken as the tackle point for improving the quality of special education via continuing to improve their professional skills and pay, formulating the standards for special education teacher recruitment and the qualification system, and ensuring the scientific and professional nature of special education services.

3.4 Diversified Support and Collaborative Development

The development and quality improvement of special education need to rely on a working mechanism that is coordinated and promoted by multiple departments, including education departments, development and reform departments, finance departments, disability federations, civil affairs departments, and health departments, in order to realize the sustainable and healthy development of special education. In recent years, China has preliminarily established a diversified support system for improving the quality of special education, and various relevant departments have issued several joint documents to plan the development of special education, reflecting the common concern for improving the quality of special education. In the future, we should continue to integrate the resources of various departments, give full play to their advantages, and perform their respective functions, further improve the support system for special education, and ensure the improvement of the quality of education and the quality of life of children with special needs in terms of education, medical care, and social services, etc.

4 Priorities and Directions for Future Development of Special Education

4.1 *Accelerating the Development of Special Education at the Non-Compulsory Education Levels*

On the whole, the achievements in the development of special education in China in recent years are mainly reflected in the compulsory education stage, with the construction of special education schools, the introduction of curriculum standards and the development of related resources, and the guarantee of schooling opportunities, all of which are mainly for the compulsory education. However, special education in the non-compulsory education stage, including preschool education and vocational education, is still relatively under-developed. At present, resources for special preschool education are in short supply, with regular kindergartens admitting children with special needs and special education schools with preschool classes (departments) both being severely insufficient. This limits the opportunities for preschool children with special needs to receive education and rehabilitation. For preschool-age children with special needs, early childhood education and rehabilitation are particularly important, highlighting the importance and urgency of developing early childhood special education. In addition, although relevant policies have established the development of vocational education at the senior high school level as one of the main tasks for the development of special education, the development of vocational education for persons with disabilities has been relatively slow in recent years, and it is difficult to meet the development needs of persons with disabilities in terms of both scale and quality. In recent years, the number of secondary vocational schools (classes) in China has not increased, but rather decreased, with 152 in 2012, 198 in 2013, but only 100 in 2015, then rising again to 132 in 2017. The number of students increased slowly from 10,442 in 2012 to 12,968 in 2017, but the number of graduates in 2017 was only 3,501, less than half of the number in 2012. In addition, the proportion of graduates from secondary vocational schools (classes) for persons with disabilities who were able to obtain a vocational qualification has been declining year by year, with nearly 80% in 2012 and 2013, but only about half in 2017, reflecting the decline in the quality of vocational education for persons with disabilities. Therefore, after special education is basically guaranteed at the compulsory education stage, efforts should be concentrated on developing special education at the preschool and senior high school levels, providing early education and rehabilitation services for children with special needs, alleviating symptoms, and developing potential, while at the same time providing high-quality vocational education for graduates with disabilities from compulsory education, so as to facilitate them to acquire a skill and improve their social adaptability, and ultimately to truly give full play to the value of special education.

4.2 Developing and Improving the Support and Guarantee System for LRC

As mentioned earlier, LRC has been the basic direction of the development of special education in China. With the promulgation and implementation of the *Regulations on Education for People with Disabilities* (revised in 2017), the enrollment of children with special needs in regular schools will soon become normalized, and LRC will no longer be promoted on project-basis or experimentally. However, in general, China's achievements in the development of special education in recent years are mainly with the construction of special education schools and the improvement of the quality of education. Resource support for LRC has yet to be further strengthened. In many regular schools, the quality of LRC is still far from ideal due to multiple reasons. Specifically, special education resources are still in short supply; effective management system and operating mechanism have yet to be established for LRC; a number of various types of professionals specializing in LRC are still insufficient; resources classrooms are not fully utilized and cannot meet the educational needs of special children; the per-student funding for LRC student is not fully allocated in some regions. Therefore, in the future, the direction of special education development in China should shift from focusing on supporting the development of special education schools to the development and improvement of the support and guarantee system for LRC, gradually streamline the management mechanism for LRC and introduce detailed implementation rules for LRC, so as to ensure the standardized and healthy development of LRC in China and ultimately improve the quality of special education.

4.3 Ensuring the Quality and Pay of Special Education Teachers

Although China has made remarkable achievements in building a team of special education teachers in recent years, teachers are still, on the whole, one of the most critical constraints in the development of special education in China. With the development of LRC, the connotation of special education teachers has gradually expanded, including not only teachers in traditional special education schools, but also itinerant mentors who provide professional support for special education in regular schools, and resource teachers who coordinate the operation of resource classrooms and the education and management of LRC students in regular schools, etc. Different types of teachers have different developmental needs at different stages. Currently, although the professional level of special education teachers is gradually improving, their workload is still relatively heavy on the whole. In addition, the level of special education allowance is extremely low, which cannot match their actual contributions. As a result, many teachers at special education schools left their position, and overall special education teacher is not a very attractive profession. In addition, regular schools lack specialized staffing for resource teachers, with most of them teachers of general subjects, whose professional competence and level of commitment can hardly meet the educational needs of students with special needs. Moreover, due to the lack of special education-related content in the pre-service training of regular teachers, most general discipline teachers lack the ability to deal with special-needs children when they start their work. According to existing regulations, special education teachers in regular schools are not entitled to the special education allowance and other benefits, making them less motivated to take LRC and highly mobile. All of these issues have restricted the rise of professional level and sustainable development of the special-education teaching force. In the future, we should continue to focus on developing teaching staff as an important tackle point of improving the quality of special education, and begin to address such issues as the training, professional title evaluation, and recruitment of special education teachers, as well as their pay and benefits, with an emphasis on the preferential treatment of special education teachers, so as to streamline the institutional mechanism for the building of special education teaching staff and ultimately build a team of high-competency and stable special education teaching staff.

CHAPTER 15

Equal School Access for Migrant Children Requires Breaking Down Double Barriers

Lan Fang[1]

Abstract

Up to now, migrant children still face a double barrier to equal access to education: first, the restrictions on enrollment and grade-progressing for migrant children; second, discrimination from different social groups. Behind the dual obstacles are both the weakness of the current education fiscal investment mechanism and the gaps among different social groups. The ultimate path to breaking down the barriers involves several measures, including establishing an education financing system where educational expenditure is shared by the government of all levels, changing the current college enrollment system where student quotas are allocated to each province, conducting broader public discussions in order to reach a consensus on urban population policy, and promoting diversified and integrated education.

Keywords

migrant children – educational equity – social status discrimination – pluralistic integration (多元融合)

The problem of migrant children's access to education has always been a problem in the area of educational equity in China.

According to a report released by the United Nations Children's Fund (UNICEF), *Population Status of Children in China in 2015 – Facts and Figures*, in 2015, there were 34.26 million migrant children and 68.77 million left-behind children.[2]

---

[1] Lan Fang 蓝方, co-founder of PlanC-Edu, a critical thinking education promotion organization, and former senior journalist of Caixin Media, focuses on issues such as education equity, social security, income distribution and civil society.

[2] Migrant children: Migrant children refer to those members of the migrant population who are aged 0–17 years. The migrant population refers to persons whose place of residence is different from the location (e.g. town/township or street committee) of their household

Although the government authorities have been actively putting efforts in properly solving the problem of migrant children's access to education, this group still faces both institutional and cultural obstacles to receiving equal education. To solve the problem of migrant children's access to education, not only do we need more active policy advocacy and a reorientation of urban population policies, but we also need active public advocacy to break down the discrimination and barriers between social groups.

1 Double Barriers for Migrant Children

1.1 *First Barrier: Institutional Conditions*

1.1.1 Enrollment Requirements for Public Schools Are Gradually Finalized

In 2001, the State Council's *Decision on the Reform and Development of Basic Education* proposed two principles to solve the problem of migrant children and adolescents receiving compulsory education. Specifically, "the Government of the inflow area should take the main administrative role, and migrant children should mainly enroll in full-time public primary and middle schools."

However, under the "county-based" compulsory education management system, local governments have set certain requirements and restrictions for migrant children to enter and advance in the local public education system.

1.1.1.1 *Enrollment Requirements*

In the process of enrolling migrant children in school, the local authorities have imposed certain requirements on the background qualifications of the parents. A child can only be enrolled in school if certain conditions are met. The conditions are usually set in two forms.

The first is the documentation system. Parents must have certain documents in order for their children to be enrolled in school. Different places have different specific requirements for documentation, depending on their financial situation and the supply and demand of the local workforce.

For example, Beijing has for many years adopted the "five certificates" as the basic enrollment requirements, including: proof of the parents' employment

---

registration (hukou), and who have left the location of their household registration for more than six months. It excludes the population whose current place of residence is different from that of their hukou registration, but is within the same city-level administration. Left-behind children: Left-behind children refer to children who live in their original domicile, but do not live together with their parents, as either one parent or both parents have migrated.

in Beijing, proof of actual residence in Beijing, the household register for the whole family, the Beijing residency card (or a valid residency registration card), and a certificate issued by the street committee or township government of their household registration that there are no guardianship conditions for the children in their original domicile. The districts and counties continue to "add" to those basic requirements. In Beijing's Tongzhou District, according to the *2018 Implementation Rules for the Review of Documents for Children and Adolescents of School Age of Non-Hometown Domicile Receiving Compulsory Education in Tongzhou District*, for migrant worker families renting in the urban-rural areas or rural areas of Tongzhou District, if their children want to enroll in school, parents must provide proof of house deeds, approval for building houses, or proof of housing conditions issued by village committees. As for "proof of employment as a migrant worker in Beijing," a labor contract and social security records must be provided.

For the group of migrant workers in flexible and informal employment, these requirements are basically unattainable.

The second is the accumulative point system. Only if the parents have a certain number of points in their background qualifications will the child have the opportunity to attend a public school.

For example, Suzhou, Jiangsu Province is currently implementing the *Implementation Rules for the Points-based Admission of Children of Migrant Parents at the Compulsory Education Stage in Suzhou (Trial)*, issued at the end of 2015. Specific enrollment measures include 35 indicators, including parents' education level, skill level, housing situation, recognition and awards, social contributions, etc., each of which has a clear scoring standard. Ultimately, the points value is used to determine the admission of children. For example, for parents' educational background, points are awarded only for junior college and above, with 30 points for junior college (senior vocational school) and 400 points for Ph.D. Sixty points are awarded for owning property, with the larger the house and the more units, the higher the score; only 10 points per year for renters who can provide a lease agreement and annual invoices.

Under such a point rule, the remaining school openings in a school district are allocated in descending order of points. The lower the points of migrant parents, the less chance their children have of enrolling in public schools.

1.1.1.2 *Restricted Schools to Enroll*

Even if the parents of migrant children meet the qualifications, this does not mean that the child will be admitted. School openings are usually first offered to children with household registration in the school district, and migrant children are accepted only when there are openings left. The district education committee usually coordinates children who cannot attend school nearby. Eventually, many children give up attending public schools because the schools are too far away.

For example, the Education Bureau of Chengdu City in Sichuan province disclosed that the shortage of public primary school openings in the central city district and the second circle layer districts reached 25,000 in 2013. With primary school students graduating year by year, the shortage of junior high school openings will continue to expand. Increases in oversized classes and situations where functional rooms are occupied as classrooms have already occurred. In a questionnaire survey conducted by the Chengdu Investigation Team of the National Bureau of Statistics, it was found that some respondents reported that "it is difficult to progress to junior high schools and they are not treated equally as local students."[3]

1.1.1.3   Restrictions on Further Education

After successfully entering the public compulsory education system, migrant children face stricter restrictions in the secondary and college entrance examinations, especially in provinces and cities where there is a risk of "college entrance examination migration." In the college enrollment system where student quota is allocated to each province, there are two types of "favorable provinces" for college enrollment: one is places with abundant higher education resources, high quality of basic education, and low local college-entrance examination admission thresholds, such as Beijing, Shanghai, and Guangdong; the other is under-developed remote places with weak basic education and fewer universities, but local candidates enjoy certain preferential policies in college entrance examination admissions, such as Hainan, Xinjiang, Qinghai, etc. In these two types of college enrollment "favorable provinces," in addition to students' consistent school records, there are also higher requirements on parents' qualifications than those for compulsory education enrollment.

For example, in Beijing, where the requirements are the most stringent, the *Work Plan for the Participation of Children of Migrant Workers Moving to Beijing to Take the Enrollment Examinations for Senior High Schools and Higher Education after Receiving Compulsory Education*, issued in 2012, is still being implemented. It requires that migrant children who have been registered for junior high school for three consecutive years and wish to continue their education in Beijing must have relevant documents proving that their parents

---

3   National Bureau of Statistics Chengdu Investigation Team, *The Problem of Guaranteed Education for Migrants Can't Be Ignored – Survey Report on Education Received by Children of Migrant Workers in Chengdu*, http://www.cddc.chengdu.gov.cn/detail.jsp?id=11306.

have been legally and stably employed and have paid social security charges in Beijing for three consecutive years. Even if the conditions are met, students can only apply for admission to secondary vocational schools, but not to a regular high school. After studying for three years in high school, parents must prove that they are legally and stably employed and have paid social security charges in Beijing for six years before students can take the college entrance exam in Beijing. And those students can only apply for higher vocational schools. Under such requirements for furthering education in Beijing, some students who are eligible to enter the public education system during the compulsory education stage may choose to return to their registered household places to study in order to get accustomed to the local test environment, thus having to be separated from their parents.

1.1.2   Gradual Reduction of Room for Privately-Run Schools

Migrant children who are unable to enter the public education system because of high barriers often have two options: study in the local privately-run schools for migrant children, or return to their household registration places and stay behind.

In the first-tier cities, the room for private schools for migrant children is continuously being compressed. In 2018, the actions to shut down schools for migrant children in Beijing and Shanghai continued to draw public attention.

Case 1: Beijing Continues to Close Schools for Migrant Children

In August 2018, Beijing's largest school for migrant children, the Beijing Huangzhuang School, which had a 20-year history of operation, was closed. The school was shut down as a direct result of the expiration of its operating license and the fact that the school site was no longer suitable for running school. The land lessor of the Huangzhuang School decided to repossess the leased land on the grounds that the school had "committed serious violations of the lease by subletting and constructing illegal buildings" during the period of leasing the land.

So far, only one school for the children of migrant workers remains in Beijing's Shijingshan district.[4]

Against the backdrop of urban expansion and the evacuation of the nonlocal people, Beijing has been closing schools for children of migrant workers

---

4 Fan Shuo 樊朔 "1800 dagongzidi gaobie Beijing Huangzhuangxuexiao: jianxiao 20 nianhou guanting, 1800打工子弟告别北京黄庄学校： 建校20年后关停 [1,800 Migrant Children Bid Farewell To Beijing Huangzhuang School: It Was Closed 20 Years After It Was Built]," August 16, 2018, http://china.caixin.com/2018-08-16/101315487.html.

for many years. According to a survey conducted by the New Citizen Project,[5] from 2014 to 2018, the number of private schools for children of migrant workers in Beijing decreased from 127 to 102, with the number of students dropping from nearly 100,000 to 47,000.

Case 2: Shanghai closed "Private-integration Primary School"

In June 2018, the operating licenses of 15 schools for migrant children in Shanghai's Qingpu District expired and were not renewed, and all 15 schools were closed.

These 15 schools for the children of migrant workers are all "Private-integration Primary Schools." "Private-integration" is the short name for the "integration into the private education system management." In 2008, the Shanghai Municipal Education Commission issued the "Three-Year Action Plan for the Compulsory Education of Children of Migrant Workers Living with Their Families," which plans to close all schools for children of migrant workers in the central city and some of those schools in suburban areas by the end of 2010. Other such schools were integrated into the private education management system in the form of "government-commissioned schools."

These schools mainly accept migrant children who are unable to attend public schools on the outskirts of the city because there are not enough openings in these schools or the schools are too far away. Under this policy, the Shanghai municipal government provides these schools with a certain amount of per-student funding. Those government funding were used as tuitions, so that migrant children receive free education. With the government's financial support, the quality of teaching, teachers' benefits, and the hardware facilities of these schools have been improved and guaranteed, and this "Shanghai model" has been recognized and appraised by academics and the media.

However, after implementing this policy, these private schools are also required to follow the government's unified regulations to set requirements for student enrollment. With the increase of population control in Shanghai, the enrollment requirements have become more and more stringent. In 2011, the requirement for migrant children's enrollment was a valid residence permit, one parent's social security charge payment record for one year or more, or a certificate of employment issued by the street or township committee for one year or more in a profession such as domestic service. At that time, the requirements for applying for a residence permit in Shanghai were relatively simple: an employment registration certificate issued by the city's labor security administration; payment of the required comprehensive insurance for

---

5   New Citizenship Project research data, as of October 2018, not yet officially published.

non-local workers; and a labor contract with an employer in Shanghai for six months or more, or a business license for an individual business.

In 2013, the requirements were raised to the parents need to hold a *Shanghai Residence Permit*, or to have completed flexible employment registration for three consecutive years and to hold a *Shanghai Temporary Residence Permit* for three years. At that time, the *Shanghai Residency Permit* required "legally stable employment and legally stable residence." It was particularly difficult for the migrant workers to get proof of "legally stable residence", because the landlords were often reluctant to help the tenants register the housing lease. Most migrant workers can only apply for the *Shanghai Temporary Residence Permit*, which only required a dormitory certificate issued by the employer or a boarding certificate issued by the neighborhood (village) committee. However, flexible employment registration was limited to specific job categories (hospital nurses in Shanghai, employees of farmers' expertise cooperatives in Shanghai, domestic service providers in Shanghai, self-employed business owners without employees in Shanghai, employees of community-based home care services for the older population in Shanghai), while workers in other industries cannot apply for the certificate.

By 2018, the requirement was adjusted to "holders of the *Shanghai Residence Permit* who have paid the city's employee social insurance for six months, or holders of the *Shanghai Residence Permit* who have registered for flexible employment for three consecutive years at the street or town neighborhood community affairs acceptance service center." The *Shanghai Temporary Residence Permit* has been canceled, but the requirements for applying for the *Shanghai Residence Permit* have not changed. This means that the requirements for school enrolment have been raised again.

As a result of the higher admission requirements, coupled with the Government's increased efforts to control the city population, the number of migrant children eligible to attend Private-integration primary schools has decreased significantly. For example, Qingpu United Private Primary School told media that the school had 700–800 students each year from 2009 to 2013; in 2014, the number dropped to around 500 at the start of the school's fall semester. Since then, the number of students has declined each year, with just over[6] 100 remaining at the start of the school year in September 2017.

---

6 A Qi 阿七 "Guanting daojishi: Shanghai 15 suo nongmingong zinv xuexiao zuihoude xueqi, 关停倒计时：上海15所农民工子女学校最后的学期 [Countdown to Shutdown: the Final Term of 15 Schools for Migrant Children in Shanghai]," May 8, 2018, https://www.jiemodui.com/N/94618.html.

The closure of Private-integration primary school seems logical because of the declining student count. However, this means that more migrant children are, in fact, being completely excluded from the urban education system and have no choice but to return to their places of origin and stay behind.

1.2   The Second Barrier: Prejudice Because of Class Status

Beyond the institutional barriers, another hidden obstacle is slowly surfacing – prejudice because of class identity.

For example, some public schools that take in children of migrant workers separate local and non-local students into different classes, with[7] "migrant children classes" and "rural classes" specifically for children of migrant workers.

In school administrators' eyes, separate classes are not a matter of discrimination, but rather for administration purposes. There are obstacles for migrant children under the current system to take the entrance exams for further education. Most of the children of migrant workers with good academic performance choose to go back to their hometowns for junior high school education. Those stayed in urban schools have poor academic performance, and even if they want to go on to further education, they can only enter vocational high school in Beijing. However, almost all local children have to prepare for the senior-high-school-entrance exams. The learning goals are different, and so are the teachers' management and teaching methods, so students "have to" be taught in separate classes or even manage separate campuses.

In some cities, when children of migrant workers start to enter public schools on the city's outskirts, the local people will complain about the deterioration of teaching quality in the local primary schools and choose to enter schools in the city. The segregation between "locals" and "non-locals" is natural, but the conflict is not acute.

But the 2018 "Segregation Wall" incident at Suzhou Qinxi Experimental Primary School blatantly dramatized this perceived segregation.

A wall was built on its campus at Qinxi Experimental Primary School (hereinafter referred to as Qinxi Primary School) in Suzhou, Jiangsu province, in August 2018. With a history of 100 years, Qinxi Primary School is a well-regarded local public school. On one side of the wall were the 400 students enrolled in Qinxi Primary School, whose parents bought a house in the school district and who were enrolled in the school according to the school district. On the other

---

7   *Chongqing Evening News*, "Nongmingong zinv zhihuo: jizhongbaohu haishi rongru chengshi 民工子女教育之惑：集中保护还是融入城市 [The Confusion of Migrant Workers' Children's Education: Centralized Protection or Integration into the City]," September 13, 2007, http://edu.people.com.cn/GB/6259996.html.

side, there were 800 students from Lixin Primary School. Lixin Primary School was a school for children of migrant workers, which was shut down due to the evacuation of the school building. After several coordination efforts by the education department, the students of Lixin Primary School were relocated to study in the unused classrooms of Qinxi Primary School.

But parents of students at the Qinxi Primary School had spoken out against such an arrangement for two main reasons.

The first reason was that such placement was considered unfair. The local school admission rules are "admission by district." In order to get access to quality educational resources, parents prepared early and purchased property. But the arrival of Lixin students broke this rule, essentially allowing students from outside the district to take over the district's educational resources.

The second reason was that they were worried that these "non-local children" would not behave properly in school and were of low quality, which would negatively affect the local children's learning. Moreover, the children in Qinxi Primary School were all in the lower grades, while those from Lixin Primary School were in the third to sixth grades. Thus, parents were concerned about possible on-campus violence and safety hazards in schools.

The education department's response to these concerns was to erect a separation wall. Lixin Primary School would be independently operated and managed, with separate teaching and activity spaces.

The erection of the separation wall has aroused widespread concerns in public, and the public has widely shared the concerns of the parents of Qinxi Primary School. Behind the wall is an unconscious public assumption that "non-local children" are of low quality and will threaten and negatively influence the "local children." This prejudice is so widespread that it is the second obstacle that migrant children have to face when they live in cities.

As a result of these two types of barriers, migrant children are unable to receive appropriate education in the city, or are forced to grow up without their parents' companion and with the self-identity of being "inferior."

2 Why the Barriers Exist

2.1 *Root Causes of Institutional Barriers*
2.1.1 Capacity Issues

Under the current financial system, local government finances at the district and county levels bear the primary responsibility for migrant children's enrollment to schools. In provinces where the issue of compulsory education for migrant children is better resolved, the central fiscal administration will "offer awards and subsidies," according to the 2008 *Circular of the State Council on the Exemption of Tuition and Miscellaneous Charges for Students at the Urban Compulsory Education Stage*. Statistics show that, from 2008 to 2015, the[8] central fiscal administration arranged a total of 61 billion yuan in awards and subsidy funds for compulsory education for children of migrant workers in cities. By rough calculation, this represents an annual average of 7.625 billion yuan over eight years. Given that the Ministry of Education announced that the annual average number of children accompanying migrant workers at the compulsory education stage was about 12 million, the per-student subsidy from the central government was a little more than 600 yuan.

In 2015, the *Circular of the State Council on Further Improving the Funding Guarantee Mechanism for Urban and Rural Compulsory Education* abolished the central rewards and subsidies policy, but proposed the unified policy of "two exemptions and one subsidy" and the benchmark per-student public funding (i.e., 600 yuan per student for primary schools in the central and western regions and 650 yuan per student in the eastern regions), which can be transferred with migrant children.

In other words, for every migrant child taken in by a local government, the central government grants a little more than 600 yuan per-student public funding. However, this amount is a drop in the bucket compared to the rising per-student expenditure. For example, in 2017, Beijing's per-student general public education expenditure was 30,016.78 yuan; Shanghai's per-student education expenditure was 20,676.54 yuan.[9] In Shenzhen, the average education expenditure per primary school student in 2016 was 16,425.18 yuan.[10]

For the inflow cities of migrant children, the more migrant children are admitted, the heavier the burden on local finances.

2.1.2 Issues of Will and Perception

Objective financial pressures make local governments reluctant to accept migrant children unconditionally. Meanwhile, some local residents are hostile

---

8   Ministry of Education: *"Response to Proposal No. 2634 (Education 258) of the Fourth Session of the 12th National Committee of the Chinese People's Political Consultative Conference* (CPPCC)," September 22, 2016.
    http://www.moe.gov.cn/jyb_xxgk/xxgk_jyta/jyta_jcys/201611/t20161117_289158.html.

9   Wang Jun 王俊 "2017 nian quanguo jiaoyujingfei zhixing qingkuang chulu, nagesheng jiaoyutouru zuida? 2017年全国教育经费执行情况出炉，哪个省教育投入最大？[2017 National Education Funding Situation Published, Which Province Spent Most on Education?]," *Beijing News*, October 16, 2018.

10 Shenzhen Education Bureau, Shenzhen Bureau of Statistics, Shenzhen Finance Commission: *"Statistical Announcement on the Implementation of Education Funding in the City in 2016,"* December 4, 2017, http://szeb.sz.gov.cn/xxgk/flzy/gggs/201712/t20171208_101536 44.htm.

to the admission of migrant children. Especially in the absence of a fundamental change in the provincial admission system for the college-entrance examination, accepting migrant children will mean not only a dilution of educational resources for local children, but also a significant increase in the intensity of competition faced by local students.

In such a context, it is natural for local governments to set thresholds for migrant children who can benefit from local compulsory education. The basic logic is not difficult to understand: children are entitled to public services only when their parents have contributed to the area's development.

Thus, under the "documentation and certification system," parents are generally required to prove that they pay taxes legally, contribute to social security, and have stable employment and residence; while under the "points system," the higher the parents' education, professional skills, the more the parents' assets and taxes contributions, the more likely their children can enjoy equal access to education.

The design of such a system, which appears to emphasize the reciprocity of rights and obligations, ignores the following two issues.

2.1.2.1 *Insufficient Recognition of the Contributions of Low-Income Workers*

Cities are ecosystems. Workers at all levels of income and class create value and contribute to the sustainability of the city.

No matter how much a city's industry is upgraded or how much the urban middle class consumes, there will always be a need for all kinds of workers. In fact, most of the time, it's migrant workers who work to meet a variety of basic needs of the urban population. From courier delivery, construction and home renovations, catering, and housekeeping to sanitation and security, the people who provide these services need roadside stands, wholesale markets, and more good quality services and products with low costs to meet their needs. While these jobs are often low-skilled, low-paying, and highly replaceable, and these people who work on these jobs may not have a stable place to live or proof of stable employment, the city would be crippled if they were not there.

When cities set school admission requirements for migrant children, the criteria used to evaluate their parents' contributions to the city are not fair and do not adequately recognize the value of low-income workers.

2.1.2.2 *Should Children Be Deprived of Educational Opportunity Due to the "Fault" of Their Parents*

Even if we accept that workers in certain occupations and jobs do contribute less to urban development, does that justify the exclusion of their children from school? In the most extreme cases, where the parents have no legal occupation in the city and live on petty theft or even crime, should that child lose equal access to the school?

For example, in Suzhou, under the migrant population points rule, violating the family planning policy, breaking the law, and having a breach of creditability will all lead to point deductions, and there is no limit to the number of points that can be deducted. When children's admission to the school is based on their parents' points, this means children will be excluded from education for their parents' fault.

It has been argued that there is nothing wrong with raising the bar for local school enrollment of the children of these migrants, and that this does not deprive them of their right to education. When these children return to their places of origin, they can receive education in the local public education system. However, in addition to the right to education, it is also a fundamental human right for children to live and grow up with their parents. For a long time in the past, the pain of parent-child separation has been overlooked in grand narratives. The first generation of children left behind, far from their parents, had grown up, and their individual suffering seemed unremarkable. In recent years, however, malignant incidents related to left-behind children happened frequently. In some cases, left-behind children are violated by criminals due to the lack of supervision; in others, left-behind children commit suicide due to psychological problems, and in others, left-behind children commit crimes. In a series of vicious social events in 2018, such as[11] the murder of a Didi Taxi passenger, one sees a series of labels such as left-behind children and lack of upbringing in the suspects. According to statistics released by the Research Office of the Supreme People's Court in 2012, the crime rate of left-behind children accounts for about 70% of juvenile crime, and is on the rise year by year. Among the juvenile crime cases handled by Sichuan provincial procuratorate in recent years, left-behind children accounted for about[12] 80% of the number of juvenile delinquents. It was impossible to predict whether the shortcomings of this generation's upbringing will evolve into resentment and revenge against society, and ultimately become a heavy price to be paid by society as a whole.

For some, the separation of parents and children is an irresponsible choice on the part of the parents. They could have accompanied their children back

---

11 On August 24, 2018, a 20-year-old young girl from Yueqing, Zhejiang province, was raped and killed by the driver while riding in a Didi Taxi. The incident caused widespread social concern.

12 Xie Wenying 谢文英 "Guan'ai liushouertong, sifabaohu fali, 关爱留守儿童，司法保护发力 [Caring for Left-Behind Children, Judicial Protection Exerted]," *Procuratorial Daily*, October 26, 2015.

to their hometowns and stayed in their places of origin to work and live. In fact, the idea of encouraging parents to return to their rural hometowns is completely contrary to the current trend of urbanization. Migrant workers choose to work in cities based on a rational weighing of the costs and benefits of working in urban and rural areas. They must choose a place with higher income and more job opportunities in order to avoid poverty and have hope of making the leap in social class level. Leaving their children behind in their hometowns is a last resort with various obstacles. The government and society should remove these obstacles so that children can live with their parents in the cities, rather than asking the migrant workers to give up better income and career development and return to their hometowns, which would be against urbanization.

2.2   *Identity-Label Related Stereotypes*

The second obstacle faced by migrant children is, in fact, also related to social perceptions.

In the case of the separation wall at the Qinxi elementary school, a large number of messages on public forums demonstrated the stereotypes against migrant children.

"Those kids' are not well educated because their parents don't have time to take care of them."

"Those kids' are involved in on-campus violence all the time. They could easily influence other children negatively."

…

Most of such statements are stereotypes that are unfairly generalized to all migrant children. However, the formation of these stereotypes is not unfounded. In a series of empirical studies, migrant children have been identified as a high-risk group for mental health and have a higher overall rate of problematic behaviors than other groups due to a range of factors, including inappropriate parenting, unstable learning, and living environments, etc.[13]

However, it is unfair to label an entire group of children because of some of their behavioral problems. Children who already exhibit some behavioral problems can still be rectified in their development, and good education and guidance are especially crucial for their healthy growth. The exclusion and

---

13   Liu Shuo, Liu Yanfang, Wang Siqin, and Liu Hongsheng 刘朔、刘艳芳、王思钦、刘红升, "Fumu jiaoyangfangshi dui liudongertong wentixingwei de yingxiang yanjiu, 父母教养方式对流动儿童问题行为的影响研究 [A Study of the Influence of Parenting Style on the Problem Behavior of Migrant Children]," *Journal of Xi'an Jiaotong University* (Social Science Edition), July 2015, Issue 35(4).

discrimination brought about by such labels only further worsen their growing-up environment.

For urban families, it is natural for parents to want their children's peers to be healthy, positive, and well-educated. While parents exaggerate and concern about the negative influences that migrant children might have on their own children, they overlook the benefits that a diverse educational environment would bring to their children's development. Children are exposed to peers from different backgrounds and share different cultural perspectives. In their daily interactions and encounters, children develop empathy, understand the complexities of society, reflect on their own privileged social identities, and develop an open mind and multiple perspectives. This is an invaluable asset for a child's life.

A segregated education system is undoubtedly harmful to the excluded non-local population. Even if such education is seemingly equal (e.g., hardware, teachers, curriculum), children are likely to grow up with a self-identification as inferior. And for those who exclude the non-locals, they lose a diverse environment to grow up in. More importantly, a segregated education system cannot foster the integration of students from different backgrounds and social groups, which is the basis for building social consensus, reducing social group conflicts, and building a tolerant and pluralistic society.

3   Removing the "Separation Wall"

3.1   *Establishing a Financial Mechanism for Education That Is Reasonably Shared by Governments at Different Levels*

There is a long-standing academic consensus on the objective of the reform of the system for the education of migrant children: to ensure that migrant children live with their parents and enjoy equal access to public education.

To achieve this goal, the first issue to be addressed is one of capacity: ensuring adequate budgets to provide qualified education in places that migrant children in-flow.

This requires first establishing a financial mechanism for education shared by all levels of government. The national, provincial, municipal, district, and county-level governments need to clarify the proportion of compulsory education expenditure, and increase the proportion of expenditure for the provincial and central government.

Secondly, the central level needs to reconsider the proportion of funds that are transferred between different regions. According to the 2018 *Report of the State Council on Promoting the Integrated Development of Urban and*

Rural Compulsory Education to Raise the Quality of Compulsory Education in Rural Areas (国务院关于推动城乡义务教育一体化发展提高农村义务教育水平工作情况的报告), the central government's education financial transfer payments (教育转移支付) increased from 281.7 billion yuan in 2016 to 306.7 billion yuan in 2018, with 80% going to rural and impoverished areas in the central and western parts of the country. The education financial transfer payments from developed eastern regions to impoverished regions in the central and western regions may seem reasonable. But the migrant population is moving in large numbers from the west to the east. Some scholars argue that if they are to be expected and encouraged to move with their children, the central government needs to appropriately increase the proportion of transfer payments to in-flow areas in the east.[14]

Lastly, although the current per-student public expenditure on compulsory education paid by the central Government has realized that "money goes with the student," the per-student expenditure of a little more than 600 yuan is far from adequate. In addition to the per-student public spending, the items and amounts of funding that migrant children can take with them need to be further increased in order to provide effective financial support to the in-flow regions.

3.2 Reform of the Provincial-Admission System for the College-Entrance Examination (分省录取的高考招生制度)

Reform of the financial mechanism for education at the compulsory education stage will remove objective obstacles for migrant children to stay with their parents for compulsory education. However, if the obstacles to further education are not abolished, migrant children will eventually have to be separated from their parents.

The current provincial-admission system for the college-entrance examination still follows the basic philosophy of the planned economy, with artificially determined admission quotas for different provinces. In provinces with abundant higher education resources, the admission quotas for colleges and universities are mostly in favor of local students, because of the constraints imposed by local financial subsidies and land supply. Meanwhile, these provinces attract a large number of the migrant population. Thus, if they opened

---

14   Li Nan 李楠, "Shujujiexi: liudongertong yiwujiaoyu caizhengzhidu de xianzhuang, wenti yu duice, 数据解析：流动儿童义务教育财政制度的现状、问题与对策 [Data Analysis: the Current Situation, Problems and Countermeasures of the Financial System of Compulsory Education for Migrant Children]," November 26, 2018, Urbanization Observation Network.

their college-entrance examinations to non-locals, the competitive pressure on local students would increase dramatically, triggering a huge conflict of interest between "locals" and "non-locals."

To remove the obstacles to the complete abolishment of area restrictions for taking the college-entrance examination, the provincial-admission system needs to be abandoned. With the implementation of the national unified college-entrance examination, colleges and universities will decide whether to admit a student based on the student's examination performance and other indicators of consideration, rather than artificially creating unfair admissions between different provinces.

3.3 Broader Public Discussion: Realizing the Value of Low-Income Workers

In addition to easing the financial burden of large cities, in order for administrators in large cities to be willing to accept migrant children, what needs to change is their basic philosophy of population management. More empirical research and public advocacy are needed to show the value of low-income workers, both to city administrators and residents.

For example, some media tracked the scavenging community's situation following Beijing's population control policy in 2017. Beijing produces around 23,000 tons of garbage per day, and non-local scavengers did most of the important job of sorting the garbage. While scavengers continued to leave the city, garbage in Beijing experienced abnormal growth. According to research by Chen Lizwen, who holds a master's degree in environmental history from the University of Southern California, the abnormal growth of garbage in Beijing in 2017 has reached 3%, almost all of which comes from waste products that have not been properly sorted and recycled.[15]

Some economists have also quantified the economic development effects[16] brought by the migrant population. Xu Xuezhen's model of the contribution of the migrant population to economic growth shows that the contribution of the migrant population to economic growth in Beijing was above 20% during

---

15   Zhao Han 赵晗 "2017 nian de yandong guohou, 20wan shihuangzhe qunaerle? 2017 年的严冬过后, 20万拾荒者去哪儿了? [After the Severe Winter in 2017, Where Have 200,000 Scavengers Gone?]," Jan. 8, 2018, https://theinitium.com/article/20180109-mainland-beijing-scanvengers-after-eviction/.

16   Compiled by Urbanization Observation Network: "*How Much Does the Migrant Population Contribute to Economic Development? 15 Economic Studies Give You the Answer*," Sept. 7, 2018, Urbanization Observation Network.

the period 2000–2011, with an overall increasing trend.[17] According to Zhang Li, although a large number of the migrant population does not participate in social security or pay individual taxes, their consumption still contributed significantly to local tax revenue.[18]

City administrators need to treat low-income workers more fairly, respect the laws of urban development and population growth, effectively solve cities' issues from the perspective of improving the level of urban management and planning. In addition, they should respect the rights and interests of low-income workers. This includes providing them with appropriate public services and infrastructure and guaranteeing their basic social and economic rights.

3.4   *Promotion of Diversified and Integrated Education*
In order to truly pull down the separation wall for migrant children, it is also necessary to break down the barriers between different social groups. Otherwise, when institutional barriers are removed, migrant children will continue to face a "segregated but equal" educational environment.

And to crack the stereotypes against migrant children, the idea of diverse and integrated education needs to be advocated more widely.

This first requires teachers to constantly reinforce and promote concepts such as equality and respect in micro-educational settings. In the relevant social study classes, teachers should help students understand the complexity of issues such as social classes and poverty. Some schools and educational institutions have already made attempts in this regard today, such as visiting urban villages and gleaning villages to enable students to understand topics such as urban poverty and urbanization in the form of PBL (project-based learning).

Secondly, breaking down the segregation between different social groups also requires top-level design at the policy level. For example, separating migrant children from local students into separate classes should be prohibited, avoiding sending a large number of migrant children in one school but dispersing them to different schools in a school district, and so on.

---

17   Xu Xuezhen 许学珍 "Beijingshi liudongrenkou dui jingjizengzhang yingxiang de shizheng yanjiu, 北京市流动人口对经济增长影响的实证研究 [An Empirical Study of the Impact of Beijing's Migrant Population on Economic Growth]," Master's Thesis, Capital University of Economics and Business, 2013.

18   Zhang Li 张力 "Liudongrenkou dui chengshi jingji gongxian pouxi: yi Shanghai weili 流动人口对城市经济贡献剖析： 以上海为例 [Analysis of the contribution of the migrant population to the urban economy: the case of Shanghai]," *Population Studies*, Issue 4, 2015.

Educational segregation due to social class stratification is not a unique problem of China's urbanization process. In the 18th and 19th arrondissements of Paris, for example, class divisions are rampant. Wealthy parents sent their children to private schools, while public schools were concentrated with children from the poorer classes. In 2016, the French Ministry of Education launched an experiment of integrated education in the 18th and 19th arrondissements of Paris. Three "mixed junior high schools" were established in these two districts to "impose" class-integration by merging public schools in neighborhoods with students from different social classes. These "mixed junior high schools" received additional educational resources due to their experimental nature. In 2018, the Centre Français de Politique Publique evaluated this experiment and found the results to be "encouraging," with significantly fewer parents sending their children to private junior high schools in these arrondissements.

Such class-integrated educational practices deserve the attention of domestic education policymakers and researchers in order to find ways of class-integrated education that are more suitable for the Chinese context.

The educational plight of migrant children is not only the objective constraints of the education finance system, but also the stereotypes against low-income workers by city administrators and residents. To break the institutional and conceptual barriers and truly promote policy and institutional reform, we still need a lot of public discussions based on empirical research, so that society can form a consensus on issues such as population management, the important value of low-income workers, and the complex causes of the problems of the poor. Only a society that truly respects every individual's value and dignity can be a fair and just society.

CHAPTER 16

Research on the Current Development State of Traditional Cultural Education in China

Bao Lige[1]

Abstract

This paper examines the current situation of various types of traditional cultural education institutions in the context of the enthusiasm in studying traditional culture in recent years using quantitative and qualitative research methods. The different characteristics and major problems in the development of colleges and universities, secondary schools, primary schools, as well as old-style private schools (私塾) and academies of classical learning (书院) were investigated. It is proposed that the functions and objectives of traditional cultural education should be defined, the "creative transformation and innovative development" of traditional cultural education should be emphasized, and an open and diversified institutional mechanism should be built.

Keywords

traditional culture education – academy of classical learning – old-style private school

Since November 2017, the 21st Century Education Research Institute, funded by the Dunwoody Foundation, has been conducting research on contemporary traditional cultural education in China. We got a basic picture of traditional cultural education in private educational institutions and universities and primary and secondary schools in multiple locations through an online questionnaire and field research.

---

1 Bao Lige 宝丽格 earned her Ph.D. degree at University of Tokyo, Japan. She is an associate researcher at the Institute of 21st Century Education. Her research interests in multicultural education.

1   Background to the Development of Traditional Cultural Education

Since the end of the 20th century, with the rise of the country's economy, China has been on a quest to find the contemporary values of its own traditions, with the fever for Chinese studies gradually emerging in the 1990s and reaching a peak in the early 21st century.

In terms of specific educational practices, the main practices in the early years were classical education, character education, and etiquette education, mainly in the form of classical reading. In 1995, nine pioneer cultural scholars, including Zhao Puchu, Bingxin, Cao Yu, and Xia Yan, proposed to offer a Chinese classical curriculum to enrich students' knowledge of Chinese literature and traditional culture. These scholars believed that there had been a gap in traditional Chinese education for a long time and wanted to remedy it, and they were convinced that the ideas of the ancient Chinese sages were still valid today. However, these initiatives remained as discussions among scholars but were not appreciated much by the public, even though both private and official classical recitation activities had been carried out. Around 2004, China underwent the second revival of traditional culture. This time, the "enthusiasm in studying Chinese traditional culture" has been more popular. Familiar examples include Yu Dan's narration of the *Analects of Confucius*, the celebration of Confucius' birthday in Qufu, the Chinese classics reading initiatives, and the revival of old-style private schools. During this period, the media played a great role in promoting the event. CCTV's *Hundred Schools of Thought* presented a series of topics such as Yi Zhongtian's "Thoughts on Three Kingdoms" and Liu Xinwu's "Dream of the Red Chamber," which all became cultural hotspots among the public. Other TV shows such as *Chinese Character Dictation Competition*, *Hero of Idioms*, *Idioms of China*, and *Poems of Chinese* were broadcast on major TV stations. Traditional culture, which was once left out, is being sought after again.

In the past two years, the most important event of traditional culture education is that in January 2017, the General Office of the CPC Central Committee and the State Council jointly issued the *Opinions on Implementing the Chinese Excellent Traditional Culture Inheritance and Development Project* (关于实施中华优秀传统文化传承发展工程的意见), which has been the highest-level national guidance for traditional culture education so far. Since then, traditional culture education has continued to be integrated into the curriculum of in-system primary and secondary schools. Meanwhile, many modern old-style private schools were also established in cities. On September 1st, 2017, the Ministry of Education published the new teaching materials, in which the content of traditional culture was significantly increased. This move attracted great public attention. Following that, the government has also issued multiple traditional culture education-related notices, such as the *Notice on the Construction of the Chinese Excellent Traditional Culture Inheritance Base*, the *Notice on the Implementation Plan of the Chinese Classical Recitation Project*, and some local governments have also issued corresponding measures.

The main venue of traditional culture education has been continuously shifting from higher education institutions to primary and secondary schools. In 2018, the research and practice education base broken through the school boundaries and expanded traditional culture education to cultural protection units, museums, and intangible cultural heritage (非遗) sites. And the content of traditional culture education has been expanding, from the initial focus on moral education, to gradually increasing contents on general cultural knowledge and traditional cultural skills. In policies, traditional culture education is often associated with patriotic education, revolutionary education, and advanced socialist culture education. In terms of the purpose of education, more emphasis is placed on the cultivation of national consciousness. Besides, the cultivation of social care and character was also brought up in policies as objectives of traditional culture education.

Classified by school education and informal education, traditional cultural education can be divided into two main sectors: school education and social education. School education can be further divided into in-system public education and private education outside the system. Thus, under the top-level planning of the Government, the different practices and interactions of the three major sectors, namely, in-system public schools, educational institutions outside the system, and social education, constitute a rich and colorful landscape of traditional cultural education in contemporary China (See Figure 16.1).

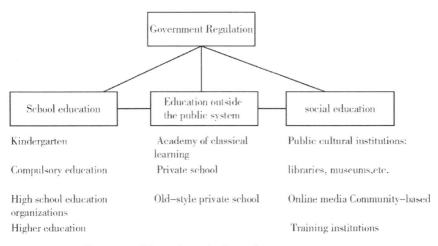

FIGURE 16.1   Illustration of the traditional culture education

2 Traditional Cultural Education Practices at the Primary, Secondary, and Higher Education Levels

2.1 *Forms of Traditional Cultural Education in Primary and Secondary Schools*

Currently, traditional cultural education in primary and secondary schools takes the following three forms.

First, campus culture development. This includes theme activities such as traditional culture knowledge contest, speech contest, traditional culture theme games, reading club, club activities, etc.

Second, classroom activities. This includes school curricula and extended activities for the Chinese language class. Integrating traditional culture into the school-based curriculum is a common practice in primary and secondary education. Different schools have different implementation methods and themes. Since the school-based curriculum takes up relatively little class time, most schools choose a single theme as the starting point, such as Chinese calligraphy, recitation of Chinese classics, Chinese paper-cutting, traditional Chinese festivals, Chinese opera, martial arts, and so on.

Third, subject integration. It mainly takes the form of project-based learning that integrates geography, history, language, mathematics, and other subjects. This component accounts for a relatively small proportion of the existing traditional cultural education.

Compared to the more diverse forms of primary and secondary schools, traditional cultural education at the senior high school level is mainly integrated into language education as well as Civics and Political Science classes. In early 2018, the Ministry of Education promulgated the *Curriculum Plan and Curriculum Standards for Chinese Language and Other Subjects for Regular Senior High Schools (2017 Edition)*. This reform of the curriculum standard covered all 14 academic subjects in China's regular senior high school education, of which the Chinese language class has undergone the most significant changes. The new standards explicitly stated that "half of the in-class reading pieces should be classic works of ancient China." The number of ancient Chinese poems for students to memorize has also increased from 14 to 72."[2] In addition, other subjects, such as ideology and politics, art, music, physical education and health, mathematics, etc., have added traditional culture component to their curricula. For example, "Chinese Calligraphy and Painting" has

---

2 Ministry of Education's Circular on the *Issuance of Curriculum Plans and Curriculum Standards for Chinese Language and Other Subjects for Regular Senior High Schools (2017 Edition)*, http://www.moe.gov.cn/srcsite/A26/s8001/201801/t20180115_324647.html.

been added to the Art curriculum, which covers the appreciation of classical works of traditional Chinese painting, calligraphy, and seal carving, as well as the theory of traditional painting. In the senior high school ideological and political science course (required courses), a culture module has been added to help students acquire the basic knowledge and ability to participate in various cultural activities. In recent years, the college-entrance examination Chinese language exams also show a remarkable increase in the traditional cultural related content.

Shandong Province is an experimental base for local curricula on traditional culture, and has been a representative example in integrating traditional culture into local curricula. In Shandong province, schools at the compulsory education level have 16 class-hours for the traditional culture curriculum per semester, which can be integrated with activities such as cultural theme education, moral education, and theme class meetings. Shandong Province defines the objectives of traditional culture education from three perspectives: emotions and attitudes, behavior and habits, and knowledge and competence. The curriculum places more emphasis on traditional cultural knowledge, ethical norms, and arts talent. Currently, ideas and teaching materials on traditional culture prosper everywhere in China. Different provinces, and even different schools, use very different traditional culture teaching materials. The traditional culture teaching materials in Shandong province have many different versions under the same guiding principle. The Shandong Provincial Education Department approved the only set of teaching material covering primary school, junior high school, through senior high school – Lujiao version of the *Excellent Chinese Traditional Culture*. This set of textbooks is divided into three sections: primary school, junior high school, and senior high school. In Shandong province, ten cities choose to use this textbook, including Weifang, Heze, Laiwu, Rizhao, Liaocheng, Jining, Binzhou, Dezhou, Qingdao, and Jinan.

2.2 *Survey on the Status of Traditional Culture Education for Primary and Secondary School Teachers*

The 21st Century Education Research Institute conducted a teachers' survey on the status of traditional cultural education in primary and secondary schools and the teachers' understanding and attitudes towards traditional cultural education. Electronic questionnaires[3] were distributed to primary and

---

3 The questionnaires were distributed through multiple venues, including: (1) the alliance schools of traditional culture education and practice of China Publishing House and the alliance schools of small-scale rural schools, who have collaborations with the 21st Century Institute; (2) conferences participants, such as the summer camp for core teachers of Chinese

secondary school teachers from May 28th to August 30th, 2018, with 2,057 valid questionnaires returned. The surveyed teachers ranged from 1,101 primary school teachers (53.5%), 612 junior high school teachers (29.8%), and 344 senior high school teachers (16.7%).

2.2.1 Content and Educational Role of Traditional Culture Education

The field of traditional culture education needs to pay attention to whether the current teachers' perceptions will lead to examination-oriented, knowledge-based, and fragmented traditional culture education, and whether the content and objectives of traditional culture education will be narrowed. Most teachers surveyed thought traditional culture education as classical education such as the Four Books and Five Classics (96.7%), etiquette (87.8%), and traditional culture talents such as music, chess, calligraphy, and painting (83.3%) (See Figure 16.2). Correspondingly, most teachers considered the top four basic functions of traditional culture education to be: passing on traditional culture (95.2%), cultivating a sense of national identity (94.8%), cultivating good moral character (88.4%), and developing good behavioral habits (86.7%) (See Figure 16.3).

The field study also showed that, due to the lack of adequate guiding theories, teaching materials, and teachers, the current traditional culture education curricula are usually taught by Chinese language teachers and teachers of moral and ethical values. The content is mostly consisting of the memorization of ancient poems and articles, learning traditional skills, and moral indoctrination. But is traditional cultural education serving its optimal purpose? For example, is it appropriate to focus the assessment of traditional cultural education at the senior high school level on ancient poetry and general knowledge? Should educational contents differ for students of different ages? For instance, could traditional cultural education at the senior high school level include more in-depth discussion and critical thinking, and minimize the fatigue and boredom that rote memorization brings to students? Also, the over-emphasis on society's collective will in traditional cultural education may overlook individual students' feelings. For younger age students, it is necessary for educators and scholars to further explore how to make traditional cultural education closer to everyday life and personalized.

2.2.2 Relevant Measures in Schools

In recent years, with the government's emphasis on traditional cultural education, schools have devoted more effort to traditional cultural education.

---

traditional culture education; and (3) texting invitations to fill in the questionnaire through the existing directory of teachers of the Institute.

RESEARCH ON THE CURRENT DEVELOPMENT STATE

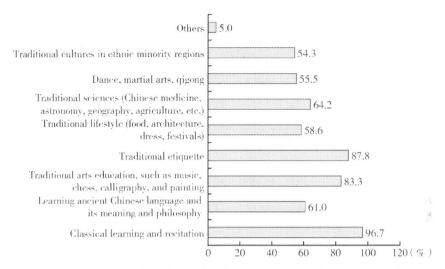

FIGURE 16.2 Percentage of teachers with different conceptions of education in traditional culture

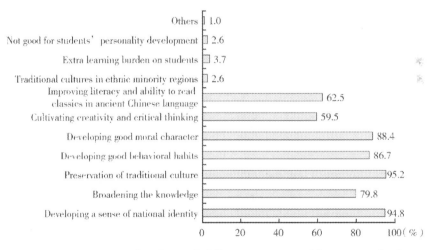

FIGURE 16.3 Percentage of teachers with different conceptions of the primary role of education in traditional culture

However, the teaching and research, as well as evaluation, still need to be improved. Among the surveyed teachers, 66.9% reported schools had dedicated work arrangements on this topic, 38.2% reported the schools had specialized evaluation system. Those who selected schools had regular teaching research activities, and full-time traditional culture class teachers were 49.8% and 34.5%, respectively (See Table 16.1).

TABLE 16.1 Measures related to traditional culture education in schools

	Specialized organization of work		Dedicated evaluation system		Regular teaching and research activities		Full-time traditional culture teachers	
	Number of people	Percentage	Number of people	Percentage	Number of people	Percentage	Number of people	Percentage
Yes	1,377	66.9	785	38.2	1,024	49.8	709	34.5
None	510	24.8	949	46.1	809	39.3	1,149	55.9
Not sure	164	8.0	315	15.3	220	10.7	187	9.1
Other	6	0.3	8	0.4	4	0.2	12	0.6
Total	2,057	100.0	2,057	100.0	2,057	100.0	2,057	100.0

2.2.3   Specific Methods of Traditional Culture Education

In primary and secondary schools, traditional cultural education is more in the form of activities and environment construction. Attention should still be paid to how to make individual activities serve a coherent educational purpose and turn the pursuit of hardware into the growth of students' body, mind, and soul, so as to avoid traditional culture education becoming a superficial form in pursuit of performance. According to the surveyed teachers, the top three forms of traditional culture education in schools are campus culture development (66.7%), integration into the curriculum of related subjects (58.8%), and club activities (52.9%) (See Figure 16.4).

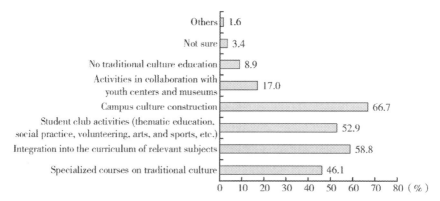

FIGURE 16.4   Percentage of teachers with different ideas about the form education in traditional culture should take

RESEARCH ON THE CURRENT DEVELOPMENT STATE 277

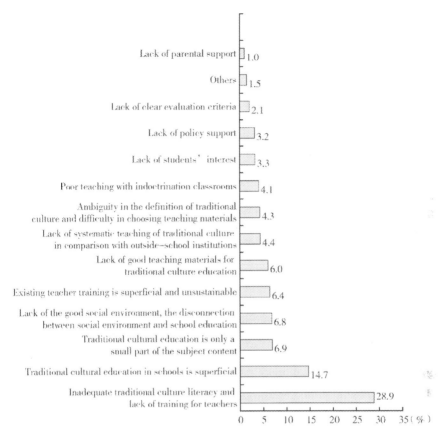

FIGURE 16.5   Percentage of teachers with different ideas about the chief impediment to promoting education in traditional culture

2.2.4   Difficulties in Traditional Culture Education

The surveyed teachers reported two outstanding problems in the implementation of traditional culture education in schools. The most prominent one was that teachers were not profoundly educated in traditional culture and lack of relevant training (28.9%). The second one was that traditional culture education in schools is a mere formality, with many slogans but difficult to implement (14.7%). Other issues with traditional culture education brought up by the surveyed teachers included: it was still only a small part of the academic content (6.9%), as well as the lack of a good social environment, which was disconnected from school education (6.8%) (See Figure 16.5).

In conclusion, the field of traditional cultural education still needs to address many questions. What is the goal of traditional culture education? What is worth passing on? What is the best way to incorporate traditional culture education in schools? What is the most appropriate way to proceed at each grade level? How to handle the conflict between traditional culture education and the existing academic teaching? How does the learning of traditional culture relate to the overall school curriculum plan and student development? How should we evaluate traditional culture education? How to develop instructional materials for traditional culture education?

In recent years, educational researchers have carried out valuable debates on several issues in the field of traditional culture education, most notably the discussion on the *Discipline for Students*. Huang Xiaodan of Jiangnan University analyzes the content of the *Discipline for Students* with detailed evidence, arguing that it does not represent the whole picture of ancient Chinese primary education. She reminded practitioners to avoid narrowing and extremes of traditional culture education. In terms of teaching methods, Ke Xiaogang at the Tongji University commented on ancient Chinese classics education: recently, some people proposed that ancient Chinese classics "should not be explained" when taught to the students. However, those arguments were not well supported by evidence. "Instead of the benefits of verbatim memorization, the real reason is the lack of enough good teachers who can teach and explain the ancient Chinese classics."[4] Currently, there are many textbooks for teaching traditional culture on the market, but the books used by many schools are only reading materials rather than truly teaching materials. The textbooks are mainly edited by scholars of literature and history, with less involvement of educational scholars. As a result, the design of the content inevitably lacks an educational dimension. And whether it is necessary to introduce it in the form of textbooks also needs further discussion. This research direction still needs the continuous attention of education researchers to guide teaching practitioners.

2.3 Practices of Traditional Culture Education in Higher Education Institutions

Traditional culture education in higher education institutions mainly includes the following approaches.

2.3.1 Discipline and Degree Training

These include universities and departments whose main purpose is to cultivate talents, such as the School of Chinese Classics of Wuhan University and the School of Chinese Classics of the Renmin University of China. In addition,

---

4 Ke Xiaogang 柯小刚 "Xiandaishehui zhong de gudianjiaoyu, 现代社会中的古典教育 [Classical Education in Modern Society]," *Culture Across the World*, No. 6, 2014.

some universities do not provide an academic education, but mostly focus on research, such as the re-established Academy of Guoxue Xia Men University, Capital Normal University's establishment of the Institute of Chinese Studies, Huazhong University of Science and Technology's establishment of the Institute of Chinese Studies, and Tsinghua University's establishment of the Institute of Chinese Studies, Shanxi University Institute of Chinese Studies, Huazhong Normal University's establishment of an academy of Chinese Studies, and Hunan University Yuelu Academy.[5] According to the internet search results, as of November 2018, there were 50 institutions for teaching and research of Chinese studies, among which 22 institutions were named after the university's Institute of Chinese Studies.

2.3.2   Curriculum
This includes the inclusion of Chinese studies in the university-wide general and elective courses. Chinese studies are also integrated into other related disciplines, such as university-level Chinese language, Chinese language and literature majors, philosophy, social sciences, natural sciences, humanities, university-level English, and ideological and political science courses.

2.3.3   Non-Curricular Methods
These include campus culture, Chinese studies clubs, and other forms. Currently, traditional culture education at the higher education level still has many problems, such as a lack of clarity in the definition of the Chinese studies and its extensions, and the knowledge structure of the existing teaching staff cannot meet the requirements of Chinese studies education.

3   Traditional Culture Education Carried Out by Socio-Educational Institutions

3.1   *Development of Traditional Culture Education outside the Public Education System*
With enthusiasm in Chinese studies since the 1990s, many social educational institutions have been established outside the school system that provides traditional culture education. Those institutions include old-style private

---

5   Zhao Xingyue 赵星月 "Gaoxiao guoxue jiaoyu xianzhuang fenxi yu duiceayanjiu, 高校国学教育现状分析与对策研究 [Analysis of the Current Situation and Countermeasures of Chinese Studies in Higher Education Institutions]," *Journal of Qiqihar University* (Philosophy and Social Science Edition), April 2015.

schools, academies of classical learning, private schools, and public educational institutions such as museums and libraries. Among them, the academy of classical learning and old-style private schools are the main institutions that provide traditional culture education. As a supplement to the education within the public system, these institutions have different school orientation, education objectives, teaching contents and methods, and have become the main practitioners in the education and development of Chinese traditional culture.

The academy of classical learning has revived as an active hotspot for studying and disseminating Chinese studies. Some historically famous traditional academies revived in the new situation. Combining tourism resources, they host educational and public welfare activities such as historical and cultural lectures and book clubs. Many are newly established academies conducting cultural research and teaching traditional culture to the public, such as the International Academy of Chinese Culture, which was established in the 1980s affiliated to Peking University, the Tongji Renaissance Classical Academy, which was founded in 2015, and the Ma Yifu Academy, which was founded in 2017 jointly by Zhejiang University and Zhejiang Dunhe Charity Foundation. In addition, there are also privately-run academies that provide traditional culture education for children and adults. Some famous ones include the Beijing Seven Treasures Academy, established in 2004, the Ni Shan Sheng Yuan College, established in 2008, the Beijing Si Hai Academy, established in 2009, and the Xiamen Yuan Dang Academy, established in 2009.

Among the privately-run Chinese studies education institutions, academies of classical learning, private schools, and old-style private schools have become the mainstay of traditional culture education for young people. Through reading the classics, they help students learn how to bring up a family, develop themselves, and promote the cultural literacy of the whole society. Most Chinese studies institutions for young children add kindergarten courses in five fields to the existing Chinese classics reading, which covers martial arts, dance, Go, calligraphy, Chinese painting, drama, and so on.

In addition, other social institutions provide traditional culture education for enterprises, and party and government cadres. They conduct educational activities and community activities in public cultural facilities such as libraries, art galleries, etc. Recently there has been an increase in the use of online social media for traditional cultural education, such as the WeChat learning group "Analects of Discourse," etc. Though differ in operating mechanisms, the content of their activities, and their scales, these institutions are all involved in the traditional culture education, and public civilization in their unique ways.

3.2 Survey on Privately-Run Traditional Culture Education Institutions

In order to grasp the overall landscape of traditional culture education institutions in China, the research team searched through the Internet with keywords "academy", "old-style private school", "private school", "Chinese studies", "Classics", "Chinese classics reading", "Traditional culture", "primary education", etc. In addition, the research team went through the traditional culture education institutions' Wechat groups and QQ groups, as well as obtained recommendation lists during the research process, and finally compiled a list of 2,319 traditional culture education institutions. During this process, we have screened out institutions that do not have an educational function or are no longer in operation. Although this may still not be a complete list of all traditional culture education institutions, they are representative of the basic characteristics and trends of this group of institutions.

3.2.1 Institutions Are Located Mainly in Large Cities on the Southeast Coast

Based on the information we collected, the top four provinces in terms of percentages of traditional culture education institutions were Taiwan (19.58%), Guangdong (10.61%), Shandong (8.11%), and Beijing (7.29%), followed by several coastal provinces, such as Jiangsu (5.39%), Fujian (5.35%), and Zhejiang (4.7%). Inland provinces accounted for a smaller share. Most of these institutions were mainly found in the large cities of the southeast coast.

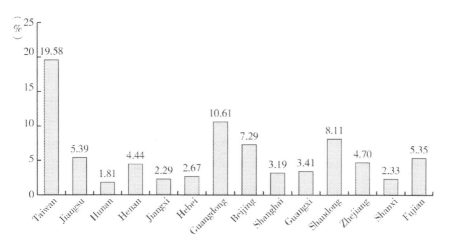

FIGURE 16.6   Provinces where privately-run traditional culture education institutions are located

3.2.2   Most of These Institutions Are Full-Time Schools, Summer and Winter Camps for Children and Teenagers

The category to which most of these institutions belong was full-time schools (47.35%), followed by winter and summer camps (34.37%), weekend interest classes (28.59%), and public service lectures and courses (16.21%) (See Figure 16.7).

These educational institutions mainly served children and teenagers. According to the survey, the highest percentage was the pre-school level (65.89%), followed by the primary education level (63.73%) (See Figure 16.8).

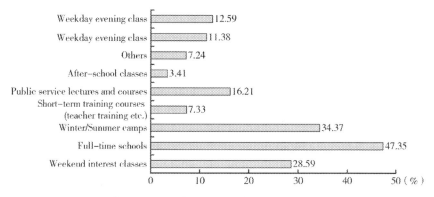

FIGURE 16.7   Types of services provided by privately-run traditional culture education institutions

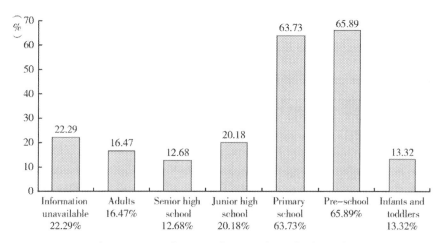

FIGURE 16.8   Student age groups that privately-run traditional culture education institutions served

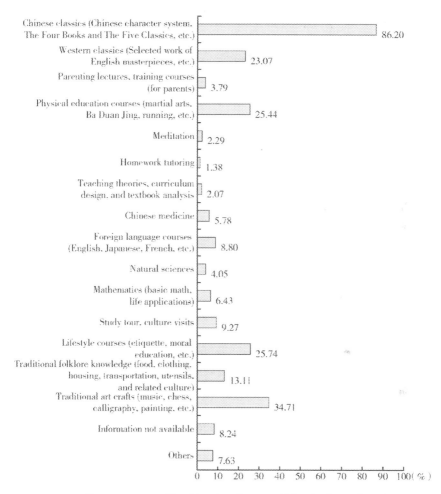

FIGURE 16.9   Course contents offered in privately-run traditional culture education institutions

3.2.3   Offer a Diverse Curriculum

The types of courses offered by the institutions were diverse, with the largest number of subjects offered to be Chinese classics (86.2%), traditional arts and crafts (34.71%), courses on lifestyle (25.74%), and sports courses (25.44%). Many schools also offered Western classics (23.07%) (See Figure 16.9).

Contrary to the public perception that traditional culture education institutions only focused on "reading and reciting many Chinese classics," their teaching methods have become more diverse, with greater emphasis on understanding and the application of knowledge and practice. The top three teaching methods (multiple-choice) were experiencing and practicing (56.9%), reading and interpreting (55.9%), and only reading many Chinese classics (48%). However, it should be noted that the implementation of the curriculum varies greatly among institutions, depending on the level of teachers.

3.2.4 Most Institutions Have Been Established since 2014 and Are Mostly Unregistered

To compensate for the limitations of online information search, the project team distributed electronic questionnaires to the heads of traditional culture education institutions from May 29 to September 10, 2018, with 102 valid questionnaires returned.[6] Survey results showed that among the surveyed traditional culture education institutions, two were founded in 1999, which were the oldest. The vast majority of institutions were founded after 2014, and the number of new institutions has increased year by year in the recent three years, which was closely related to the policy on traditional culture education.

Thirty percent of the institutions were unregistered. In terms of the registration status of the institutions, the top three categories were unregistered (33.0%), registered as an enterprise (26.8%), and registered as private non-enterprise units (20.6%).

3.2.5 Teachers Were Mainly Trained by Their Own Institutions, with a Shortage of Teachers and a High Degree of Mobility

The top three ways institutions recruit teachers were: the institutions' own training (64.7%), referrals from acquaintances (61.8%), and teacher self-referrals (54.9%). Due to the limited amount of salaries private educational institutions were able to offer, teacher shortages and high mobility were common.

3.2.6 Graduates of These Institutions Face Risks and Challenges with Their Career Paths

Survey results showed that the top three main career paths for institutional students after graduation are: to return to primary and secondary schools (57.1%), continue to study in academies of classical learning (57.1%), and work directly in traditional culture education institutions (36.5%).

---

6   The distribution period was from May 29 to September 10, 2018, and 102 valid questionnaires were collected. The distribution channels were quite diverse, including the WeChat groups and QQ groups of traditional culture education institutions such as old-style private school associations and the Forum of Chinese Studies; and published on the official websites of major traditional culture content media such as Tencent Confucianism and Buddhism Channel, Chinese Studies Channel of IFENG News, https://www.rujiazg.com/, shuyuanchina.org, and http://www.guoxue928.com/.

Combined with the field research data, the students' main career paths were the following. (1) Return to the in-system schools. It is easier for students to transition to in-system schools if the teaching content of the old-style private schools is in line with in-system education. Some students choose to apply for colleges and universities through taking self-taught higher education examination and graduate school entrance examinations. Some universities in China recruit students who graduated from old-style private schools through independent admission examinations. (2) Continue their studies in traditional cultural educational institutions. For example, the Wenli Academy, which mainly focuses on reading Chinese classics, accepts students over the age of thirteen to further their Chinese classics studies. Some academies of classical learning and old-style private schools offer "Chinese classics studies classes," which accept young people aged 13 to 20 who have read the Chinese classics for ten years and want to further their studies and better understand the classics. (3) Study abroad. This is mainly an option for families with good economic conditions. (4) Find a job: Students from privileged families may enter their family business after graduation. Some schools may have collaborations with companies and offer career programs or internship opportunities. Depending on each institution's situation and the social resources it possesses, as well as students' own social resources, graduates of the institutions have different career paths. In many cases, students will face great challenges.

3.2.7 The Institutions Need to Obtain School Qualification and Financial Support

Most of the funding of privately-run traditional culture education institutions came from tuitions (i.e., 72.9% of total income). Most modern old-style private schools were at the borderline of barely breaking even in terms of financial situations, with 33.3% had a slight deficit and 30.4% at a break-even position. The top two items of expenditure were salaries (54%) and expenditures on school premises (30.4%).

The reported most urgent needs for the healthy development of traditional culture education institutions include: obtain government-recognized qualifications to run schools (79.4%), receive financial support from the Government and enterprises (52%), and build a platform for exchanges information and communication among traditional culture education institutions (47.1%). At present, old-style privately-run schools are not recognized by the government for their legitimacy in providing full-time Chinese classics reading education at the compulsory education level. Their academic qualifications are not recognized, and they can be banned at any time because of "running schools illegally." This greatly restricts parents' free choice of schools.

4   Recommendations for the Healthy Development of Traditional Culture Education

4.1   *Functions and Objectives of Traditional Culture Education*

In the environment of examination-oriented education, many school principals and teachers are not motivated to work on traditional culture education due to its marginal status. In most schools, the teaching of traditional culture lacks a holistic design, the educational contents are not coherent, and the teaching materials are scattered and fragmented. Regions and schools often work in isolation, with much enthusiasm but poor teaching effectiveness. In addition, there is a tendency towards focusing on knowledge memorizing in traditional culture education for test-taking purposes.

Learning traditional culture is not just about knowing the past, but more about helping students to create the future. In terms of the contents and objectives of traditional culture education, it is necessary to gradually reconcile the differences and contradictions between globalism and nationalism, especially from the perspectives of the individual and the other, the nation and the global, the traditional and the modern, and individual and social values. Traditional culture education should focus on harmonizing Chinese Han culture, ethnic minority cultures, and the cultures of countries around the world. Meanwhile, the values of individual and social values need to be reconciled. Specifically, if too much emphasis is placed on the collective will of society in traditional culture education, students may feel their individual feelings are ignored. Traditional culture should be integrated into students' life so that the abundant resources of traditional culture education can enrich students' life experiences. Students should be cultivated to understand, express, communicate and create traditional cultural values.

4.2   *Emphasis on the "Creative Transformation and Innovative Development" of Traditional Culture Education*

In order to bring traditional culture education into modern society and contemporary life, and be truly welcomed by young people of the new generation, the most important thing is, as stated in the *Opinions on Implementing the Chinese Excellent Traditional Culture Inheritance and Development Project*, to "insist on creative transformation and innovative development." Specifically, we should "uphold an objective, scientific and respectful attitude to take the best of what is good, remove the dross, and transform and innovate traditional culture. We should not constrain ourselves to the ancient culture and strictly copy from it; neither should we simply deny traditional culture. Instead, we should constantly give meanings reflected the new era and modern forms of expression, constantly supplement, expand, and improve the traditional culture. In this way, the most basic cultural component of the Chinese nation is compatible with contemporary culture and harmonious with modern society."

During our research, we found a series of vivid forms of traditional culture education that broke the stereotype of traditional culture education, which was limited to the study of ancient classics. For example, the "Enlightenment of All Creatures" course enables students to "experience the beauty of oriental humanities and arts, as well as the rational spirit of natural science" through the exploration of all living creatures. With Chinese culture and philosophy at its core, Aurora Academy International (AAI) is a school that is in alignment with the diverse realities of the world. Compared to traditional education, which is "lecture-based," "teacher-centered," "subject-based," "unified teaching," and "Lack of reflection on learning objectives and strategies," the curriculum at AAI has more emphasis on methods and approaches such as "self-constructed," "student-centered," "project-based learning," "differentiated teaching and elective classes," and "understanding the learning process and learning to reflect." These approaches are of great relevance to the forms of traditional culture education. The Daohe Academy adds the beauty of local features in education "to integrate the philosophy of Confucianism, Buddhism, and Taoism into Chinese education philosophy; integrate the traditional music, Chinese chess, calligraphy and painting into Chinese educational aesthetics; integrate the Chinese Taiji, health-promoting theories, martial arts, archery into Chinese education of physical intelligence, and integrate the Chinese health science into Chinese children's nutrition." Fuxi Education relies on the vast fields and lakes as well as rural folklore, accompanied by traditional culture education in Chinese classics, calligraphy, and martial arts, to implement a people-oriented, all-round education. All of these show us the innovation and creative transformation that gives vigor to traditional culture education.

4.3 *Building an Open and Pluralistic Institutional Mechanism*

The development of contemporary traditional culture education is characterized by two mechanisms: top-down and bottom-up. The advantages of government-led initiatives are that it provides institutional, policy, and financial support to facilitate holistic and systematic cultural development in all aspects such as curriculum, teaching materials, teaching staff, discipline development, and internship bases, so that school education becomes the main channel for passing on cultural heritage. Outside of in-system school education, privately-run educational institutions, such as old-style private schools, mass media, social cultural institutions, provide diversified and enriching educational content and venues, and have a strong drive for self-growth and development.

People are easy to go extremes regarding traditional culture education, either to be extremely censured or extremely celebrated, and hold biased opinions on the development of traditional culture education. The fact is, we do not have definite answers to many of the challenges and problems in the current cultural heritage processes. Our possible solution is to compare and select in practice through diverse explorations to reach progress and evolution. This requires an open attitude and mechanism, not settling on one idea, but taking an inclusive approach, tolerating, and recognizing the value of learning from the people. We should allow enough room for diverse privately-run education. By integrating bottom-up and top-down approaches, we can create different models, programs, methods, and pathways, so that traditional culture can take root and revive its vitality in the social environment of the new era.

4.4 Issuing Relevant Policies to Address the Legitimacy of Privately-Run Traditional Culture Education Institutions

Under the national compulsory education system, we should create a feasible, legal, and free space for the operation of traditional culture education institutions that meet the requirements. The government should recognize their qualifications as soon as possible, and guide their healthy development. In addition, the legitimate rights and interests of students, parents, and teachers of privately-run schools, such as the old-style privately-run classics reading schools, should be effectively protected through supervision and management. We should ensure the quality of teachers and teaching effectiveness, and parents and students should be involved in the evaluation and monitoring system. These institutions should be guided to avoid such defects and shortcomings as a narrow nationalism that favors Chinese culture over Western culture, an emphasis on the humanities but the exclusion of the natural sciences, nonstandard reading of the ancient classics, neglect of children's interests and feelings, a single and dull curriculum setting and teaching activities, the growth of students disconnected from the real world, and excessive pursuit of commercial profits.

Some privately-run traditional culture education institutions have established alliances in some regions to promote communication among institutions, such as the National Old-style Private School Fellowship Association and the Chinese Studies Network. These alliances aim at solving common problems, sharing experiences, and providing support. In the process of establishing alliances, the industry standards are established to ensure that the practices of institutions follow the educational principles, and the curriculum is in line with children's physiological and psychological characteristics, so that the quality of education is improved.

4.5   *Cultivating Teachers of Traditional Culture Education*

The lack of professional knowledge among teachers in educational institutions requires a set of systematic measures to promote teacher training, recruitment, and evaluation. At the same time, there is a need to ensure that a unique system and standards are established to select and train teachers. In terms of teacher training, experts from other disciplines, such as education, psychology, sociology, anthropology, and cultural studies, should be brought in to maximize the interdisciplinary effectiveness of traditional culture education.

Index

13th Five-Year Plan for National Education Development 233
211 Project 13, 167, 169, 174
985 Project 167, 168, 169, 170

academic performance 99, 108, 109, 115, 116, 130, 219, 221, 223, 225, 258
academies of classical learning 269, 280, 284, 285
Administrative Provisions on the Participation of People with Disabilities in the National College-entrance Examination (Interim) 233, 234, 246
all-around education 224
all-round development 70, 88, 94, 224, 229
all-round development of children 94
all-round education 287
annual household consumption expenditure 184
arts courses 203
assessment system 2, 62, 83, 226

basic education system 17, 19, 20, 26, 28, 29
basic literacy courses 202
behavioral problems 263
Beijing's population control policy 266
Buddhism 284, 287
burden of schoolwork 143, 161, 219, 225
burden reduction 134, 135, 136, 137, 138, 139, 140, 141, 142, 143, 144, 145, 146
burden reduction order 142, 143, 144, 145–146

campus culture development 272, 276
categorized management 31, 32, 33, 34, 35, 36, 37, 38, 40, 41, 43, 44, 45, 46, 47, 48
central fiscal administration 259, 260
child health 157
children's education 143, 258
children with special needs 52, 232, 233, 234, 235, 236, 237, 238, 243, 244, 246, 247, 248, 249
China College Students Survey 96
China Homeschooling Alliance 198
China National Knowledge Infrastructure 52
China's education system 180

Chinese classics 198, 270, 272, 278, 280, 281, 283, 284, 285, 287
Chinese studies 270, 279, 280, 281, 284, 288
class divisions 5, 268
classroom activities 227, 272
college enrollment system 251, 254
college-entrance examination 55, 99, 100, 101, 109, 110, 111, 120, 121, 123, 124, 132, 155, 160, 208, 233, 234, 246, 254, 261, 265, 266, 273
college entrance examination migration 254
compensation schemes 30
comprehensive improvement of school facilities in poverty areas project 54, 63
compulsory education 1, 3, 4, 5, 6, 7, 8, 9, 25, 40, 43, 45, 48, 54–55, 62, 65, 66, 67, 68, 69, 123, 135, 136, 137, 139, 141, 142, 146, 148, 150, 151, 155, 159, 160, 178, 179, 180, 186, 187, 188, 189, 193, 196, 219, 220, 223, 228–229, 232, 234, 235, 236, 237, 238, 248, 249, 252, 253, 254, 255, 256, 259, 260, 261, 264, 265, 273, 285, 288
Confucianism 284, 287
consumption expenditure 183, 184, 185
Core Competencies and Values for Chinese Student's Development 2
courses on lifestyle 283
cramming education 129
curriculum standards 2, 142, 202, 221, 230, 233, 235, 248, 272
Curriculum Standards for Compulsory Education in Schools for Students with Intellectual Disabilities (2016 Edition) 235
Curriculum Standards for Compulsory Education in Schools for the Blind (2016 Edition) 235
Curriculum Standards for Compulsory Education in Schools for the Deaf (2016 Edition) 235

Decision of the State Council of the Central Committee of the Communist Party of China on Winning the Battle against Poverty 50, 51

Decision on the Reform and Development of Basic Education 252
diverse curriculum 283
diversification of education service supply 195
diversified resource supply 193
documentation system 252
Double First-Class 166, 167, 168, 169, 170, 171, 172, 173, 174, 175

early education 147, 159, 249
early parenting 157
economic growth 178, 266, 267
educational development environment 187
educational ecology 129, 135, 166
educational evaluation 132, 219, 229
educational gains 95, 96, 111, 113, 114
educational innovation 4, 5, 15, 197
educational opportunity 31, 261
educational philosophy 173, 175, 198, 200, 201, 208, 215, 230
educational plight 268
educational practice 21, 106, 164, 220, 224, 231
educational practices 105, 106, 108, 109, 115, 116, 197, 198, 268, 270
educational quality 1
educational reform 10, 15, 26, 58, 92, 129, 132, 149, 166, 173, 176, 197
educational resources 67, 78, 92, 93, 95, 98, 99, 115, 120, 122, 125, 130, 137, 144, 148, 159, 160, 165, 170, 174, 187, 189, 219, 227, 228, 230, 233, 259, 261, 268
educational segregation 268
education and training institutions 136, 138, 144, 145, 226
education and training market 134, 135, 138, 139, 145, 146
education evaluation system 219, 229
education expenditure 177, 178, 179, 181, 182, 183, 184, 189, 190, 191, 192, 260, 264
education financial transfer payments 265
education financing system 177, 187, 251
education funding 62, 66, 177, 178, 180, 182, 187, 193, 260
education governance 1, 2, 5, 9, 14, 15, 132
education industry 1, 9, 30, 34, 44, 186

education system 4, 5, 9, 13, 15, 17, 18, 19, 20, 21, 22, 23, 24, 25, 26, 27, 28, 29, 31, 34, 46, 60, 135, 166, 180, 187, 188, 189, 193, 197, 208, 218, 225, 228, 233, 234, 247, 252, 254, 255, 256, 258, 262, 264, 279, 288
elementary school 4, 19, 22, 29, 140, 202, 204, 263
examination-oriented education 1, 2, 3, 4, 14, 15, 18, 25, 26, 70, 79, 80, 81, 82, 83, 84, 87, 93, 94, 117, 118, 123, 125, 129, 130, 131, 132, 133, 139, 143, 148, 157, 161, 173, 208, 286
extracurricular activities 78, 86, 93, 95, 104, 105, 114
extracurricular tutoring 1, 143, 147, 225

financial mechanism for education 264, 265
first-generation college students 95, 96, 97, 98, 99, 100, 101, 102, 103, 104, 105, 106, 107, 108, 109, 110, 111–112, 113, 114, 115, 116
fiscal education expenditure 178, 181, 182, 183, 189, 191, 192
fiscal investment in education 180, 181, 185, 188, 189, 191, 193
fiscal revenue 191, 192
fiscal revenue growth rate 191
for-profit private schools 33, 37, 38, 39, 40, 43, 44, 47, 48
full-time schools 198, 282
full-time special education teachers 241, 242, 243, 247
full-time teachers 68, 240, 241

Gansu province 50, 53, 55, 56, 57, 59, 60, 63, 64
Gansu Province Precision-targeted Poverty Alleviation Pre-school Education Special Support Plan (2015–2020) 59
Gansu Province Precision-targeted Poverty Alleviation Rural Teachers Special Support Plan (2015–2020) 59
GDP growth rate 191
governmental financial support 36, 188
governmental investment increases as the private investment recedes 177
government funding 182, 236, 256
growth in GDP 191

INDEX

Guidance on Further Promoting the Reform of the Senior High School Entrance Examination 2
Guidelines for Regular Schools on Special Education Resource and Classrooms Constructions 233, 235, 246

Happy Activity Days 141
Hengshui High School 117–132
Hengzhong Model 117–132
higher education 5, 6, 12, 13, 14, 33, 34, 36, 39, 45, 52, 55, 68, 95, 96, 100, 103, 114, 115, 117, 129, 130, 161, 167, 168, 169, 170, 171, 172, 174, 175, 178, 179, 190, 193, 194, 204, 224, 234, 236, 237, 244, 254, 265, 271, 272, 278, 279, 285
higher education institutes 236
high-income countries 12, 189, 190
high school entrance examination 1, 2, 119
human capital theory 149, 163

Implementation Plans for Educational Support Plans for Precision-targeted Poverty Alleviation 52
inclusive education 232, 233, 235, 237, 246
innovative education 1, 15, 198
Innovative Small and Micro Schools 197, 198, 199, 200, 201, 204, 205, 206, 207, 208, 209, 212, 214, 215, 216, 217, 218
innovative teaching methods 215, 228
in-system public education 271
in-system traditional schools 208, 209, 212, 215
intangible cultural heritage 271
investment in education 146, 177, 178, 179, 180, 181, 185, 187, 188, 189, 191, 193, 195, 196, 227

junior college 20, 71, 76, 77, 78, 154, 242, 253

Law of Investment Securities 43
Law of the People's Republic of China on the Promotion of Privately-run Schools 30, 31, 120, 148
learning in regular classrooms (LRC) 232, 234, 235, 236, 246, 247, 249, 250
left-behind children 6, 7, 8, 55, 56, 57, 152, 251, 252, 262

legal person 37, 39
letter grade 137, 139, 141, 142
life education 149
Lixin Primary School 259
local policy innovations 47
low-income workers 261, 266, 267, 268

mentorship system 203, 208
middle-income trap 152, 162
migrant children 7, 9, 45, 152, 251, 252, 254, 255, 256, 257, 258, 259, 260, 261, 263, 264, 265, 266, 267, 268
migrant parents 253
migrant population 9, 48, 159, 251, 262, 265, 266, 267
migrant workers 7, 8, 9, 157, 253, 254, 255, 256, 257, 258, 259, 260, 261, 263
military-style management 123, 124
modernization of education governance 1
monitoring system 141, 230, 288
moral education 65, 220, 221, 222, 223, 227, 229, 231, 271, 273
moral education environment 222
multi-channel funding for education 181
multiple education systems 22, 28

National People's Congress and Chinese People's Political Consultative Congress 19, 135
national school operation resources 170
New Citizen Project 256
nine-year continuous education system 25
non-compulsory education 180, 186, 189, 193, 232, 234, 248
non-fiscal education expenditure 178, 181, 182, 183

old-style private schools 269, 270, 280, 285, 287
Opinions on Implementing the Chinese Excellent Traditional Culture Inheritance and Development Project 270, 286
outdoor exercise 203
overall development 91, 106, 132, 179, 187, 206, 228, 229
Overall Plan for Promoting the Construction of World-Class Universities and World-Class Disciplines 167
overburdened with schoolwork 134

parental satisfaction   70, 73, 74, 75, 76, 77,
   85, 86, 92, 93
parent education   70
physical education (PE)   54, 203, 204, 221,
   222, 223, 224, 228, 229, 231, 272
pluralistic integration   251
population growth   267
poverty alleviation   6, 50, 51, 52, 53, 54, 55,
   56, 57, 59, 60, 61, 62, 63, 64, 67, 68, 151
poverty alleviation through education   6,
   50, 51, 52, 53, 55, 56, 57, 59, 64, 151
precision-targeted measures   50
precision-targeted poverty alleviation   6, 50,
   51, 52, 53, 54, 55, 56, 57, 59, 61, 62, 63,
   64, 67, 68, 151
pre-college characteristics   96, 97
preschool education   29, 45, 54, 55, 56, 60,
   61, 64, 66, 68, 234, 248
primary and secondary schools   5, 11, 20, 21,
   24, 25, 58, 59, 65, 66, 134, 135, 137, 138,
   140, 141, 159, 223, 269, 270, 271, 272, 273,
   276, 284
Private-integration Primary School   256, 258
private junior vocational school   31
privately-run schools   30, 31, 32, 33, 34, 35,
   36, 37, 38, 39, 40, 41, 42, 43, 44, 45, 47,
   64, 70, 71, 85, 120, 122, 123, 137, 148, 189,
   194, 255, 285, 288
private preschool education   60
Private School Promotion Law   31, 32, 33, 34,
   36, 38, 39, 40, 41, 42, 43, 46
private schools   5, 9, 31, 33, 35, 36, 37, 38, 39,
   40, 41, 42, 43, 44, 47, 48, 49, 85, 86, 87,
   88, 93, 120, 121, 137, 139, 142, 144, 145,
   146, 148, 180, 181, 183, 195, 216, 255, 256,
   268, 269, 270, 279, 280, 285, 287
professional knowledge   222, 227, 230, 236,
   289
Professional Standards for Special Education
   Teachers (Trial)   236
professional training   208, 236, 241, 242, 247
property rights system   35, 43
Provincial-admission System for the College-
   entrance Examination   265
public education expenditure   191, 260
public education system   4, 5, 15, 21, 252,
   255, 262, 279
public finance   188

public schools   4, 5, 8, 37, 44, 45, 70, 71, 85,
   87, 88, 93, 120, 121, 136, 144, 146, 147, 148,
   189, 195, 205, 216, 217, 252, 253, 254, 256,
   258, 268, 271
public service lectures and courses   282

reasonable profit return   32, 33, 34, 36
reflective education   149
reform of the education system   17, 18, 19,
   25, 26, 27, 28, 29, 188, 189, 193
Regulations on Education for People with
   Disabilities   233, 235, 249
rehabilitation services   232, 233, 243, 249
Rozelle's talk   149, 150, 153, 157, 159
rural education   1, 2, 3, 6, 7, 8, 9, 10, 14, 15,
   50, 65, 67, 149, 150, 154, 157, 158, 159, 161,
   162, 165, 180
Rural Education Action Program   149
rural high school students   160
rural students   10, 12, 15, 130, 131, 151, 157, 158,
   159, 160, 161

school admission requirements   261
school culture   222
school curriculum   139, 226, 278
school dropout   149, 152, 159
school for life   164, 165
schooling experiences   96
school learning and life   210, 212, 213
school management   9, 10, 78, 79, 86, 93, 142,
   217, 229, 231
school operation qualification   214
schoolwork burden   4, 135, 141, 226
school workload   219
secondary school   11, 15, 19, 20, 21, 25, 59, 60,
   67, 117, 119, 132, 134, 135, 136, 138, 139,
   140, 141, 146, 154, 160, 200, 203, 207, 216,
   273, 274
secondary vocational education   29, 67, 152,
   154, 155, 156, 159, 193, 196
Second Phase of the Plan for Promoting
   Special Education (2017–2020)   233, 234,
   235, 237, 246
senior vocational school   253
separation of management, operation, and
   evaluation   9, 15, 216
Shanghai Residence Permit   257
social educational institutions   279

INDEX

social status discrimination   251
special education   65, 66, 232, 233, 234, 235, 236, 237, 238, 240, 241, 242, 243, 244, 245, 246, 247, 248, 249, 250
special education schools   65, 232, 233, 234, 235, 236, 237, 238, 240, 243, 244, 246, 247, 248, 249, 250
special education services   247
special education system   233, 234
special education teachers   232, 236, 240, 241, 242, 243, 247, 249, 250
special education teaching staff   237, 240, 245, 250
sports courses   283
State Council   6, 8, 14, 24, 38, 50, 51, 55, 150, 156, 167, 180, 186, 214, 237, 260, 264, 270
Stock Act   43
student recruitment   10, 215
student-retain-rate   150, 151, 179
student school registration records   215
students with disabilities   234, 235, 236, 237, 238, 239, 240, 244, 245, 246
subject integration   272
Super Secondary School   117, 118, 119, 122, 123, 125, 129, 131, 132

Talents for Three Districts   58
Taoism   287
tax-sharing system   187
teachers' quality   78, 92, 219, 230
teacher training   53, 54, 59, 60, 61, 64, 208, 218, 226, 289
teaching methods   89, 206, 207, 208, 215, 228, 230, 233, 258, 278, 283
teaching staff   36, 48, 58, 68, 79, 207, 237, 240, 245, 250, 279, 287
technical secondary school   154
test-taking training   123, 125, 148, 161
the 21st Century Education Research Institute   5, 70, 197, 198, 269, 273

the Dunwoody Foundation   269
the Four Books and Five Classics   274
theme-based/project-based learning   202
The Ministry of Education (MOE)   1, 2, 24, 38, 41, 51, 117, 123, 148, 150, 169, 202, 223, 234, 235, 236, 260, 270, 272
the Ministry of Finance   169
the National Curriculum Program   228
the National Development and Reform Commission   169
the United Nations Children's Fund (UNICEF)   251
traditional arts and crafts   283
traditional Chinese painting   273
traditional cultural education   269, 270, 271, 272, 273, 274, 276, 277, 280
traditional cultural knowledge   273
tuition schemes   30, 35
tuition standards   44, 194

undergraduate education   166, 171
universal upper secondary education   155
universities construction   166, 167, 169
university admissions system   147
urban and rural residents   183, 184
urbanization process   7, 268
urban middle class   261
urban population   251, 252, 261

vocational education   6, 27, 28, 29, 50, 52, 55, 66, 67, 152, 154, 155, 156, 157, 159, 193, 196, 204, 234, 248, 249

weekend interest classes   282
well-rounded education   117, 129, 132, 133, 134, 148
Western classics   283
winter and summer camps   282
World Trade Organization (WTO)   187

zero starting point   137, 139, 141, 142

Printed in the United States
by Baker & Taylor Publisher Services